Educational Policy and th

Governments around the world are trying to come to terms with new technologies, new social movements and a changing global economy. As a result, education policy finds itself at the centre of a major political struggle between those who see it only for its instrumental outcomes and those who see its potential for human emancipation.

This book is a successor to the best-selling *Understanding Schooling* (1988). It provides a readable account of how educational policies are developed by the state in response to broader social, cultural, economic and political changes which are taking place. It examines the way in which schools live and work with these changes, and the policies which result from them.

The book examines policy-making at each level, from perspectives both inside and outside the state bureaucracy. It has a particular focus on social justice.

Both undergraduate and postgraduate students will find that this book enables them to understand the reasoning behind the changes they are expected to implement. It will help to prepare them to confront an uncertain educational world, while still retaining their enthusiasm for education.

Sandra Taylor is Associate Professor and **Miriam Henry** is Senior Lecturer in the School of Cultural and Policy Studies at the Queensland University of Technology. **Bob Lingard** is Associate Professor in the Graduate School of Education at the University of Queensland. **Fazal Rizvi** is Professor of Educational Policy and Administration in the Faculty of Education at Monash University.

Educational Policy and the Politics of Change

Sandra Taylor, Fazal Rizvi, Bob Lingard and Miriam Henry

London and New York

First published 1997
by Routledge
11 New Fetter Lane, London EC4P 4EE

Simultaneously published in the USA and Canada
by Routledge
29 West 35th Street, New York, NY 10001

Typeset in Palatino by Routledge
Printed and bound in Great Britain by TJ Press (Padstow) Ltd, Padstow,
Cornwall

British Library Cataloguing in Publication Data
A catalogue record for this book is available from the British Library

Library of Congress Cataloguing in Publication Data
Educational policy and the politics of change / Sandra Taylor . . . [*et al.*].
   Includes bibliographical references and index.
   1. Education and state. 2. Politics and education. 3. Educational change. 4.
   Education and state – Australia. I. Taylor, Sandra.
   LC71.E346 1997   96–9720
   379–dc20   CIP

ISBN 0–415–11870–0 (hbk)
ISBN 0–415–11871–9 (pbk)

Contents

Preface

The origins of this book lie in our efforts – both individual and collective – to understand policy processes in education. For more than a decade, we have been researching the ever-changing landscape of education policy both in Australia and elsewhere. As governments around the world try to come to terms with new technologies, new social movements and the politics of difference, a global economy and the postmodern condition, education policy finds itself at the centre of a major political struggle between those who see it only for its instrumental outcomes, and those who see its potential for human emancipation. At the same time, there has never been greater uncertainty about the intellectual resources with which to consider issues of politics, culture and education.

In these 'new times', we have looked at educational policy processes both from inside the state bureaucracies, as policy advisers, and from the outside, as members of educational communities trying to figure out how policies sent down from head office might change the way our educational practices are structured. We have been involved in conducting workshops and in-service courses, and have witnessed the exasperation felt by teachers and administrators as they try to respond to the policy imperatives of the new times. We have been in meetings where, with others, we have sought to develop strategies to resist policy prescriptions that we have known to be educationally inappropriate.

During this time, we have taught policy analysis in education to undergraduate and postgraduate students, trying to prepare them to confront an uncertain educational world, and trying to provide them with an understanding of policy processes in such a way that their enthusiasm for education remains undiminished. In this we have stressed the importance of thinking about the relationship between policy and change, not only because educational policy may be viewed as a response to broader social, cultural, economic and political change, but also because it prescribes changes which our students are expected to implement. Change has therefore been a central concept in our courses.

To teach these courses, we have searched in vain for a suitably critical and accessible text. Existing texts either tend to focus at a 'macro' level on how educational policy development has now become subordinated to economic concerns (for example, Marginson 1993), or alternatively they provide a more 'micro' level account of how educational policies are received and rearticulated in schools (for example, Bowe *et al.* 1992). Both approaches provide insights which no student of educational policy can afford to ignore, but what they do not provide is an account of how questions of political economy and cultural practices of schools are related. This book attempts this task, and may be viewed as located in the space between political economy and cultural studies of policy. It looks at policy processes in order to discuss the ways in which educational policies are developed by the state in response to the broader social, cultural, economic and political changes taking place around the globe. It examines the ways in which schools 'live' and 'work' with these changes, and with the policy prescriptions of the state. We focus on the processes of policy making at each of its various levels, making issues of power central to our analysis.

In writing this book for the purposes of teaching, we have made extensive use of examples, drawn mostly from Australia, but applicable to policy making processes in other Western countries as well. Though our examples are taken from most areas of education, it is to issues of social justice that we have paid the greatest attention. This not only reflects our own experiences of educational policy, but also our conviction that it is in the framing of social justice issues that the tensions between the economic and cultural imperatives of educational policy are most clearly revealed. As critical policy analysts, we do not believe that it is possible to eschew normative questions in educational policy analysis, and have therefore attempted to show how values enter into the processes of policy making, making our own commitment to democracy and social justice explicit. We have written this book, not attempting to provide definitive answers to the problems of educational policy, but to generate dialogue about the complexities of policy and change. We suggest therefore that readers use the vignettes in Chapter One as examples with which to think about the more substantive issues of educational policy raised in later chapters.

It is something of a convention in jointly authored books to declare the responsibility each of us has taken for the various chapters in this book. We cannot, however, make such a declaration because this book is the outcome of a genuinely collaborative project, in which efforts have been shared equally. It has been a joy to write this book, and we hope that our enthusiasm can be captured by the students of policy who will use it. No book, however, stands on its own, but is built upon the work of others.

There are many friends, colleagues and students who have influenced

our approach to policy analysis. There are too many to name individually, but they may recognise their influences in this text.

Finally, we would like to thank Joy Dougherty, Merle Warry, Merideth
Sadler and Janine McAlpine for their administrative and editorial support. Without their help, and the support of friends, this book would not
have been possible.

Chapter 1

The policy phenomenon

Much of the collective effort of policy makers, researchers and administrators is aimed at making the school reality conform to the rational model. We then bemoan the fact that the schools fail to conform to the model. It just may be that we need a new paradigm.

(Arthur Wise 1984: 86)

INTRODUCTION

This book is concerned with issues of policy in education. We are interested in discussing a whole range of questions. What is policy? What, if anything, is distinctive about educational policy? How do educational policies affect us as parents, teachers, students, administrators and citizens? How is policy made and by whom? How are policies implemented? And how should they be analysed and evaluated? As we will see, these are complex questions to which there are no easy answers. The issues they raise have been much debated over the past three decades, because the way we think about educational policy making is linked to the ideological or philosophical positions we hold, not only in relation to education, but also to the nature of civil society. More specifically, they are linked to our beliefs concerning the manner in which the decisions about education should be made and implemented. The study of policy thus represents a highly contested field.

Let us begin with the concept of 'policy', now a widely used word in our vocabulary. According to the Oxford Dictionary, policy means 'plan of action' or 'statement of aims of ideals'. In everyday language, we often use the word policy to refer to the promises we make to ourselves – such as in the sentence, 'My policy is never to lend money to anyone.' But this is not the kind of policy we will be examining in this book. Our concern is not with personal policies but with policies made by organisations. However, the scope of this book has some further limitations. We are concerned with *public* policies, that is, those policies which are made on behalf of the state by its various instrumentalities to steer the conduct of individuals, such as teachers or students, and organisations, such as schools or universities. We are thus interested in those aspects of governmental activity that are positive and directional, as distinct from the activities of private enterprise which are often motivated by self-interest alone.

This book focusses, then, on public sector activity in education, though later we will suggest that the distinction between public and private has become less clear in recent years. Nevertheless, it is useful to look at the distinction which is ideally drawn between the public and private sectors. The public sector represents a group of institutions which rely in some way on, or justify their activities in terms of, the authority of the state. At the same time, the public sector is more exposed to political direction and scrutiny than the private sector. It is characterised by public accountability, which extends to the performance of all state functions, and is enforced in a variety of ways ranging from the administrative to the electoral. Theoretically, at least, the public sector is based on the principle of equality of treatment of citizens. The concepts of ownership of enterprise and profit have been traditionally missing from the public sector. Finally, the idea of a public sector embodies the principle that all public authority must only be used in the public interest. In contrast, individuals and companies in the private sector can usually do anything that is not forbidden by the law to maximise their personal advantage.

If private sector activity is motivated largely by profit, then what is the motivation for the development of public policies in education? One answer to this question may be that public policies in education exist in order to ensure that education occurs in the public interest. Before mass schooling, education was a private business available only to a small section of the community. But since the creation of government schools for whole populations – a trend which began in nineteenth-century Europe and which is captured in the phrase 'mass schooling' – public policies in education have stipulated the conditions under which schools must operate. The earliest policies in education outlined a range of requirements that governed the administration of government schools. These included not only prescriptions for curriculum, pedagogy and assessment but also such matters as the conditions of teacher employment and the physical maintenance of school buildings, as well as the requirements concerning student attendance. Many of these policies were written down in documents that teachers and administrators needed to consult in order to perform their duties. Public policies in education thus had two main functions: to provide an account of those cultural norms which were considered by the state as desirable in education; and to institute a mechanism of accountability against which student and teacher performance could be measured.

These remain two of the most important functions of educational poli-

cies. However, since the 1960s, policies in social areas, including education, have increasingly performed yet another significant function: that
of marshalling and managing public calls for change, giving them form
and direction. As society has become more complex, and interest groups
more assertive, governments have had to construct policies which
attempt to respond effectively to their demands. Educational policy has
thus become a bureaucratic instrument with which to administer the
expectations that the public has of education. Stephen Kemmis (1990b: 1)
has suggested that policy is increasingly replacing educational theory as
a source of guidance for practitioners. What Kemmis means by this is
that education is no longer discussed in terms of broad visions and ideals
but in terms of what governments believe to be possible and often expe-
dient, and what interest groups feel they can persuade governments to
do. The language of educational policy, according to Kemmis, is thus
linked to political compromises between competing but unequal interests.

Many of the most significant changes in educational policies over the
past thirty years or so have been due to the political work of organised
social movements like the civil rights movement and the women's movement. Each of these movements has been dissatisfied with the role education plays in the maintenance of the existing social order. Each has
exerted a considerable amount of pressure for change. Thus, in the 1960s,
calls for action on poverty and other social inequalities faced by women,
minorities and people with disabilities led governments in most developed countries to formulate a swag of policies and programmes in education which sought to provide greater equality of educational
opportunity. New policies were developed to cater for the increasing
number of students who wanted to stay longer in schooling, partly as a
vehicle for social mobility. In line with changing social values, a more
social welfarist policy regime in education was established – but only
after a long political struggle. The economic context also favoured the
development of these policies, as new industries established after the
Second World War matured into making large profits, giving nations revenue they needed to expand educational provision.

However, the social democratic settlement in education, as it has been
called, never did enjoy universal public support. Those opposed to its
universal access orientation seized upon the economic difficulties most
Western countries have faced since the mid-1970s to call for a different
way of funding and organising education. As a result, many of the
achievements of the 1960s and 1970s have begun to be eroded as, in
changed economic circumstances, new policy regimes are established,
guided by a different set of interests exerting influence on governments –
though perhaps more so in the UK and the US under conservative governments than in Australia under Labour governments. Thus while it

might have been difficult to imagine how educational policies that resulted in greater equality of access and opportunity, in recognition of women
and minority rights, could be abandoned, many past initiatives have
been disbanded, especially in the UK and the US. Even in Australia, a
great deal has already happened to suggest that many of these social
democratic reforms in education are now being watered down and made
secondary to the economic agendas for education. For example, the idea
of a curriculum more responsive to cultural diversity, enshrined in the
notion of multiculturalism, has been attacked. Global economic restructuring has led to calls for the creation of an educational system more
responsive to the changing labour market needs of nations. The collapse
in the youth labour market has led to calls for educational policies
designed to ensure greater student retention in senior secondary schools
and curricula that are more vocationally responsive.

Economic restructuring has not, however, been the only factor responsible for a changed policy climate in education. Technological changes
have also demanded revision to educational policy, and in particular to
curriculum priorities and pedagogical styles. If the emergence of new
technologies has changed the patterns of everyday life and powerfully
restructured work and leisure as dramatically as many suggest, then
education cannot remain oblivious to these changes. Similarly, changes
in social attitudes towards authority, particularly among young people,
have also created new pressures for education. As Willis (1990) has
argued, students brought up on the cultural values of the globalised
mass media are unlikely to be comfortable with the requirements of
bureaucratically defined regimes of discipline. Such cultural and attitudinal changes have demanded policy shifts in education.

At the same time, people are no longer prepared to leave policy making to politicians and bureaucrats. They wish to be involved in the steering of policy processes. Powerful social movements have developed over
the past few decades which demand democratic engagement in policy
processes. These movements form alliances to pressure systems and
organisations to change, to ensure that policy makers do not ignore their
voice. For example, the feminist movement will not permit issues of gender inequalities in education to drop off the state's policy agenda.
Similarly, indigenous groups and ethnic minorities want a direct say in
the policy making processes. This in itself constitutes a major cultural
change which no discussion of educational policy can afford to ignore.

What this brief discussion indicates is that educational policies do not
emerge in a vacuum but reflect compromises between competing interests expressed by the dominant interests of capitalism on the one hand
and the oppositional interests of various social movements on the other.
While it is true that policies are responses to particular social changes, it
is also the case that these changes may themselves be represented in a

variety of different ways, and accorded contrasting significance. Recent educational policy initiatives may thus be viewed as responses to the struggle over particular constructions of social, political, economic and cultural changes. The state itself puts forward its policy initiatives in the rhetorical language of reform, often presented as the only plausible response to the social and economic changes described. Indeed, the term 'reform' has become one of the most over-used ideas in the political vocabulary. It presupposes legitimacy and invites support for the ideas propagated in the particular policy. In this way, therefore, the state is not neutral with respect to the changes occurring in society, and its own interest in sponsoring some changes and preventing others is reflected in policy.

References to change have now become ubiquitous in politics and policy. At the same time few, if any, policies are entirely new: most are shaped by the characteristics of previous policies. As Hogwood and Peters note: 'Policies are rarely written on a *tabula rasa* but rather on a well-occupied and even crowded tablet of existing laws, organisations and clients' (1983: 1). Policy is thus an instrument through which change is mapped onto existing policies, programmes or organisations, and onto the demands made by particular interest groups. To put forward a policy is to acknowledge that a new policy was needed or that the old policy needed to be revised in response to the changes occurring in society.

However, this is not the only way in which change and policy are related. While it is possible to *initiate*, to put on to the public agenda, issues that are poorly understood or ignored and to *bring about* or *implement* change with the development of new policies, it is also possible to use policy as an instrument with which to *exclude* certain issues from the realm of public debate; or indeed *resist* certain claims made by interest groups. With policy it is also possible to *articulate, re-articulate* or *institutionalise* the manner in which particular issues might be understood. In short, policies serve to manage change, but exactly how this management occurs varies greatly from policy to policy and site to site. The relationship between policy and change is indeed complex. In this book, our aim is to provide an introduction to educational policy studies which highlights some of the ways in which the ideas of policy and change are related.

VIGNETTES: POLICIES IN PRACTICE

To explore the relationship between policy and change, we want to begin with a series of vignettes of education policy making in a number of different policy domains and settings to demonstrate some of the complexities of education policy and policy analysis. The vignettes are located in our experience as teachers of educational policy in the various States of

Australia, but we have little doubt that they apply equally to the experiences of policy making in other Western countries as well. They are illustrative of policy experiences, and attempt to show the various ways in which education policy is received and enacted by practitioners, and the various ways in which it is produced, disseminated and implemented. They demonstrate the value-laden nature of policy making and policy analysis, and highlight the various levels at which education policy making occurs and the links which exist between education policy and other policy fields. They also demonstrate the significance for policy analysis of the location of the analyst.

The first of the vignettes concerns teachers' experience of policy. We begin with a story of a teacher because many education policies end up in schools: on principals' desks, buried in libraries, in teachers' pigeon holes, the subject of innumerable staff meetings. Teachers are expected to put these policies into practice, so the issue of the ways in which teachers understand policies is of utmost importance.

Mark's story

Mark has been teaching in an inner-city primary school in New South Wales for more than fifteen years. He has always regarded himself as a highly committed teacher who, in the mid-1980s, participated actively in the work of his union. He enjoyed teaching and felt himself to be at the vanguard of the social democratic reforms in education which were being attempted in the 1980s. But in the last few years things have begun to go wrong, so much so that Mark now considers the profession he joined has been totally transformed – for the worse. He believes that the system no longer supports the educational values to which he is committed. At the same time, the attempts by governments to 'reform' education with a plethora of policies which are simply 'thrown at' teachers, has made teaching unattractive to him. In the State of New South Wales, the educational bureaucracy has been restructured no less than three times in the past ten years. Curriculum advisers upon whom he could rely are no longer available as curriculum has been continually revised. Class sizes have increased significantly. New assessment regimes have also been introduced which serve in a real sense to undermine the professionalism of teachers.

Of course, Mark recognises that changes in society demand new educational policies, but what concerns him is the confused way in which policy shifts are explained to teachers who have to implement them, and the manner in which teachers have effectively been frozen out of policy making processes. Mark finds the current rhetoric of devolution particularly confusing because it promises responsibility for decision making to be devolved to the school level, and yet, from his point of view, it has placed more restrictions on teachers' work than ever before. Severe financial cut-backs have produced an intensification of teachers' work. The morale at his school is particularly low, and many of his friends have already left teaching. What concerns Mark the most is that whereas once the economic and vocational uses of schooling were just part of its purpose, they are now vaunted as its primary purpose. He feels that the cultural and critical role of education in the transformation of society is now being diminished.

Mark's story raises a number of issues concerning policy processes in education. To begin with, it raises the question of who should determine education policy and what role should teachers play in policy processes. In recent years, teachers have increasingly felt excluded from processes of policy development, as the system seeks to make stringent demands on them for greater accountability to externally devised policies. They are expected to produce change of the kind prescribed by particular policies, but are seldom given an opportunity to explore these policies in relation to their own values and traditions. Their understanding of policies is therefore often either limited or skewed, and what is subsequently produced in practice often bears little resemblance to the original intentions. Policies are thus often refracted to suit local circumstances. While many feel anxious about how new policies might have implications for their practice, others simply reject the idea that policies are important and thus find little reason to change existing practices. These features highlight some of the limitations of the so-called rational model of educational change which separates policy processes into two distinct stages of policy development and policy implementation. This model assumes that, given a set of perfect conditions, policies can produce the desired outcomes. But given human diversity and organisational complexity, this assumption is fundamentally flawed. Implementation can never be achieved in a vacuum. Since policies are part of a social environment, they can be expected to be ignored, resisted, contested or rearticulated to suit local circumstances. Mark's story thus underlines the political nature of policy processes and the compromises between different interests which are involved. This applies to all public policy making, but in education it is particularly relevant because the purposes of education are always contested and teachers claim some professional autonomy.

Maria's story

Maria was first appointed as a principal of a high school in a provincial town in Victoria in 1987. She is convinced, with some justification, that the last ten years have been the most difficult time to be a principal in the history of public education. Policy changes in education have been rapid, and have come not only from the State government but also increasingly

from the federal government in Australia. When Maria was first appointed principal, social democratic education policies were still in place in
Victoria. The ideas of community participation in decision making and
equality of educational opportunity were flourishing. However, within
two years of Maria's appointment, things began to change. First, there
was the fear that in the face of a government policy of rationalisation, her
school might be closed because of declining numbers. Only an intense
political struggle saved the school – but the reprieve was only temporary: two years later, it was forced to amalgamate with a neighbouring
school. Second, the school had to respond to a range of new policies on
curriculum change, especially in the post-compulsory years, coming
from both the Victorian government which wished to overhaul its
Victorian Certificate of Education, and national moves towards competency based approaches to education and national curriculum statements
and profiles. According to Maria, the two sets of policy prescriptions did
not always keep in tandem, creating much confusion. Finally, following
the election of a conservative government in Victoria, a new schools policy was introduced which drastically cut funding, sacked a large number
of teachers and changed the ways in which schools were to relate to the
State educational bureaucracy and to the community. The policy, *Schools
of the Future*, introduced many market principles in the administration of
schools, transforming the role principals were expected to play. They are
now expected to administer schools as managers of an enterprise, in
competition with other schools, raise private sponsorship to supplement
school budgets and run their schools as fiscal units which are none the
less accountable to the central office.

Maria's story reveals the extent to which changes in government ideology have the capacity to transform school administration. In a new policy environment, Maria is expected to become a pivotal figure in driving
change in line with policies determined by the system, policy trends to
which she is personally opposed. As a principal, however, she has to
somehow reconcile her personal views with the directions she is given
by central administration. She is thus faced with a range of difficult
issues concerning contemporary policy making and school leadership in
a political climate of turbulence, complexity and teacher resistance. How
should she manage policy at her school in refocussing it to market principles? Maria's story also highlights the fact that administrative practice in
schools has to respond to often conflicting policy agendas, ranging from
those of federal and State governments to the expectations that local
communities and teachers and students have of schools.

From these two accounts of how policy changes affect the work of
those at the school level, let us now move to look at the ways policies are
developed. The first story is that of Shakila, a teacher who was pulled

into the central bureaucracy to provide a representative voice on a committee developing anti-racism policy.

Shakila's story

Shakila had been a science teacher at a suburban secondary school for almost five years when, in 1992, she was asked by the principal of her school to join a State-wide advisory committee established to develop the Queensland Department of Education's anti-racism policy. Shakila was flattered but at the same time surprised as she had had no previous direct dealings with the Department and felt she knew very little about policy making processes. She guessed that the reason for her nomination to the advisory committee was that her family had immigrated to Australia to escape racism in South Africa some ten years ago, and that the principal had presumably thought that this gave her some special insights into the nature of racism and educational programmes appropriate to combat it. At her first meeting, three things became clear to Shakila: that the Department's commitment to the development of anti-racism policy was at best tepid; that the impetus to have such a policy came from a single determined senior officer in the Department who had been able to convince her colleagues on the Executive Management Committee that Queensland needed a policy similar to those which existed in two other States in Australia; and that the composition of the committee was quite arbitrary and consisted of representatives from various interest groups. Many of these people had little expertise or interest in matters concerning racism in Australian schools – so much so that a number of general remarks Shakila made at the first meeting saw her joining the group appointed to draft the policy.

Shakila took on this task with all the commitment she could muster. She read widely, attended a number of conferences and consulted with a large number of parents, teachers and students, as well as members of the ethnic and Aboriginal communities. In the end, the writing group produced a policy that met the concerns of most of its members, though Shakila felt that the consensus process was itself conservative because many of the members of the group opposed anything they considered radical in her proposals. The draft was then presented to the whole advisory committee which, according to Shakila, watered it down further. But the most significant setback came when the draft endorsed by the advisory committee was presented to the Department of Education's Executive Management Committee, which asserted that the policy had to be 'revenue neutral' and that the Department was not in a position to support recommendations which involved a major injection of funds. Also, it was thought that the draft policy was too long and that all that was required was a short policy document simply stating the

Department's opposition to any form of racism. The policy was then revised, and reduced to one page lacking any clear statement of rationale. Shakila had hoped that the policy document itself would have an educative function, but in its brief form it appeared no different from most bureaucratic documents. At this stage, in frustration, Shakila resigned from the advisory committee in protest. Many months later, the policy was diluted further at the Premier's Department level, where the Office of the Cabinet sought to bring it into line with the government's political agenda and ensure that it was consistent with its various legal obligations. After three years the policy is still awaiting release.

Shakila's story suggests that radical policy statements are difficult to achieve through the policy making processes that most educational bureaucracies currently employ. It shows that policy is not rationally made but is achieved in tentative and incremental steps, each of which involves exercise of power. It also demonstrates that public policies are often located within the broader legal and political framework. Governments develop policies not only in response to public pressure but also because they can secure some electoral advantage in taking the lead on some issues. Shakila's story also indicates that there are many different kinds of policies, some material since they involve allocating resources for their implementation, others symbolic since they are designed to create a social climate in which educational work can proceed, around a commitment to a particular set of values.

In the processes of educational policy development, participation is often encouraged. But this may take a number of different forms. In the case of the Queensland Department of Education's anti-racism policy, participation was achieved through a representative structure which enabled various interest groups to have a voice in decision making. Shakila's committee included a parent association representative, primary and secondary school representatives, a teacher union representative, representatives from various regions of Queensland, as well as representatives of the Aboriginal and ethnic communities. What remains unclear in such a model, however, is the extent to which that participation in fact influences final policy documents given other bureaucratic agendas and associated internal politics. Some of these features are also present in Susan's story, which follows.

Susan's story

Susan is employed as a policy officer in a State education department. Mainly in response, she thought, to concerns which had been raised about the department's legal liabilities, she was asked to develop a policy on distance education. The task was to be completed in six months and required extensive research, particularly into legal matters. Susan had to make decisions about policy content and format, and the draft policy had to be scrutinised and approved at various levels within the bureaucracy, a task involving some degree of negotiation and in-house politics. Formulating the content involved consultation and negotiation with many interest groups, some more powerful than others, though Susan wanted to ensure a voice for the less powerful – a task involving her in difficult community politics at times. She was not at all clear about how to develop criteria for judging how much weight to give the various voices in her final document beyond a rather vague notion that equity for all students was her guiding concern. As the task progressed, and contrary to her initial understanding of policy development, she became acutely aware that the politics of getting through an acceptable document was becoming more important than the substance of the document itself. She also became aware of, and frustrated by, her remoteness at the centre from other groups involved in the policy process. This was because the policy making model used within the department, and the public service generally, separated policy formulation from implementation and evaluation stages. Hence she would have no input into the implementation of the policy, nor would she have an opportunity to modify the policy as problems emerged elsewhere in the policy chain.

What further does this story tell us about policy processes? First, it expands our understanding of problems with so-called rational policy processes which formally separate formulation–implementation–evaluation stages. Teachers' frustrations at being at the receiving end of policy are echoed by the frustrations of a senior policy officer working in isolation – consultation processes notwithstanding – in head office. Second, it once again highlights the value-laden nature of policy making and, related, the fact that policy processes are often highly political rather than merely technical in nature. Finally, the vignette raises the important question of why it is that issues 'hit' the policy agenda at particular times. In this instance, as in many policy developments, questions of legal liability had forced the pace. But further probing would reveal other pressures, so the general point here is to acknowledge that policies do not exist in a vacuum: an understanding of the context in which policies emerge is critical to an understanding of policies themselves.

For a clearer illustration of this latter point, we will move to another vignette, this time relating to the university sector.

Peter's story

Peter, a university lecturer, was selected to participate in one of his university's 'quality teams' as part of a quality assurance audit – a process set in train by the Commonwealth Department of Employment, Education and Training (DEET) as part of a broader accountability agenda. After a number of rehearsals, the group was able to create some agreed upon accounts to tell the audit team. In doing this, members of the group realised they had no clear idea about how to define 'quality', let alone how the audit team might interpret the term. No guidelines had been provided. The end result was a rather glowing account of the university's record, which was apparently met with some scepticism from the audit team. Originally, the task of the audit teams covering the country's thirty-six universities was to make recommendations to the government about the allocation of $200 million of 'quality money' to the top 50 per cent of the universities. However, a last-minute change of minister plus intense lobbying from the universities during the process resulted in new guidelines, so that ultimately all universities received some funding, ranging from $50,000 to $8 million, with one of the oldest and wealthiest receiving the largest amount, and one of the newest and least wealthy receiving the smallest. Peter's university came somewhere in the middle.

The story usefully highlights some further aspects of policy processes. For a start, the connections between the micro setting (in this case, the university) and policy making at the macro level are more obvious. Clearly the DEET quality agenda itself is embedded in a wider set of pressures or contexts – historical, political, economic – which would need to be understood to make sense of this story. The vignette also illustrates a rather different kind of feature of policy: its at times *ad hoc* nature. Initially, the bid for quality money was interpreted as a ploy by the then higher education minister to obtain extra funding for his portfolio. However, the quality argument must have resonated with other agendas in Cabinet for, somewhat unexpectedly, the money came through and a system for allocating it then needed to be rather hastily put in place. The notion of 'policy on the run', which this vignette to some extent exemplifies, is a recurring theme in the policy literature, as are related notions of policy distortion or unintended consequences of policy. For what this story also shows is how an originally modest idea of providing universities with some financial carrots developed a more powerful momentum to the point, some argued, of becoming a significant mechanism for recreating a divide between first- and second-class institutions that, in theory, had been eradicated with the creation of the unified national system of higher education in 1988.

Another significant feature of policy making and policy processes evident in this vignette relates to the language and discursive context of policy documents. For example, a term like 'quality', deriving from modern management discourse in the corporate world, had no taken-for-granted meaning within the university context. Hence an integral part of the quality audits process was the struggle to define that term to support the particular educational or political agendas of varying interest groups. So, for example, our somewhat cynical interpretation of the quality agenda as serving to shore up a traditional divide between old and new universities would most likely not be shared, publicly at least, by a DEET policy analyst. Similarly, as debates at the time showed, the Vice-Chancellor of Melbourne University (a winner) and the Vice-Chancellor of Murdoch University (a relative loser) had very different views about the legitimacy and usefulness of this policy process. Finally, this vignette says something about national policy making, an issue of particular significance in the Australian federal context with its complex division of roles and responsibilities between Commonwealth and State governments. We will say much more about this in later chapters. Suffice to mention here that the development of national policies in education is a relatively recent phenomenon, and to understand this we need to consider yet another dimension of policy making: the international context.

To illustrate the significance of the international context of national policies, we turn to vocational education and training which involves, as well as the three educational sectors (schooling, technical and further education (TAFE) and universities), areas sometimes not traditionally seen as part of the education arena: industry and private training providers. The complexity and scope of this policy agenda will be examined in more detail in Chapter Six, but it is illustrated briefly in the following and final vignette.

Jack's story

Jack is the project officer for an Australian Vocational Training System (AVTS) pilot project in the automotive industry, one of several hundred pilots funded by the Commonwealth government to trial a new system of vocational education and training in Australia. The new AVTS aimed to improve the quality and accessibility of education and training for young people in the post-compulsory stages of schooling. To this end, amongst other things it aimed at converging vocational and general education, creating credentialled pathways between schools, TAFE and workplaces, and replacing the dual system of (male-dominated) apprenticeships and (female-dominated) traineeships with a uniformly recognised AVTS credential. Involved in this particular pilot project were a TAFE college, a local high school, a nearby Catholic boys' school and another private boys' college, the Vehicle Builders' Union and the Australian Automotive Industry Training Council. In order to get funding for the project, Jack had to show how convergence would be achieved and what kinds of pathways and credentials would be offered. He also had to ensure that all curriculum was offered in modular, competency-based mode, and he had to indicate how the project would contribute to the Commonwealth government's equity objectives.

The task turned out not to be as forbidding as it sounded. Both the

n and the Industry Training Council were helpful in offering ideas
out the competencies required in the industry and for making existing
curriculum content more relevant. Links between a number of local
industries, the TAFE college and the schools involved in the project had
already been in operation for several years (another reason Jack was able
to get the project up and running quickly), and Jack was confident some
kind of credentialling system would be worked out in time. Convergence
was also well in hand, as all the schools involved already required students in vocational tracks to take at least two general education subjects.
As for equity – well, as he indicated in his submission, the project did not
discriminate against any applicant on the basis of gender, race or disability. Jack's project was funded, though a year down the track a satisfactory credential still had not been worked out. Of the twenty-six students in
the first-year intake, ten were from the Catholic boys' school, eight were
from the private boys' school and eight were from the local high school.
The one girl applicant withdrew in the first week and there were no
Aboriginal or Torres Strait Islander students enrolled.

What additional policy issues are raised by this story? These are perhaps best presented as a series of questions. The new directions and
emphasis on vocational education and training are part of a world-wide
trend. What forces – political, economic, ideological – are driving this
trend and what is the relationship between policy making at the national
level and at the international level? Indeed, what is meant by 'national
policy making' and how does this process work? What factors contribute
to the slippage between the formal objectives the projects were supposed
to meet and the early outcomes? Even this brief vignette provides a few
clues: tensions between national objectives and existing local practices?
Ineffective monitoring procedures? Different interpretations of terms
such as convergence or pathways? Another point: this is a complex policy agenda attempting to bring together many different and even competing interests or imperatives. Which of these prevail over time, and under
what circumstances? And what about the gender dimensions involved
here, or the approach to equity matters more generally? Why have the
private schools become so involved in vocational education?

SOME GENERAL OBSERVATIONS

The point of these vignettes is not so much to raise specific issues –
school administration, anti-racism, distance education, vocational education and training – but rather to give some insight into the scope and
complexity of education policy and to our approach to policy analysis.
These issues are taken up in more detail in the following chapters, but it
is worth making some brief general observations here.

Policy is more than the text

When we talk about policy, we are certainly referring to more than just a policy document or text. To analyse policies simply in terms of the words written in formal documents is to overlook the nuances and subtleties of the context which give the text meaning and significance. Policies are thus dynamic and interactive, and not merely a set of instructions or intentions. They represent political compromises between conflicting images of how educational change should proceed. As we have noted, the words chosen to be included in the policy text are carefully selected and much revised in light of the objections of the various interests. The anti-racism policy upon which Shakila worked went through a number of drafts, and even when the writing group was satisfied, the officials of the Premier's Department felt it necessary to alter the text. Much thought was given not only to the words but also to the form (paper size, font and print size, etc.) in which it was to be printed.

Policy is multi-dimensional

Each of the stories here could have been presented from many different perspectives. For example, Jack the project officer's story could have been told from the point of view of the girl who withdrew from the project, from an OECD official charged with evaluating international trends in vocational education and training, from a Commonwealth department bureaucrat trying to formulate funding guidelines, from someone charged with formulating equity guidelines, and so forth. Each of these policy players in some way contributes to the way this policy develops and 'works' – in other words, to policy outcomes. Not all influence this process equally; often there is conflict and contradiction between the perspectives or interests of those involved, and not all players benefit equally.

Policy is value-laden

Values permeate policy processes. For example, the restructuring of education bureaucracies is often justified on the grounds of efficiency and effectiveness. But whose definition is this? And in whose interests? Certainly, from their different positions in the education bureaucracy, neither Mark nor Maria seemed to concur with that view. On the other hand, what values held by either Mark or Maria underpinned their rejection of the changes taking place?

Policies exist in context

It is not possible to understand any of the stories in isolation. A school does not decide to develop a discipline policy out of thin air. State policies on anti-racism, or national policies on vocational education and training, do not materialise from nowhere. There is always a prior history of significant events, a particular ideological and political climate, a social and economic context – and often, particular individuals as well – which together influence the shape and timing of policies as well as their evolution and their outcomes.

Policy making is a state activity

While many corporations and private organisations, including private schools, make policies of one kind or another, education policy making as seen in the vignettes belongs to the realm of public or social policy – a state (or government) activity. However, the state is a complex beast. As Susan and Shakila's stories showed, for example, the state is not a single entity and policies often have to run the gauntlet of the differing agendas, interests and expectations of different departments or even units within departments. Further, as Jack's story hinted, the state has a complicated relationship with the private sector and, as Shakila's story showed, an equally complicated relationship with civil society. Policies are therefore often shaped by these interactions between the state, the economy and civil society.

Education policies interact with policies in other fields

This is not always self-evident, but even seemingly self-contained school-based policies can usually be seen to be connected in some way with broader policy developments. It does not take too much imagination, for example, to see links between distance education and rural development projects, between anti-racism policies and international forums on human rights, between vocational education and training and labour market policies.

Policy implementation is never straightforward

Implementation of policy is often viewed as the link between policy production and policy practice. It occurs in a highly complex social environment, with official policy agendas seldom intersecting with local interests. Mark and Jack's stories demonstrate in different ways how a linear model of policy implementation does not work, and that government edict alone cannot produce desired changes. In schools, the role of the principal is central to an understanding of the processes of policy implementation. But principals increasingly encounter a fast changing and confusing policy environment in which, as we saw in the case of Maria, they have to somehow work strategically with particular policy prescriptions. Exactly how they might do this depends on the view of educational policy analysis to which they subscribe.

Policies result in unintended as well as intended consequences

Policy making is a precarious business, the consequences of which are unpredictable given the complex interrelationship of contextual factors, different and sometimes opposing interests, linguistic ambiguities and the variety of key players involved in policy processes. Look at what happened to the quality processes alluded to in Peter's story, or the accessibility principles of the AVTS pilots in Jack's story, or the noble ambitions of the anti-racism policy Shakila helped to develop.

CRITICAL POLICY ANALYSIS IN EDUCATION

Given these general insights, then, how should we approach policy analysis? This raises the question of the purposes of policy analysis. Why do policy analysis? This is not an easy question to answer, since much depends on the views we might hold about the nature of knowledge, the way it is justified and the ways in which we should use it politically. Our values are thus inextricably linked to the way we might approach policy analysis, particularly in a field like education, where the very notion of education is linked to moral purposes and is thus highly contested. Also contested are the various views we might hold about the importance of democratic participation in public policy making. Before we say something about our own approach, it might be worth giving a brief account of how policy analysis has been approached in the past. This traditional model of policy development and analysis is often referred to as the 'rational' model (Wise 1984).

The formal study of public policy, or the policy sciences as it is also sometimes called, emerged in the 1960s to assist governments in the task of policy development. The history of the concept of policy sciences is to be found in the development of welfare economics and in the wartime problems of resource allocation. The main objective of policy sciences was to determine the technically best course of action to adopt in order to implement a decision or achieve a goal. The policy scientist was not only expected to clarify the possible outcomes of certain courses of action, but also to choose the most efficient course of action in terms of available factual data. What the policy sciences aspired to, then, was a

technology of decision making in the public sector to enable governments to make the most cost-effective decisions.

The problem with this aspiration, however, was that it was based on
an assumption that decisions in the public sphere could somehow be
made in a value-neutral manner – effectively in a way which could avoid
or simplify the political complexities involved in public policy making.
Moreover, in its assessment of costs and benefits of particular policy
options, the policy sciences assumed the axioms of welfare economics, an
area of economics concerned with estimating individual welfare. More
fundamentally, it assumed that the welfare of the community depended
on the welfare of the individuals comprising it, and nothing else. The
issues of power and the ways in which the state might exercise it were
largely ignored. Also overlooked in the area of education was the idea
that education was a highly contested endeavour about which members
of the same community had widely differing views. The state could not
therefore calculate in some neutral fashion the costs and benefits of particular policies, but rather had to negotiate them with various interest
groups holding competing views of education.

This traditional view of policy analysis was thus based on a particular
view of knowledge, and the way it might be applied to solve social problems. This view, often referred to as 'positivist', stipulates that, for it to be
of any use, knowledge must be scrupulously value-neutral, grounded in
the essential facts provided by the most systematic observation possible.
Only with such an approach to knowledge, it is claimed, can we add a
measure of rationality to the hurly burly of policy making and thus
counteract the special pleading and special sectional interests which
might otherwise dominate the political processes. Policy analysis,
viewed in these terms, assumes an 'underlabourer's' job to the more up
front task of policy advocacy and implementation. This job involves careful, rigorous and reasoned collection of data about the social processes in
order to be able to advise policy makers on such matters as the likely
options and possible consequences of particular policy choices. Analysts
qua analysts, according to this view, can advise policy makers on the
most efficient course of action to take to achieve a particular goal, but
they are not seen as qualified to assess the morality or the legitimacy of
the goal itself. Policy analysis is thus sharply distinguished from policy
advocacy.

Our own view of policy analysis differs quite markedly from this traditional view. To begin with, we reject the positivist assumption that
social scientific knowledge can be value-neutral. We thus deny the fundamental distinction between facts and values. In our view, observations
are inevitably informed by our theories and values in ways which make
any absolute distinction between policy analysis and policy advocacy
hard to sustain. What we 'see' when we examine the processes involved

in the development and implementation of any particular policy is framed by larger questions, which are themselves linked to the normative positions we might adopt about education and its role in creating conditions for social reproduction or transformation. That normative questions cannot be excluded from the province of policy analysis can be demonstrated by looking at one of the key notions in the armoury of the traditional view of policy analysis – efficiency. As Fay (1975) has pointed out, the idea of 'the most efficient means to a given end' begs the question – efficient in terms of what? Furthermore, the very emphasis on efficiency, at the exclusion of such other virtues as thoroughness, creativity, imagination and so on, indicates that a particular value is already preferred as more worthwhile than others.

If values cannot be avoided in policy analysis then we believe that they ought to be declared and argued for up front. The critical view of policy analysis to which we are committed conceptualises education as a moral idea linked to the concerns of social justice. In our view, education has both individual and social purposes – it seeks both to instil those capacities and qualities in students that help them to lead creative and fulfilling lives and to create conditions necessary for the development of a caring and equitable society. These two purposes converge around the idea of active and informed citizenship, implying the important role education has in the formation of cultural practices and communities in which the interests of individuals and society become indistinguishable. In many ways, this conception of education is consistent with the views articulated in the early part of this century by the American educator John Dewey. For Dewey (1958), education is essentially about the development of democratic communities in which everyone can feel free and capable of participating.

Of course, this view of education is stated at a very general level. Not only is the idea of education contested, but so are the ideas of both social justice and democratic participation open to a wide variety of interpretations. Moreover, these ideas do not admit universal definitions, and can be used in a variety of different ways. If this is so, then the question of which interpretation is most appropriate and morally justifiable becomes an open question which can only be resolved in its particular expression, and in its particular context. It is in particular policies and practices that the meanings attached to terms like social justice and participation are revealed. Clearly, then, a major task of critical policy analysis must be to investigate the ways in which key terms are used, and the extent to which particular policies and practices are consistent with our moral vision for education. In this way, critical analysis is overtly political – it is anchored in a particular vision of a moral order.

If the values of justice and participation are central to education, then critical policy analysis must pay attention not only to the content of the policy, but also to the processes of policy development and implementation. In relation to the processes of policy making, we need to observe politics in action, tracing how economic and social forces, institutions, people, interests, events and chance interact. Issues of power and interests need to be investigated. Questions of who is involved in policy making, how processes of consultation are arranged and whose interests they serve thus become critical. An examination of the manner in which power is exercised in the making of political choices is thus central to critical policy analysis.

To ignore issues of power is to ensure our own powerlessness. On the other hand, when we understand relations of power, we are better situated to shape policy making processes, to help improve the quality of policy decisions and perhaps even to empower community action. This observation highlights how critical policy analysis can contribute to policy advocacy. The traditional view of policy analysis implies that it is conducted solely for the benefit of the bureaucracies and those in power – as a technology of control. In contrast, we feel that critical policy analysis has a somewhat different purpose. It cannot afford to ignore the technical issues of planning, but it must also be political and strategic. It can help anticipate political pressures and mobilise countervailing support. It can expose the ways in which agendas are set and framed in favour of dominant interests, and it can identify and overcome obstacles to a democratic planning process. It can reveal the ways in which information provided for consultation might be distorted or false or misleading. However, it can do all this only if it clarifies the nature of the context in which particular policies are made and implemented. Without an understanding of the context in which a policy emerges, it is neither possible to adequately understand the policy nor to strategise a response to it.

If critical policy analysis is to understand the context in which a policy arises, to evaluate how policy making processes are arranged, to assess its content in terms of a particular set of educational values, to investigate whose interests the policy serves, to explore how it might contribute to political advocacy, to examine how a policy has been implemented, and with what outcomes and so on, then it is clear that policy analysis cannot be located in any particular disciplinary tradition. Hence, in our view, critical policy analysis represents a synthesising, interdisciplinary field of study, which is relevant to the work of both the state and civil society. It can contribute to an understanding of a policy already in place or help create pressures towards a new policy agenda. In this way, critical policy analysis can be both reactive and proactive. Its technical role lies in the assessment of the available information in order to identify new options. It can promote an understanding of the policy by explaining the links between local practices and external contexts.

These, then, are the matters taken up in this book. In the following

chapter we provide an overview of the *dimensions and scope* of public policy – and the position of education policy within this – while in Chapter
Three we focus on methodological issues, in particular exploring *critical
approaches* to educational policy analysis. In Chapter Four our analytical
focus shifts to the *international and global dimensions* of policy making and
the relationship between these and policy making at the national level.
These three chapters provide the theoretical grounding for the book. In
Chapters Five, Six and Seven we turn to more substantive arenas of policy: educational restructuring, vocational education and training, and
social justice respectively. In these chapters, the focus is more explicitly
Australian though in all cases the *policy issues* raised have broader application. Chapter Five examines the impetus for, and various manifestations of, *educational restructuring* which have occurred in Australia, as
elsewhere, over the past decade or so, while Chapter Six explores the
imperatives driving policy trends in *vocationalising general education*.
Again the Australian experience is used to point to more general policy
issues. Chapter Seven, drawing on some policy case studies, canvasses
some of the complexities of policy development in the area of *social justice* given the predominant economic framing of education described in
previous chapters. In the final chapter we examine the complex and
problematic *relationship between educational policy and social change* alluded
to in this opening chapter, looking at policy practices in terms of the
question, Does policy matter?, and exploring the various ways in which
policies can lead to, and also sometimes inhibit, educational change.

Chapter 2

What is policy?

Social policies, it becomes clear, are not responses to social problems already formed and 'out there'. Social policies constitute the problems to which they seem to be responses. They are involved in problem-setting, the setting of agendas.

(Anna Yeatman 1990: 158)

INTRODUCTION

In the previous chapter we illustrated a number of types of educational policies, ranging from Commonwealth policies, through those developed by State Departments of Education to those produced in schools by school communities, including administrators, teachers and parents. In our discussions of policy and policy making in this book we include all these types of policies. While there are some differences in policy making at these different levels, they also have much in common in terms of the policy processes involved. The traditional political science and public administration literature which deals with policy tends not to take such a broad approach. Rather, that literature focusses mainly on what is referred to as *public policy*, meaning government generated policies which are developed and implemented through state bureaucracies. This is reflected in one of the simplest definitions of policy as 'whatever governments choose to do, or not to do' (Dye 1992: 2). With Dye, we want to emphasise the area of non-decision making in the policy domain, as this may be equally significant in terms of the effects of government action.

Public policy, then, refers to all areas of government action stretching across the spectrum from economic policy to those policies usually referred to under the rubric of social policy, covering education, health and welfare areas. It is important to understand, though, how these different policy domains are interrelated in various ways. First, we need to note how economic policies and their effects, along with government attitudes to the budget process – for example, a commitment to the creation of an expansive welfare state (Keynesianism), or alternatively a commitment to a minimally interventionist and small state (monetarism) – frame and shape the possibilities in the other areas of public policy. More specifically, policy decisions in one area may have significant intended or unintended impacts in another. Take for example the case of Australia when, in the late 1980s in the face of high levels of youth unemployment, the federal government abolished unemployment benefits for sixteen and seventeen year olds which effectively raised the school leaving age.

Alternatively, government departments may work together to address particular issues. For example, in Queensland in the early 1990s the State government established an interdepartmental working party, with representatives from the Women's Policy Unit from the Premier's Department, the Health Department and the Education Department, to develop a strategy to address violence against women. Such collaboration may also occur across levels of government, State and Commonwealth, as in the case of the *Common and Agreed National Goals for Schooling in Australia* (Hobart Declaration) (Australian Education Council 1989), as well as *The National Policy for the Education of Girls in Australian Schools* (Commonwealth Schools Commission 1987), which we discuss further in the next chapter on policy analysis.

Keeping all of this in mind, in this chapter we attempt to define policy as both product and process and discuss various ways in which policies may be classified. Additionally, we elaborate upon some central concepts, practices and institutions which are crucial to understanding both conceptions of policy.

DEFINING POLICY

There is a vast literature within a number of disciplines, including political science, public administration and policy sociology, which attempts to define policy. The one thing all of these attempts have in common is their recognition that achieving such a definition is not an easy task. As Cunningham (1963: 229) suggests, policy is a bit like an elephant – you recognise one when you see it, but it is somewhat more difficult to define.

In a traditional introduction to policy analysis, Hogwood and Gunn (1984: 13–19) distinguish between 'policy as a label for a field of activity', 'policy as a general expression of general purpose or desired state of affairs', 'policy as specific proposals', 'policy as decisions of government', 'policy as formal authorisation', 'policy as a programme', 'policy as output', 'policy as outcome', 'policy as a theory or model' and 'policy as process'. Also operating within a traditional framework, Harman defines policy as:

the implicit or explicit specification of courses of purposive action being followed or to be followed in dealing with a recognised problem or matter of concern, and directed towards the accomplishment of some intended or desired set of goals. Policy also can be thought of as a position or stance developed in response to a problem or issue of conflict, and directed towards a particular objective.

(Harman 1984: 13)

However, we think there are several shortcomings with this definition in relation to how policy works in practice. We would want to stress the notion of policy as process, to refer to the politics involved in the recognition of a 'problem' which requires a policy response, through the formulation and implementation stages, including changes made along the way. Harman's definition appears to give the impression that there is general agreement when policies are generated and that they are implemented in a straightforward and unproblematic way, feeding into an oversimplified way of viewing policy. This view reflects functionalist assumptions about the way society works, that is, that society is underpinned by a value consensus and that the various institutions in society contribute to the ongoing stability of the whole. In contrast, our view of society draws on a conflict approach which sees society as consisting of competing groups having different values and access to power. Thus in relation to policy we need a definition which reflects the political nature of policy as a compromise which is struggled over at all stages by competing interests. As well as being imbued with functionalist ideas, the definition reflects a positivistic approach, that is, a particular approach to knowledge which purports to apply scientific method to solve policy problems. Our view is that policy problems are too complex to be solved in simple technicist ways.

Additionally, it must be recognised that the courses of action outlined in Harman's definition do not sit in a simple linear relationship with each other. Thus knowledge from practice may feed into ongoing modifications to the policy text, and policy processes are often complicated by the reality that they are occurring at a number of levels and within a number of arenas (Fulcher 1989). Wendy Johnson (1992), for example, in writing about the five-year phasing in of the abolition of corporal punishment in South Australian government schools, demonstrates how a directory of good practice from schools was an important component of the policy process. We would also emphasise that policy processes are ongoing and dynamic. When we describe policy we are thus attempting to capture and pin down something which is continually in process. This helps to explain why policy is so difficult to define.

In summary, then, we would stress that policy is much more than a specific policy document or text. Rather, policy is both process and product. In such a conceptualisation, policy involves the production of the text, the text itself, ongoing modifications to the text and processes of implementation into practice. Considine has nicely encapsulated such a view of policy in his statement that policy has more to do 'with recipes rather than blueprints, with cooking rather than engineering' (1994: 3). Hence, in contrast to the more prescriptive traditional approaches in policy, sometimes called *rational models*, which conceptualise policy in distinct and linear phases (policy development or formulation, implementation and evaluation), we see policy processes as being more complex, interactive and multi-layered. The South Australian example referred to above is an indication of a two-way interactive, top-down and bottom-up approach to policy development processes. Bowe *et al.* (1992: 20) refer to these relationships as the 'policy cycle'. Within this cycle, they refer to three interrelated contexts: the context of policy text production, the context of practice and the context of influence. In a more recent study, Ball (1994a: 26) has added two further contexts to the policy cycle conceptualisation. The first is the context of outcomes, which has two components, namely outcomes in policy practice, measured against the articulated goals of the policy, and outcomes in terms of social justice goals. The second additional context is that of political strategy, which operates in terms of our evaluations of the former two sets of outcomes. Taking all this into account, Ball is concerned to emphasise that:

> Policy is both text and action, words and deeds, it is what is enacted as well as what is intended. Policies are always incomplete insofar as they relate to or map on to the 'wild profusion' of local practice.
>
> (Ball 1994a: 10)

In emphasising policy as process in addition to policy as text, we have highlighted the political character of both the process and the text. Our position thus differs substantially from those who prescribe a rational approach to policy making. Such approaches usually require a set of chronological steps in policy development. These include: problem definition; clarification of values, goals and objectives; identification of options to achieve goals; cost/benefit analysis of options; selection of a course of action; evaluation of the course of action; and modification to the programme. While this might be a useful way to work through the policy processes, we would suggest that in reality most policy is developed in a more disjointed, less rational and more political fashion. Carley (1980), who advocates a rational approach to policy making, acknowledges that there are three elements to policy, namely political decisions about which values will be allocated, then a rational determination through steps similar to those listed above, and finally the need to recognise that the bureaucratic structure will also impact upon the actual policy achieved.

Our view of policy differs from Carley's in that we believe that, in practice, it is not possible to delineate and separate the elements so clearly. For example, one of us was involved in the development of a classification system for disadvantaged schools for a State department of education in Australia. We were required to utilise Australian Bureau of Statistics (ABS) data on a range of socio-economic measures to develop an index of disadvantage to classify schools so that equity monies could be distributed to those schools serving the most disadvantaged communities. Supposedly, we were the 'rational' experts employed to carry out the technical work after the political decision to initiate the Disadvantaged Schools Program had been made. What we very quickly found, however, was that the seemingly rational process of creating indices of disadvantage was fraught with political questions of which statistics would be used – income, occupation, educational levels, housing, Aboriginality and so on – to measure disadvantage. Further, one index meant that certain schools would receive benefits which would be denied to other schools, while different indices derived from different components from the ABS had different effects. In the end we accepted an index which most closely confirmed the 'expert' view of those who worked in the various regions of the State on the programme, indicating very clearly the ongoing and interactive rational/political character of the policy development process.

In terms of the stages of policy formulation, Rein (1983: 211) has suggested that at least three steps are involved. These are problem setting, the 'mobilization of the fine structure of government action' and the 'achievement of settlements in the face of dilemmas and trade-offs among values'. The latter trade-offs are manifested in the actual policy text. Rein's observation is a recognition of the politics involved in policy formulation and is more in line with the stance we are adopting. In terms of policy implementation, or the processes which occur after the creation of a policy text, Rein argues that implementation processes are best seen as an attempt 'to resolve conflicts among authoritative, rational and consensual imperatives' (1983: 135). This is why he also speaks of 'the politics of implementation' (p. 113). Raab's comment about policy processes – 'the pudding eaten is a far cry from the original recipe' (1994: 24) – nicely captures the slippages and refractions involved in policy implementation. In a similar fashion, McLaughlin (1987), after reviewing the implementation literature in education in the US, notes that bargaining and negotiation are involved at all stages. This is also in line with our position: that it is important to recognise policy processes as inherently political in character and involving compromises, trade-offs and settlements.

We have already mentioned that there are competing interests in the policy process and that policies represent compromises over struggles.

This highlights the value laden nature of policies and again emphasises the highly political nature of policy processes. In an old but influential formulation, Easton defines policy as 'a web of decisions and actions that allocates values' (1953: 129–30). Prunty (1984, 1985), whose work has been influential in critical educational policy analysis, builds on this approach by defining policy as 'the authoritative allocation of values' (1985: 136), in recognition of the fact that policies are never value free and that power and control are central in policy processes. Within traditional sociology, authority is recognised as the legitimate right to exercise power. In Australia and other comparable societies, it is governments that 'control' state institutions (following election victories) and that have the legitimate right to allocate values through policy development.

There are debates within sociology about whose values are allocated in the policy process and whose interests these values represent. First there are those accounts which accept a dispersal of values and power throughout society and argue that governments attempt to please as many interest groups in the policy process as possible. This is the *pluralist approach*. In contrast, the *elitist approach* sees governments as acting in relation to the values and interests of dominant groups. *Neo-marxist approaches* take this position even further in arguing that those who 'control' the economy have more political influence than others. Within such accounts there is a distinction between those who see this relationship as tightly deterministic and those who see it as more indirect – acknowledging that governments sometimes act against the interests of the economically powerful. *Feminist approaches* may be pluralist, elitist or neo-marxist but all see the state as operating to reproduce male interests and power.

Our position is that dominant groups in society, for example big business, are more likely to be able to influence governments in their exercise of power. Indeed, certain groups achieve formalised – institutionalised – access to policy making. For example, under federal Labour governments in Australia in the early 1990s, the Business Council of Australia and the Australian Council of Trade Unions became part of the policy process in the development of the national training reform agenda, while women's groups and indigenous people were marginalised. As Ball comments, 'Policies embody claims to speak with authority, they legitimate and initiate practices in the world and they privilege certain visions and interests' (1990: 22). We would add that there will always be political struggles over whose voices will be heard and whose values will be reflected in policies.

Some recent approaches to policy draw on post-structuralism, and particularly on Michel Foucault's theory of the relationship between power and knowledge in which discourse is a key concept (Fulcher 1989, Ball 1990, Bowe *et al.* 1992, Ball 1994a). From this perspective, policy making is seen as an arena of struggle over meaning, or as 'the politics of discourse' (Yeatman 1990). The emphasis is on policy processes and policy is seen as 'struggle between contenders of competing objectives, where language – or more specifically discourse – is used tactically' (Fulcher 1989: 7). For example, in her study of the development and implementation of integration policy in Victoria, Fulcher found that within the overarching discourse of 'integration' were embedded two competing discourses: the 'rights' discourse articulated by parents of students with disabilities, and the discourse of professionalism of the special educators. Struggles such as these are viewed as occurring at all levels and in all arenas of policy making. For example, Fulcher (1989) identified policy arenas at six different levels in the Victorian education system, ranging from School Council Subcommittees on Integration to the Regional Board. Such contestation and struggle is often reflected in the form of tensions and contradictions, or competing discourses, in the resulting policies themselves.

Within a politics of discourse framework, then, policy texts represent the outcome of political struggles over meaning. Codd argues that: 'Fundamentally policy is about the exercise of political power and the language that is used to legitimate that process' (1988: 235). He further elaborates:

> policy documents can be said to constitute the official discourse of the state (Codd 1985). Thus policies produced by and for the state are obvious instances in which language serves a political purpose, constructing particular meanings and signs that work to mask social conflict and foster commitment to the notion of universal public interest. In this way, policy documents produce real social effects through the production and maintenance of consent.
>
> (Codd 1988: 237)

Ball (1994a) makes a distinction between policy as text and policy as discourse. He utilises the distinction in relation to the agency of *policy actors*, the name often given to significant agents in policy making, and the structural constraints under which they work, with both agency and structure implicit in each other. Within a literary theory approach he sees policy as text as allowing for agency in the policy cycle, with the readers of policy being able to interpret the text in a variety of ways. In contrast, drawing on Foucault's approach to discourse analysis, Ball sees policy as discourse as a way of indicating the significance of power relations in framing interpretations of policy texts.

In summary, then, we want to stress that policy is more than simply the policy text; it also involves processes prior to the articulation of the text and the processes which continue after the text has been produced, both in modifications to it as a statement of values and desired action, and in actual practice. Furthermore, contestation is involved right from the moment of the appearance of an issue on the policy agenda, through the initiation of action to the inevitable trade-offs involved in formulation and implementation. Contestation is played out in regard to whose voices are heard and whose values are recognised or 'authoritatively allocated' in the policy and which groups ultimately benefit as a result of the policy. At the same time, however, we acknowledge the complexity – 'the messy realities' (Ball 1990: 9) and 'the evolving chaos' (Brieschke 1989/90: 305) – of policy and policy processes.

POLICY AND THE STATE

In understanding the power issues involved in policy processes, we need to recognise the importance of the state, which consists of political, judicial and administrative institutions which have a complex relationship with the government of the day. While judges are government appointed, there is a tradition of judicial independence, and while public service departments and the bureaucrats who work within them are supposedly there to enact government agendas, at the same time they are expected to provide independent advice to the government. This tension is nicely encapsulated in the TV series *Yes, Minister*, where we see the different and often conflicting interests of the politicians and senior bureaucrats.

It can clearly be seen, then, that the state is not a unitary entity to which can be ascribed purposeful action, nor is it a straightforward instrument of powerful groups external to it such as transnational corporations. Rather, the state can be conceptualised as a set of processes which collectively have particular outcomes. Furthermore, the state consists of a large number of entities – public service departments and statutory authorities of various kinds – which often have conflicting interests; for example, compare Treasury with Social Security. Indeed even within the same public service department there can be very real disagreements and struggles over policy directions. In the Australian policy context there is the added complexity resulting from a federal political structure. Painter refers to policy making in federalism as 'politics with extra vitamins' and suggests that federalism 'distorts, enlarges, diminishes, confuses, frustrates and stimulates' (1988: 65) all at once. Federalism draws our attention to the existence of two significant arenas of educational policy making within the Australian polity, federal and State governments. However, as we elaborate in more detail in Chapters Four and Five, these arenas in turn form part of a larger – international or global – polity, which has implications for educational policy making at the level of the nation state.

What salience then should we accord to the state in policy processes? We would agree with the observation of Davis and his coauthors that:

The state is a complex structure which defies precise definition, but which remains of crucial importance in understanding the contours of public policy. It is a crucial starting point because the state translates values, interests and resources into objectives and policies.

(Davis *et al*. 1993: 19)

However, some feminist, post-structuralist and postmodernist writers have argued that the idea of the state is too abstract to be of value, or that the significance and political impact of the nation state is diminishing (Allen 1990, Crook *et al*. 1992, Hoffman 1995). Others argue in a normative sense against a state-centred politics (Hinkson 1991, Yeatman 1994). Related to this playing down of the state by these theorists is their conceptualisation of power. Drawing on Foucault (1980), they work with a conception of power as diffuse and productive rather than centralised and oppressive, as in more traditional approaches. For various reasons, then, such writers focus instead on specific sites and instances of policy making – similar in some respects to policy cycle theorists. However, for Hatcher and Troyna the policy cycle approach 'distorts understandings of the policy process, especially in the relative powers which it assigns to the central apparatus of the state and to the schools' (1994: 156), a position with which we would largely agree.

Offe's (1975, 1984) work is useful in helping to clarify the relationship between the state and policy development. It provides an account of the state in capitalist societies as a set of institutions which has to balance irresolvable tensions between the need to ensure that the economy continues to function in a satisfactory fashion so that state revenues can be generated, and the need for the state to respond to political and democratic demands upon it for policy coverage. Offe's view is that the state can never 'solve' this problem, but simply comes to settlements which seek to manage the tensions between what he calls *accumulation* and *legitimation* functions of the state. As Castles puts it: 'The state is at one and the same time the guardian angel of the capitalist economic process and the chosen instrument for protecting society from the corrosive impact of that process' (1988: 4). Furthermore, Offe argues that state structures mediate the policy process, 'determining' to some extent what issues get on to the policy agenda and how, the possible policy options available and policy outcomes.

Offe's account, then, is really about the mediation of the policy process by state structures. State structures refer here to the political organisation of the state (for example, federal or unitary forms of government) and to the administrative structure of particular departments. So, for example, having a social justice division within a state department of education makes it more likely that social justice issues will be taken up in policy development than might be the case in a department which simply has a junior officer to handle Commonwealth monies for social justice purposes. This symbiotic relationship between policy processes and state structures is picked up in Offe's observation that:

> it is not only true that the emergence of a social problem puts into motion the procedural dynamics of policy formation, program design, and implementation, but also, conversely, the institutionalized formal mode of political institutions determines what potential issues are, how they are defined, what solutions are proposed, and so on.
>
> (Offe 1975: 135)

Ball has argued there is a third field of problems for the state in addition to those encapsulated by Offe as accumulation and legitimation. These are 'the technical and managerial problems of the state itself' (1994a: 5). As will be shown in Chapter Five, states in the so-called advanced industrial nations have significantly reorganised their management structures, with considerable impact upon educational systems and educational policy. We would additionally argue, following Jessop (1990), that the state itself is a 'strategic-relational' terrain upon which state actors (bureaucrats) also struggle over policy texts and processes (see also Lingard 1993b). Consequently, the state is not only a mediator of policy via its structures, but also a terrain upon which individual policy actors struggle to achieve desired political outcomes. Lingard (1995), for example, has shown how femocrats – feminists employed by the state – 'strategised', that is acted politically, to achieve desired gender equity goals. Tripcony (1995) has offered a similar account of the internal and external pressures experienced by Aboriginal people employed by the state. Thus state policy actors are not simply neutral conduits for policy pressures placed upon them, but are involved in micropolitics inside the state. Policy actors are also linked into 'issues networks' (Weiss 1986) comprised of academics, consultants and interest group representatives, which form part of what is sometimes referred to as the *policy community*. Our view, then, is that both state structures and state policy workers rearticulate policy pressures in the move from the articulation of a problem on to the policy agenda to the generation of the policy text.

The work that bureaucrats do inside the state is often referred to as *administration*. In the traditional public policy literature, a distinction is often made between policy making which is deemed to be legislated by politicians, and administration of policy which is deemed to be the responsibility of bureaucrats. However, while recognising the significance of legislation as a framework for policy making, we do not regard such a distinction as useful. The state today is so large and complex that much policy has its gestation within the bureaucracy, rather than from a legislative framework or from a minister or political party. Thus politicians and bureaucrats both administer and formulate policy or, as

Anderson puts it, 'Policy is being made as it is being administered and administered as it is being made' (1975: 98).

We have been discussing the role of policy bureaucrats working within central administrations. Lipsky (1980) has developed the concept of *street level bureaucrats* to refer to other state workers – those at the 'coalface' who are responsible for the actual delivery of a policy into practice. Street level bureaucrats develop strategies in order to cope with the myriad pressures they face in the work situation, which result in the *adaptation* of centrally imposed policies rather than their straightforward implementation. Clearly there are some parallels here with the position of teachers who are asked to implement policies emanating from head office at the 'chalkface'.

Earlier, we noted Offe's suggestion that the state does not so much solve policy problems, as arrive at what we might call 'settlements', which provide a temporary solution to a policy problem. We find this concept of *settlement* quite useful in understanding how, at different historical moments, the state comes to large-scale settlements which then frame up the options in specific policy domains. So, for example, we can compare the Keynesian welfare state settlement from the postwar period until the mid-1970s with the subsequent search for a post-Keynesian settlement which has witnessed a resurgence of liberal economic ideology, and which seeks to give precedence to the market over the state as the major steering mechanism in societies like Australia (Pusey 1991). This has seen the establishment of what Cerny (1990) has called the 'competition state', a post-Keynesian settlement where the state grants policy priority to internationalising the economy with consequent implications for education.

Terri Seddon's definition of settlement is useful for our purposes. She notes:

> A settlement is a truce or compromise which establishes a framework for policy and practice. Within this framework disagreements and conflicts occur, but there is agreement over what to disagree about, over the mechanisms for resolving that conflict and over the range of what might be acceptable resolutions. Contesting and reconstructing the framework is not a major agenda item.
>
> (Seddon 1989: 18)

It should be noted, however, that the word settlement has been used in a number of ways. Jane Kenway (1990) has used the concept in a narrower sense in relation to policy texts and their surrounding pressures to indicate the suturing together of different interests. She observes that: 'Policy represents the temporary settlements between diverse, competing, and unequal forces within civil society, within the state itself and between associated discursive regimes' (Kenway 1990: 59). Thus Kenway, unlike some discourse theorists, acknowledges the significance of the state to policy making.

Hence we see an understanding of the state as important in theorising policy. We emphasise that the state is not a unitary entity, while also rejecting a view that it is a straightforward instrument of powerful groups external to it. However, as we argued earlier, some groups have more influence in setting policy agendas than others. In this context, we need to recognise the gendered (Franzway *et al*. 1989) and racialised (Troyna and Williams 1986) nature of the operation of the state and its bureaucracies.

TYPES OF POLICY

A number of different ways of classifying policies utilising binary distinctions are distinguished in the policy literature. In this section we illustrate some of these different categories with reference to specific policies, noting that these distinctions may be somewhat arbitrary or overly simplistic, and that their meanings may change over time and in different contexts. Additionally, it is sometimes possible to classify an actual policy as manifesting characteristics of the two arms of the binary distinction within a category.

Policies can be analysed as *distributive* or *redistributive* according to how any allocation of resources or benefits is made. Distributive policies involve straightforward allocation of resources or benefits or entitlements, for example if an allowance is provided for all students for school books or uniforms. However, if such an allowance is provided to a targeted group through means testing, the policy could be said to be redistributive in character. Many special needs policies are of this redistributive nature, for example additional resources granted to schools under the Disadvantaged Schools Programme in Australia. Other redistributive policies would include special allowances made available for geographically isolated students to attend boarding schools.

The *symbolic* and *material* distinction refers to the extent of commitment to implementation by those responsible for formulating a given policy. Regarding this distinction, Rein (1983) has written that the implementation of a given policy will be affected significantly by three factors: the clarity of the goals of the policy, the complexity of the implementation process and the extent or otherwise of the resource commitment to the policy. Material policies include a commitment to implementation through the provision of resources, whereas these are absent for symbolic policies. A good example of a symbolic policy is the Queensland Education Department's 1981 policy *Equality of Opportunity in Education for Girls and Boys* – just half a page in the *Education Gazette* (Lingard *et al*. 1987). This policy was developed in response both to the availability of

Commonwealth funding and to pressures on the State department to develop such a policy. No State government funds were allocated and initially there was little attempt to implement the policy in schools. Symbolic policies tend to have broad, vague, ambiguous, abstract goal statements with little or no resource commitment and little thought given to implementation strategies. Indeed, the extent of resource commitment will often tell us much about the extent of political support for a given policy. In general, then, symbolic policies are weaker than material policies. However, it should not be thought that symbolic policies are necessarily unimportant. Symbolic policies can have a strategic function in legitimising the views of certain groups and altering the political climate in which issues are discussed (Rein 1983: 131). For example, the Queensland policy referred to above legitimated the actions of feminist teachers in schools throughout the State. Another example is the case of the Reconciliation Process with Aboriginal and Torres Strait Islander people in Australia, an initiative of the Keating Labour government, operating at a cultural level to change broader societal attitudes. The development of a symbolic policy may be the first stage of an ongoing political strategy. Once an issue gets on to the policy agenda, pressure can be subsequently directed at strengthening the policy and the financial commitment to it – depending upon the extent of political support for the policy in the electorate.

In the traditional public policy literature, a distinction is made between *rational* and *incremental* approaches to policy and policy development. As indicated earlier, rational advocates outline a set of prescriptive stages for the development of policy. On the other hand, incrementalists argue that policy development works over time by building on currently existing policies and practices. Even with a change of government, incrementalists argue that policy usually defines itself in relation to what went before. For example, in their policy analysis of the Hawke government's Participation and Equity Programme in Victoria, Rizvi and Kemmis (1987) show how the existing discourses, practices and structures related to the earlier Transition Education Program, thus ensuring that some incrementalism occurred in policy development. Our discussion of the history of gender equity policies in Australia in the next chapter also provides examples of incrementalism.

A further distinction is made in the policy literature between *substantive* and *procedural* policies. Substantive policies deal with what governments are intending to do, and procedural policies with how things are to be done and by whom. For example, the Queensland Department of Education's Social Justice Strategy was developed in the early 1990s in the form of a brief rationale and statement of principles. As such, it could be said at that stage to have been a substantive policy. When it was fully developed with resources and guidelines for implementation, it could

also be classified as a procedural policy because it outlined re
ties for implementation across the system.

Policies in the equity and social justice area tend to be of a reg
character, that is, they are about controlling practices. Thus, for exai
sexual harassment policy seeks to prohibit certain behaviours. By c
trast, *deregulatory* policies are usually associated with an ideological con-
mitment to minimal government – or state intervention – often
associated with the release of market forces. Such policies are not concerned with overt control, though more subtle mechanisms of control
may emerge in devolved systems. Deregulatory impulses have underpinned much policy development in recent years, for example in vocational education and training in order to encourage more industry
involvement, and in the funding of higher education in order to reduce
levels of government support.

We have already mentioned the distinction between *top-down* and *bottom-up* approaches in policy development in relation to the abolition of
corporal punishment in South Australia. Top-down approaches are those
where the policy is formulated, say, in a central department of education
and then disseminated and distributed 'down' through the system to
schools. In contrast, a bottom-up policy builds on currently existing practice and pressures for change. Thus, for example, the National Schools
Network seeks to document good practice for reforming schools from
current good practice in schools.

CONCLUSION

Throughout this chapter we have provided an account of policy as text,
but also as process. Policy processes accrue both prior to the production
of a policy text and afterwards, through the stages of implementation
and reinterpretation. Policy is rearticulated as it is recontextualised
across the policy cycle. This is why it is difficult to pin policy down and
give it a simple definition. We have also argued the significance of the
state in policy processes and considered different categories of policy. At
the outset of the chapter we noted Dye's simple definition of policy as
'whatever governments choose to do, or not to do' (1992: 2). Building on
this definition of policy, a simple definition of policy *analysis* might be,
'the study of what governments do, why and with what effects'. It is
these matters and the interactive processes involved that form the focus
of policy analysis and to which we next turn in Chapter Three.

Chapter 3

Doing policy analysis

[T]he problem always remains that by focusing on the figures which move across the policy landscape we may neglect the geomorphology of the land-scape itself and changes in its terrain and substructure. On the other hand, a preoccupation with dominant modes of political rationality and global eco-nomic forces may lead to a misleading neglect of transformative activities and the possibility of surprise.

(Stephen Ball 1994b: 118)

INTRODUCTION

This chapter attempts to provide an introductory framework for thinking about the practices of policy analysis in education. The working out of this framework will become clearer in subsequent chapters when the focus will turn to specific policy developments. What we want to empha-sise at this point, however, is that there is no recipe approach for doing policy analysis. For example, there is a substantial difference between broad system-wide policy frameworks for, say, vocational education and training, and the processes involved in the development of a school dis-cipline policy. Thus the approaches to policy analysis will depend at one level on the actual nature and site of production of the policy. Clearly there are other relevant factors here, including the position and institu-tional location of the analyst, and the purposes for which the analysis is being carried out. These issues will be elaborated further throughout this chapter.

Perhaps a useful way to begin this discussion is to ask, What are the purposes of policy analysis? The answer to this will help frame the sorts of questions we ask. Some traditional policy literature makes a distinc-tion between *analysis of* and *analysis for* policy (Gordon *et al.* 1977). The former is viewed as a more academic task, while the latter is usually regarded as referring to the policy research conducted within education-al bureaucracies in the process of policy production and evaluation. However, Cibulka (1994: 107) conceptualises policy research as operating on a continuum between academic and applied policy analysis. We would not want to see academic policy analysis as simply a critical academic exercise with no political value; thus we would reject any absolute distinction between *analysis of* and *analysis for* policy as being somewhat artificial, though in some circumstances the distinction may be conceptually useful. Academic policy analysis can be utilised by teachers, teacher unionists, politicians and workers within the state to various political ends. While making this point, we would also acknowledge the argument proffered by Richard Smith (1982) that the more critical the analysis is, the less likely it is to have an impact in the short term. We would also support his argument that because of their position and location it is probably more difficult for those within educational bureaucracies to offer more critical analyses. However, many state workers strategise towards progressive policy outcomes within the constraints of their positions. Such workers often utilise critical policy analysis carried out in more academic arenas in these internal political struggles, and as Rein (1983) notes they will often have to 'play politics' to achieve policy gains. These issues are highlighted when academic policy researchers undertake consultancies for government departments and they too have to take account of political constraints. So, to reiterate, the sorts of questions asked in policy analysis depend on its purpose, the position of the analyst and the presence of any constraints which may be operating on him or her.

Our stance is that in critical policy analysis there must be a concern with reform and change, recognising of course that these are value-laden terms. Thus Henry, for instance, has argued that critical policy analysis is 'a value laden activity which explicitly or implicitly makes judgements as to whether and in what ways policies help to make things better' (1993: 104). Consequently, we have an interest in exploring the values and assumptions which underlie policies and the related issues of power, leading to questions such as, 'In whose interests?' and 'Who are the winners and losers?' in any particular policy initiative. Feminist policy analysis, for example, will ask these questions with a particular focus on the implications for women and girls and for broader gender relations (see, for example, Williams 1989, Blackmore and Kenway 1993).

QUESTIONS FOR POLICY ANALYSIS

There are different approaches to policy analysis within the literature, with each approach tending to ask different questions. For example, we have just referred to feminist policy analysis and the kinds of questions which characterise such an approach. In addition to feminism, the major traditions in policy analysis are positivism, interpretivism and critical policy analysis. The North American literature refers to the 'policy sciences', a term first used by Lasswell in 1949 (Deleon 1994: 77). Most of this early literature tended to be positivistic in its methodology and functionalist in assumptions. While this work continues, and is particularly evident in political science, some more recent work in the US is critical of this tradition and is generally referred to as *interpretive* – meaning that it takes an anti-positivist methodological stance (Hawkesworth 1988, Marshall 1993). In the British and Australian literature, work taking a similar methodological stance tends to be termed *critical* and includes neo-marxist approaches utilising conflict rather than functionalist perspectives. Critical sociological approaches are informed by more radical European theoretical traditions, drawing on the work of the social theorists known collectively as the Frankfurt School, and more recently on the work of Habermas. As Prunty (1985) has explained, critical theorists have only relatively recently extended their analyses of schooling processes to examine educational administration and policy. Recent work within a broader critical tradition in policy analysis also includes post-structuralist and feminist approaches.

There is another distinction between the North American context and the European and Australian contexts which it is probably useful to make. In the US, educational policy analysis as an academic field has tended to fit within the politics of education, while in Europe and Australia educational policy has traditionally been located within educational administration, with more recent critical work developing out of the sociology of education. Some of this critical work in the educational policy literature uses the term *policy sociology* which Jenny Ozga suggests is 'rooted in the social science tradition, historically informed and drawing on qualitative and illuminative techniques' (1987: 144).

Troyna (1994: 81–2), however, rejects any dichotomy between policy sociology and other approaches using a social science perspective, basically because he believes that the former under-emphasises feminist and anti-racist work, and fails to provide analyses which offer strategies for change. Troyna emphasises the need for linkages between critical policy analysis and critical social research and for an approach which is interested not only in what is going on and why, but also in doing something about it. Thus drawing on Harvey (1990), Troyna stresses that 'critical social research includes an overt political struggle against oppressive social structures' (1994: 72) and, we would add, practices. To be most useful in this context, policy analysis needs to concern itself with the question of how progressive change might occur and the desirability of alternative policy options. We agree with Troyna's position; this is the approach we take throughout the book, and which is illustrated in the case studies in this and later chapters.

In reflecting on critical policy analysis, Stephen Ball (1994a) advocates an open and creative approach which emphasises finding the appropriate theory and concepts for the task at hand, rather than narrowly applying a particular theory which may close off possibilities for interpretation. According to Ball: 'The task, then, is to examine the moral order of reform and the relationship of reform to existing patterns of social inequality, bringing to bear those concepts and interpretive devices which offer the best possibilities of insight and understanding' (1994a: 2). Similarly, in recent North American policy literature there has been a concern to recover the 'Lasswellian tradition' of the development of an interdisciplinary 'policy sciences of democracy', an approach which it is claimed has been lost as a result of the dominance of positivism (Fischer 1989).

Moving from these broader issues, Jane Kenway's (1990: 24) 'what', 'how' and 'why' questions are most useful as a way to begin to think about policy analysis. More specifically, Kenway asks, 'what is the approach to education?' in terms of curriculum, assessment, and forms of pedagogy; 'how are such proposals organised?' in terms of funding and staffing arrangements, authority and administrative structures; and 'why have they been selected?' This last question relates to more general sociological questions such as:

Why was this policy adopted?
On whose terms? Why?
On what grounds have these selections been justified? Why?
In whose interests? Indeed, how have competing interests been negotiated?

(Kenway 1990: 24)

We would want to add a further question, namely, 'Why now? Why is this particular policy on the agenda at this particular time?' This moves our focus to issues of policy production and to the broader policy context. Policy analysis is also concerned with exploring the impact of a particular policy when it is implemented, and so we also need to ask a final question: 'What are the consequences?' In relation to this question, Ball (1994a: 26) distinguishes between first order (practice) effects which relate to the goals of the policy, and second order outcomes relating to social justice.

In doing policy analysis, we need to keep in mind a distinction between policy *per se* and the substantive issues with which a specific policy deals. These matters are dealt with in Kenway's 'what' and 'how' questions. Some analysts suggest that the very first task in policy analysis is to focus on the issue itself. There is a need to do this so that we are able to assess how the policy is likely to work in relation to the problems it is addressing. For example, Gil suggests the first task in 'unravelling social policy' is 'to gain understanding of the issues that constitute the focus of a specific social policy which is being analysed or developed.

This involves exploration of the nature, scope and distribution of these issues, and of causal theories concerning underlying dynamics' (1989: 69). However, given that policy is often as much about problem setting as problem solving, there are often difficulties in separating the policy and the issues, because policies frame policy issues in particular ways. This point is taken up later in the chapter.

RESEARCH FOR POLICY ANALYSIS

Although some attention has been given to the development of 'policy oriented qualitative research' (Finch 1984), there has not been much of a focus upon research methodology for policy analysis within the educational policy literature. As Ball (1990: 9) has noted, the field of policy analysis has been dominated by commentary and critique rather than empirical research. It would appear that methodological questions about what data or material we need for analysis and how we collect that material, have been less important in critical policy work than the theoretical frameworks which are used and the questions which are asked. Until recently, therefore, not much attention has been given to methodological questions in policy literature – except in the US where there is an extensive body of literature dealing with policy evaluation and implementation studies. Much of this has been technicist and uncritical in approach, although, as we have mentioned, a more critical literature has emerged in recent years (see, for example, Hawkesworth 1988). In the British context, Halpin and Troyna's (1994) edited collection has helped to redress the lack of concern for methodological issues within critical educational policy analysis.

Different research traditions in policy analysis have grown up in different national contexts. For example, as noted above, policy research in the US has tended to focus upon evaluation and implementation studies within a positivist, pluralist and largely functionalist framework (McLaughlin 1987). In the UK some policy research also fits within pluralist assumptions utilising a case study approach (McPherson and Raab 1989). However, other studies are influenced by neo-marxist perspectives focussing on the workings of the state (Dale 1989). Some of these studies are of the commentary and critique type, while others are studies of elites using ethnographic approaches to explore the role of 'key players' in the processes of policy formulation (Ball 1990). It is interesting that in Australia, notwithstanding some case study work conducted at Deakin University (for example, Rizvi and Kemmis 1987), much critical policy work has tended to highlight at an abstract level the operation of the state without investigating actual operations at local sites. In this way these studies have been state-centric. This may well be related to the particular contexts of educational policy making, that is, the greater control over education policy which the Commonwealth and State governments have in Australia compared with the situation in the UK, where policy making has occurred more at the local level – although this has changed significantly since the centralising impact of the 1988 Education Reform Act. The state-centric character of much critical educational policy analysis in the Australian context also reflects the traditionally state-centric character of Australian political culture. In addition, until recently Australia has had federal and State Labour governments and, as a result, critical academics have not been excluded from policy processes in the same way as has occurred in the UK under a lengthy period of Conservative political hegemony.

We have briefly discussed the variety of approaches to policy research and considered the sorts of questions we might ask in critical policy analysis. The particular questions we ask will influence the kind of information or data we will need to collect in policy research. For example, if we were concerned with the gestation of a given policy we might interview key policy makers within the state and perhaps some relevant pressure groups. If we were interested in the content of a policy text, we might only need the particular policy document itself and associated documentary material, including minutes of meetings, perhaps submissions and other cognate policies. If we were more interested in implementation issues, we might conduct several case studies at school sites of the policy in practice.

It will be evident that all of the examples given above utilise qualitative methods. This reflects the fact that policy research is aiming to unravel the complexities of the policy process, a task for which qualitative approaches in our view are better. This is not to deny a place for quantitative methods within critical policy research, either alone or in combination with qualitative methods. For example, the statistical data provided by Teese *et al.* (1995) demonstrate the complexity of the relationships between gender and social class in school subject choices and school performance, and have contributed in important ways to an understanding of the issues and subsequent policy development.

There are some additional challenges which accompany the pursuit of qualitative methods which are related to the politics of research. Qualitative approaches within policy research require access to key players in the policy process who are very often powerful politicians, political advisers and senior bureaucrats. Questions of access to such people can become an issue, particularly for students conducting research. There is also a politics which goes on in the actual interview situation, or indeed in participant observation of meetings. Whereas in the past researchers tended to gloss over the impact of their presence within the research situation, more recently there has been a trend towards exploring and addressing the position of the researcher. These are issues which hàve been highlighted by feminist researchers for some time (Roberts 1981), but have lately been raised within the general qualitative research methodology literature (Le Compte *et al.* 1992). In addition, Ozga and Gewirtz (1994) have written specifically about their experience as women policy researchers interviewing past and present senior policy makers. We also need to remember that when people are being interviewed, they will provide an account from their perspective which may include a distorted or magnified perception of their role in relation to a particular policy. For this reason, it is important to access as many accounts and sources as possible in order to move towards as complete a picture as possible. There are also many related ethical issues here to do with anonymity of informants and confidentiality of the information they provide.

Maguire and Ball (1994) have usefully outlined three orientations to qualitative work in policy research in the UK. The first of these is elite studies, which involve either a focus on long-term policy trends through life history methods involving past and present senior policy makers (Gewirtz and Ozga 1990), or interview-based research on specific contemporary educational policy developments (Ball 1990). The second category of policy research they classify as 'trajectory studies' which involve elite studies of policy text production as the first stage in the research agenda. Trajectory studies thus follow a specific policy through the stages of gestation, the micropolitics inside the state involved in text production, and through case studies of the implementation of the policy into practice. Thus, for example, in their study of the Assisted Places Scheme in the English context, Edwards *et al.* (1989) began their research with detailed interviews with key players in the policy process, examined documentary material and moved through to case studies of implementation at the school level and interviews with parents. In an Australian example of a trajectory study, Henry and Taylor (1995a) documented refractions in various levels of the policy process in the first stages of the implementation of the Carmichael Report on the Australian Vocational Certificate Training System. The third category identified by Maguire and Ball is implementation studies, which focus on 'interpretation of and engagement in policy texts and the translation of these texts into practice' (1994: 280). These studies tend to use participant observation methods together with interviews within critical, ethnographic case study traditions. An example of this kind of study is Mac an Ghaill's (1991) research on teacher responses to the implementation of vocational education policies in an inner-city comprehensive school in the UK, and the resistance of those who felt that equal opportunities policies were more important.

Much education policy research, as Maguire and Ball (1994) note, has been methodologically unsophisticated, with issues of language and

meaning taken for granted. However, recent theoretica.
around post-structuralism have been useful in offering 'a ᴵ
to begin to try to explain things' (Ball 1990: 18). Post-struₗ
gest that there is a close nexus between power and knowle
meaning is constructed historically in contested social domaι
1980). This has led to an increasing emphasis on matters of n
a related shift towards exploring the effects of policy, rather tₗ ₋. simply
focussing on policy intentions (Codd 1988, Ball 1990). For example, in the
previous chapter we discussed the influence of discourse theory on policy studies and its value in conceptualising policy processes as the 'politics of discourse'. Applications of discourse theory allow valuable
fine-grained analyses of policy documents to be undertaken within a
broader structural analysis. The approach is also useful in highlighting
values and teasing out competing discourses, both in the development
and implementation stages of the policy process. Discourse analysis can
be used to help answer many of the major questions we have outlined
above by highlighting the subtleties of the ways language is used in policy making and illuminating how the policy process may work – particularly in relation to change.

Some fine-grained analyses of policy texts focus on language – exploring linguistic strategies used to position readers (McHoul 1984, Luke *et
al.* 1993), as well as the key words used (Kenway 1990: 63). For example,
Rizvi and Kemmis (1987: 276–7), in their analysis of the Participation and
Equity Programme policy statements and related documentation in
Victorian education, utilise Bourdieu and Passeron's (1977) notion of
'magisterial discourse' to describe the character of the language used.
They describe magisterial discourse as a style in which the speaker's
authority is demonstrated, which is 'unidirectional' in nature – 'it com-
mands and instructs' – and in so doing requires the reader to take note of
what is being said. Rizvi and Kemmis suggest that this type of language,
'which implies that the speaker is not only in authority but is also an
authority' (1987: 277), is now conventional in many government policies
and programmes. Bowe *et al.* (1992: 10–11) , drawing on the work of the
literary critic Roland Barthes, make a distinction between 'readerly' and
'writerly' texts, with the former limiting the possible readings, while the
latter are more open to multiple readings.

However, it is important that such fine-grained textual analyses are
placed in a broader context. Codd's formulation is useful here: 'Policy
documents . . . are ideological texts which have been constructed in a
particular context. The task of deconstruction begins with a recognition
of that context' (1988: 243–4). Discourse theory can be helpful in relation
to this task, for example in exploring the historical context of specific
policies and how policy 'problems' are constructed. It is also useful in
highlighting how policies come to be framed in certain ways, in other

words in pointing to the ways in which economic, social, political and cultural contexts shape both the content and language of policy documents. For example, discourse theory can be used to analyse significant changes in the framing of approaches to educational inequality, and in key concepts which have been used in education policies (Rizvi and Kemmis 1987, Connell and White 1989). Differences in terminology used reflect the particular historical and cultural context, and have implications for the ways in which relevant concepts are used and understood. As Apple puts it: 'Concepts do not remain still for very long. They have wings, so to speak, and can be induced to fly from place to place. It is this context which defines their meaning' (1993: 49). We utilise some of these newer approaches to methodology within our broader framework for critical policy analysis which we outline in the next section.

EXPLORING CONTEXTS, TEXTS AND CONSEQUENCES

In terms of levels of analysis of the policy process, some analysts make a distinction between 'macro' and 'micro' levels, while others use a 'macro', 'meso' or 'micro' distinction. Macro issues are seen as those which impact upon the whole policy making apparatus, for example global economic pressures; 'meso' is used to refer to the intermediary levels of policy making, for example, a state education department implementing a national policy; while 'micro' usually refers to policy making at the level of schools and classrooms. While these distinctions may sometimes be useful analytically, they will not always be appropriate as they are somewhat arbitrary and tend to oversimplify policy processes. In our view, there is a need to explore the multi-levelled character of policy processes, with particular emphasis on the articulations or linkages between the different levels. Bowe *et al.* (1992) emphasise the need to take account in policy analysis of the interactive, non-linear nature of the relationship between what they see as the three elements of the policy cycle – contexts of influence, text production and practice. Likewise, Ham and Hill (1993) point to the interconnections between more conventionally defined stages of policy formulation and implementation.

Policy analysis can be concerned with one or all of the stages or levels of the policy making process. However, analysis involves more than a narrow concern simply with a policy document or text. We need to understand both the background and context of policies, including their historical antecedents and relations with other texts, and the short- and longer-term impacts of policies in practice. A useful framework which encompasses this breadth distinguishes between contexts, texts and consequences of policy.

In the following sections we illustrate our framework as it might be applied in the case of one particular policy, *The National Policy for the Education of Girls in Australian Schools* (Commonwealth Schools Commission 1987). This policy was promoted by the Hawke Labour government as part of its *National Agenda for Women* – a long-term plan to improve the position of women in Australia by the year 2000 (Department of Prime Minister and Cabinet/Office of the Status of Women 1988). It is a particularly interesting example because it was the first national policy to be developed for Australian schooling, and it was developed as a result of extensive consultation with the States.

Context

At its broadest, context simply refers to the antecedents and pressures leading to the gestation of a specific policy. These include the many economic, social and political factors which lead to an issue being placed upon the policy agenda. Related to these factors are the influences of pressure groups and broader social movements which force governments to respond through the articulation of a policy statement (Rein 1983). As well as these more contemporary aspects of context, an analysis also needs to consider the historical background of a policy, including previous developments and initiatives upon which a policy is built. Such considerations of both the contemporary and historical contexts of policy help to illuminate the 'why' and 'why now' questions we ask in critical policy analysis.

In considering the historical antecedents of *The National Policy for the Education of Girls in Australian Schools*, one noteworthy feature was the fortuitous alignment of the development of the women's movement in Australia, with global developments such as the United Nations' International Women's Year in 1975, and the election of the progressive Whitlam Labour government in 1972. While educational inequality between the sexes had been raised as an issue in the past, it was the combination of particular cultural and political factors which led to the issue being placed on the policy agenda and to the production of the landmark discussion paper *Girls, School and Society* (Schools Commission 1975). This report was produced for the Schools Commission, a statutory authority established by the Labour government to advise the federal government on education, and provided the first serious review of the position of girls and schooling in Australia. The extensive discussion paper comprised a review of existing research on the topic and made recommendations to improve opportunities for girls. Some developments resulted but were short lived following the dismissal of the Whitlam government, highlighting the significance of political context in relation to education policy issues.

Following the publication of *Girls, School and Society* in 1975, most of the State governments issued their own reports on sexism in schooling and subsequent policies. However, at the federal level little progress was made until the election of the Hawke Labour government which replaced that of the Fraser-led Liberal–National coalition in March 1983, illustrating the differences in approach to inequality traditionally taken by Labour and Liberal governments. While the Fraser government took little action in respect of girls and schooling, in 1981 the Schools Commission established a Working Party on the Education of Girls which resulted in the publication of *Girls and Tomorrow* (Commonwealth Schools Commission 1984a). This report noted that: 'A comprehensive national policy which contains a strategic commitment to equality of educational outcomes for girls is urgently needed to change rhetoric into reality' (1984: 9). This goal was finally achieved in 1987 in the form of *The National Policy for the Education of Girls in Australian Schools* (NPEG) (Commonwealth Schools Commission 1987).

The way this policy built upon the earlier developments is an example of *incrementalism* in policy production. Policies are also *intertextual*, that is, they are often related to the development of other cognate policies. The same political, social and cultural context which witnessed the development of the NPEG also resulted in the development of other policies for women and, more broadly, the Hawke government's *National Agenda for Women* (Department of Prime Minister and Cabinet/Office of the Status of Women 1988), of which the NPEG was a component. Similarly, the requirement that Queensland schools develop sexual harassment policies followed the development of the Queensland government's anti-discrimination legislation in 1991.

Also significant in a consideration of policy antecedents is the role of what are often referred to as the *key players*. In the case of the development of the NPEG, it was particularly opportune that during the late eighties the Schools Commission was headed by Lyndsay Connors and the federal minister was Susan Ryan. Both these women were feminists and strongly committed to ensuring more than symbolic status for the NPEG, highlighting the significance of the personalities and beliefs of individuals involved in 'high education politics' (Archer 1985: 40).

We have already mentioned the fact that the NPEG was the first national policy for Australian schooling. 'National' carries particular salience here, for schooling is constitutionally the prerogative of the States, while the Commonwealth can only play a policy and strategic function in relation to schooling. Great care was taken to articulate the nuances of the usage of 'national' in the NEPG:

There is a necessary distinction between *Commonwealth* and *national* policies in education. Commonwealth policies relate specifically to the objectives of the Commonwealth government, such as those addressed through the Commonwealth's general resources programs and its specific purpose programs. In contrast, a *national* policy in education addresses matters of concern to the nation as a whole in which a comprehensive approach to policy development and implementation is adopted by school and system authorities across the nation. A national policy, based on principles of collaboration and partnership, necessarily involves commitment and agreement from the various parties responsible for schooling, including Commonwealth, State and Territory governments and non-government school authorities.

(Commonwealth Schools Commission 1987: 11, original emphasis)

Implicit in the NPEG, then, as a school policy, was the expectation that education authorities would develop their own plans and strategies within the overall framework.

The Schools Commission played a significant role in the formulation of the NPEG. However, given its advisory role to the federal minister, it did not have the political authority or power to endorse a national policy which carried any weight with school systems in the States. It was the Australian Education Council (AEC), an intergovernmental council consisting of Commonwealth, State and Territory ministers for education, which pursued and endorsed the policy and which ensured that it carried some political weight. It was significant that, from the late 1980s, the AEC became more involved in policy making, reflecting an increasing ministerialisation of educational policy making, and the congruence for a short period of a majority of State Labour governments with a federal Labour government.

The NPEG sits at the cusp of the transition between the era of Susan Ryan as federal minister and the John Dawkins period, which saw substantial restructuring of the federal department with the creation of the new mega Department of Employment, Education and Training. This restructuring heralded the increasing influence of economic rationalism on education policy, with an associated reframing of equity in education, and some impact on the way the NPEG was implemented (Kenway 1990, Henry and Taylor 1993).

A further question for consideration in analysis of policy contexts deals with what we call *production questions*, that is, the more proximal and tangible processes involved in the development of the policy itself. For example, very often policy documents are produced in two stages: green (discussion) papers and white (policy) papers. A different set of production processes was followed in the case of the NPEG: an interim report was produced after extensive consultation with parties in all States, including relevant members of the policy community (for example, teacher unions, women's groups). Subsequently a final report incorporated minor changes. Neither the Commonwealth nor the State governments were willing to accept a formal programme of implementation strategies tied to funding as had been proposed in the interim report. Hence in the final report the proposed national plan of action was replaced by a set of illustrative strategies (Connors and McMorrow 1988), weakening the ability of the policy to make strong requirements upon the State systems of schooling.

The final report of the NPEG was produced by the Schools Commission and was granted the political imprimatur of the AEC. Mentioned above was the significance of the conjunction of a majority of Labour governments in the AEC's endorsement of the National Policy. Queensland's position was particularly interesting during both the development and endorsement of the policy. The National Party government there officially opposed the policy, while government bureaucrats remained involved with its development in an attempt to have some influence over the policy and to remain eligible for any associated funding. Formal endorsement only came with the election of a Labour government in Queensland in late 1989.

It should be clear, then, that many pressures and interests were involved and influential in the development of the NPEG, particularly relating to the political context. We now trace the ways in which that complexity is actually reflected in the document itself.

Text

Mention was made above of the significance of the usage of 'national' in the NPEG. In turning to the text, one can analyse the work that national does in terms of the very structure of the policy itself. Because of the complexity of federalism in schooling policy in Australia, any national policy for schools needs to provide as much direction as possible, while allowing flexibility for individual States to develop their own priorities. This is illustrated in the case of the NPEG where the principles, objectives and priorities are agreed upon within the framework of the policy, but where States have some freedom in terms of what is supported in schools. There is an attempt to strengthen the policy through the inclusion of reporting and review processes, even though these are not as strong as some had hoped.

As mentioned above, the NPEG comprises a Schools Commission Report, including a one-page policy framework which was endorsed by the AEC as the actual policy statement. The NPEG has features which allow us to classify it as a material policy, in contrast to some policy statements which are merely symbolic in character. These features include: a comprehensive framework for action, illustrative implementation strategies, reporting and review arrangements and some funding made available for implementation. In addition, enough background material is provided for the policy to fulfil an educative function for administrators and teachers. In relation to the NPEG, Kenway comments that:

> Simplicity, informed by clear thinking, is the name of the game, and it works – to a large extent. Rather than overwhelming its readership with long lists of recommendations, the policy framework gives a short set of educational values and principles, identifies only four objectives and within these a number of priority areas.
>
> (Kenway 1990: 66)

As well as making the ideas accessible to teachers and administrators, the report and subsequent related materials were produced using feminist colours of purple, green and white, making them easily identifiable and indicating their political provenance.

Analyses of policy content may be conducted at various levels, answering the 'how' and 'what' questions of the policy. For example, we can examine the assumptions underlying policies. In the case of the NPEG, the assumptions are explicitly outlined in a set of values and principles, for example: 'gender is not a determinant of capacity to learn', and 'girls and boys should be valued equally in all aspects of schooling' (Commonwealth Schools Commission 1987: 28). The approach to feminism which underpins the policy could also be the focus of critical policy analysis. Several feminist policy analysts (Kenway 1990, Yates 1993) have indicated that the dominant ideology informing the policy is liberal feminism, indicated by the way the approach focusses on girls gaining access to existing educational structures rather than a commitment to more radical change. Other feminist discourses exist in the policy and sit in a contradictory relationship to the dominant liberal feminist ideology. For example, the influence of socialist feminism is apparent in the recognition for the first time in educational policy of the fact that girls are not a homogeneous group. The educational barriers faced by girls from Aboriginal, Torres Strait Islander, ethnic minority and working-class backgrounds are discussed, together with the particular needs of girls with physical disabilities. Radical feminist discourses are also reflected in the policy, for example in the concerns with sexuality and sexual harassment, and in the affirmation of female culture and experiences and a critical view of the education of boys (Kenway 1990: 68).

At yet another level, drawing more on discourse theory, we can move to the area of language and explore further the way equity issues are framed within the document. Unlike earlier policies, there is a focus on equal outcomes as well as on access and participation. At another level still, one could focus on the linguistic strategies used by the text, for example the devices used to address the reader (Luke *et al.* 1993). In the one-page policy framework, and particularly in the statement of educational values and principles, the language is clear and directive with frequent use of the verb 'should' to indicate that action is impera-tive. In a linguistic sense what is not said is often as important as what is said. Thus an analysis of the *silences* of a policy may be very telling. In the NPEG, for example, the recognition of diversity amongst girls does not extend to lesbian issues. Here we see again the impact of the compet-ing interests impacting upon the policy. Because of its collaborative and national character, inclusion of lesbian issues would likely have been a sticking point in the acceptance by all State governments, especially con-servative ones. What we see here is an example of *policy as settlement*, that is, policy attempting to suture together and over matters of difference between the participating and competing interests in the processes of policy text production.

Consequences

To this point, we have indicated some of the contextual complexities and competing interests involved in policy making which may actually be manifested as ambiguities in the policy document itself, with implica-tions for how the policy is read and implemented. Sometimes the sutur-ing of difference within the policy settlement means that very different things can be done legitimately in the processes of policy implementa-tion. Different interests can give very different emphases to various aspects of the policy. Furthermore, when we are looking at a national policy within a federal political structure in which the States have responsibility for running schools, there is very real potential for distor-tions and gaps in policy implementation – sometimes referred to as 'poli-cy refraction' (Freeland 1981). And we must remember that, even *without* any obvious ambiguities in a policy text resulting from competing inter-ests, there will be no single interpretation of a policy document. This means that predicting the effects of policy is never easy.

It is important to recognise that contexts, as well as affecting policy production, also often distort policy goals in various ways and so have a very real impact on policy implementation. This was certainly the case with the NPEG, where the constraining influence of economic rational-ism was evident in the publications, materials produced and initiatives funded as a result of the policy. The curriculum objective of the policy narrowed from a broad approach to one which emphasised getting girls into mathematics and science courses and encouraging them into non-traditional areas of training. Further, while the report itself defined post-school options broadly and paid some attention to girls' and boys' future child rearing roles, implementation initiatives focussed more narrowly on employment options only (Kenway 1990, Henry and Taylor 1993). Kenway commented that the government had made a 'highly selective' reading of the NPEG: 'Gender justice is coming to mean an education designed to prepare girls for the sort of vocations that the government believes will enhance the economy' (Kenway 1990: 73). New approaches to public sector management also impacted upon the implementation of the policy through the requirement introduced into the reporting process of measurable outcomes through performance indicators.

Of course, as well as measurable outcomes, a policy may have all sorts of less tangible impacts or effects on school practice in both the short and long term. For example, the many publications resulting from the NPEG, such as the *Gender Equity Network* newsletter, and the *Girls in Schools* reports, helped to disseminate material about strategies for change and good practice in schools. In this way, a top-down national policy served to reinforce and legitimate bottom-up gender reforms in schools which were already under way, while at the same time helping to raise awareness about the issues in other locations. Initially, there were uneven developments across the States with different levels of awareness among teachers, reflecting different levels of commitment and policy developments by State governments of differing political persuasions (Henry and Taylor 1993). However, these differences have to some extent evened out because of subsequent changes in government, and the fact that liberal feminism crosses party lines – serving to reinforce the point that we need to consider both the short and long terms in analysing policy consequences.

After almost ten years, the effects of the NPEG continue: the review process built into the original policy ensured that the policy was reviewed after five years. The *National Action Plan for the Education of Girls 1993–97* (Australian Education Council 1993) which resulted from the review process recommended the need for the NPEG to continue, outlined eight new priority areas and gave renewed emphasis to questions of sexual harassment (Yates 1993). The plan also reflected changes in developments in post-structural feminism and an increasing interest in the construction of gender, with the latter named as a priority area. One result was that issues to do with masculinity as they relate to the education of girls were moved onto the agenda. At this time policies for the education of girls were increasingly being questioned in the media in the light of the 'What about the boys?' debates, which argued that policies for the education of girls had 'gone too far' and policies focussing on boys were now needed. The review of the NPEG incorporated these concerns without losing the primary focus upon the education of girls. As such, it helped to 'hold the line' in the face of a media-generated antifeminist backlash. This is a clear reminder of the political character of both policy texts and policy processes.

As with the development of the original policy, the strategies involved in the development of the National Action Plan were consultative and

ised. Some significant issues are illustrated by the use of
ɔ inform policy production processes. For example, the
ɔ *Girls* report (Milligan and Thomson 1992) provided powerful
of the extent of sexual harassment experienced by girls in
ı schools, and helped to establish a strong case for the policy to
continue, as well as for sexual harassment to be a priority area for investigation. This is a specific example of the utilisation of research to
mobilise policy development (Weiss 1989).

The case study of the NPEG has demonstrated that any analysis of the
effects and consequences of policy needs to consider many levels of the
policy process, interactive top-down and bottom-up relationships, as
well as the short and longer term. Such analysis also needs to acknowledge the ongoing character of the processes of policy implementation so
that any assessment at a specific point does not provide, in any sense, the
'final word' on the topic.

PROBLEMATISING POLICY ANALYSIS

Earlier in the chapter we differentiated between the policy construction
of an issue and an adequate understanding of the issue itself. We stressed
this distinction between the issue and the policy *per se*, suggesting that
the first stage in policy analysis ought to be to gain an understanding of
the issues which constitute the policy being analysed. That distinction is
also significant in relation to assessing policy consequences. Thus we can
measure consequences in terms of the policy's construction of the problem, or in terms of the effectiveness of the policy against our understanding of the issues. We might like to make a distinction here between
analysing a policy on its own terms or, alternatively, against a set of criteria we establish as policy analysts.

Critical social science makes a distinction between the making and
taking of problems for research and analysis (Dale 1994), arguing that a
critical approach requires a more sceptical engagement with social problems as constructed by governments and the media. This is an insight
which has particular relevance to policy analysis, given that policies are
developed ostensibly to 'solve' social problems. For example, if youth
unemployment is conceptualised simply as a problem of lack of skills,
when in fact it has more to do with structural changes in the labour market brought about by a globalising economy, the resultant policy is likely
to be ineffective. It is thus extremely important that policy problems as
constructed are carefully scrutinised. Within some recent policy literature
(for example, Beilharz 1989, Yeatman 1990, Griffin 1993) the need to
problematise how policy problems are constructed and how they are
framed within policy documents has been emphasised. For example,
Schram (1993) shows how social welfare policy in contemporary post-

industrial US maintains old distinctions and helps to recreate problems of the past – especially in relation to reproducing women's poverty. She argues that by continuing to define single parent families as 'deviant' and outside the mainstream, welfare policy helps to construct the reality it confronts.

Even context is not a given in policy analysis, and policy contexts are often constructed within their recommendations (Seddon 1994). A good example here would be the way in which arguments about the effects of an emergent, global economy are utilised to justify numerous national policies aiming to produce multi-skilled, flexible and more productive workers. International agencies such as the Organisation for Economic Co-operation and Development (OECD) and the World Bank have utilised such a construction of the context of contemporary education policies, resulting in some convergence of policy developments within western economies. Thus policy analysis must scrutinise the ways in which a given policy constructs policy problems and their context, including the way the context has been framed, more recently, in terms of global imperatives. The next chapter focusses specifically on the processes of globalisation and what they mean for education.

Chapter 4

Globalisation, the state and education policy making

What is distinctively Australian about our culture is under assault from homogenised international mass culture.

(Commonwealth of Australia 1994: 1)

A GLOBAL CONTEXT?

In the previous chapter, we talked about the importance of the context of policy, at the same time recognising the point that contexts are also policy constructs which need to be treated with some caution. Policy rationales often argue the imperative for a particular position because of pressing concerns or problems within 'the context'. So to the subject matter of this chapter. Much is written these days about the global context, and the rhetoric of 'global imperatives' now underpins a host of policy prescriptions, from the study of Asian languages and cultures in Australia, to computers in schools, administrative reform or increased participation in higher education. As Waters has pointed out, globalisation appears to have become a key idea with which many social theorists are now attempting to 'understand the transition of human society into the third millennium' (1995: 1). Yet, as a conception upon which so much explanatory weight has been placed, it remains poorly understood and inadequately utilised in policy research generally.

While we would accept that the notion of globalisation needs to be approached cautiously, it is none the less the case that there is something new about the manner in which the world is constituted and the ways in which local communities and nation states relate to each other. Every day we participate in social processes which are transnational in character: in our offices, reading e-mails; in our libraries, consulting CD-ROM catalogues; surfing the net in coffee bars; using slivers of plastic in automatic telling machines to extract Italian lire from Australian bank accounts; watching movies financed in the USA, located in a Brisbane Gold Coast movie studio, shot by a multinational crew and processed in the Philippines; eating hamburgers cloned in Brussels, Belgrade and Bangkok. The list could go on. It may be that globalisation is simply a term that refers collectively to these complex processes which occur in ways that are uneven, even chaotic.

So, what is globalisation? Put simply, globalisation could be described as a set of processes which in various ways – economic, cultural and political – make supranational connections. In his discussion of a world economy, Hobsbawm distinguishes between international and transnational dimensions, the latter being characterised by 'a system of economic activities for which state territories and state frontiers are not the basic framework, but merely complicating factors' (1994: 277). He goes on to suggest that:

> In the extreme case, a 'world economy' comes into existence which actually has no specifiable territorial base or limits, and which determines, or rather sets limits to, what even the economies of very large and powerful states can do. Some time in the early 1970s such a transnational economy became an effective global force.
>
> (Hobsbawm 1994: 277)

According to Giddens (1994: 4), globalisation is really about the transformation of time and space. More precisely, Giddens defines globalisation as 'action at a distance', and suggests that its intensification over recent years owes much 'to the emergence of means of instantaneous global communication and mass transportation'. Action at a distance refers to the 'interconnectedness' of economic, political and cultural activities across the globe. As Giddens notes, this results not only in 'the creation of large-scale systems', but also in 'the transformation of local and even personal contexts of social experience' (pp. 4–5). Waters' definition is generally in line with this understanding. According to Waters, globalisation 'is a social process in which the constraints of geography on social and cultural arrangements recede and in which people become increasingly aware that they are receding' (1995: 3). Under globalisation territoriality remains significant, but is no longer the most fundamental organising principle for social and cultural life it once was. To some extent 'deterritorialisation' has occurred and been augmented by the existence of a non-territorially bounded cyberspace. People in distant geographic locations are able today to form relationships almost as easily as those living in the same locality.

There are thus two aspects of globalisation: first, the facts concerning transnational processes and communication; second, an increasing awareness of this reality. The result, Giddens (1990) suggests, is that many individuals now have been disembedded from local contexts and the constraints contingent upon time and space, enhancing a conception of the world as an integrated whole. In summary, as the Commission on

Global Governance has observed: 'The shortening of distance, the multi-plying of links, the deepening of interdependence: all these factors, and their interplay, have been transforming the world into a neighbourhood' (1995: 42–3). It is these changes and the awareness of them to which the concept of globalisation refers.

It has to be recognised that the notion of globalisation is not the same as internationalisation, though the two concepts may be closely related. Internationalisation embodies relationships and transactions between nations rather than those which transcend national borders. Nor is glob-alisation the same as universalisation. Globalisation does not impinge on all nation states in exactly the same way. Nor does it entirely determine how nation states relate to their awareness of its salience. In this respect, Robertson (1992) notes that globalisation is neither necessarily a good nor a bad thing, reflecting Waters' observation that it is simply 'the direct consequence of the expansion of European cultures across the world via settlement, colonization and cultural mimesis' (1995: 3). It is also linked to the development of capitalism. This does not imply that the entire globe has or must become capitalistic or Westernised, but it does suggest that all spheres of social life must establish their position 'in relation to the capitalist West' (Waters 1995: 3). Western capitalism has become a ref-erence point against which nation states entertain their policy options. Of course, the manner in which different nation states relativise their poli-cies and cultural practices to globalising trends varies enormously, depending on their specific histories, political institutions, cultural tradi-tions and the economic constraints within which they operate. China, for example – the largest nation in the world and one of the fastest growing economies – remains committed to communist ideology, despite moves towards market liberalisation.

GLOBALISATION PROCESSES AND THE STATE

We can talk about three interrelated dimensions of globalisation, namely: economic, relating to social arrangements for the production, exchange, distribution and consumption of goods and services; political, to do with social arrangements for the distribution of power, of centres of policy development and of institutional practices of authority and control; and cultural, relating to social arrangements for the production, exchange and expression of signs and symbols – meanings, beliefs and preferences, tastes and values (Waters 1995: 7–8). Much of the globalisation literature suggests that these dimensions are structurally independent. While we would agree that analytically the distinctions are useful, in practice the categories do not always work discretely, as the following discussion will show.

Waters (1995) argues that in an ideal-typical pattern of economic globalisation, trade would move in the direction of free exchange between localities. Some of this has occurred, for example in the economic relationships between British Columbia and the west coast states of the USA, or in relationships between the Northern Territory in Australia and parts of South-east Asia. (The maps on the walls of Northern Territory government ministers' offices depict the Territory as part of Asia rather than the Australian land mass!) The present reality, however, has witnessed more the emergence of regional trading blocks, for example the Asia Pacific Economic Community, the North American Free Trade Area or the European Union, manifestations of the borderless economy which puts pressure on the nation state. In addition, the emergence of transnational corporations with budgets larger than those of many nation states, and with operations spread across the globe, is an important component of economic globalisation.

It is, however, in the domain of 'instantaneous' and 'stateless' financial markets that Waters suggests globalisation is most advanced. Globalised financial markets are very difficult for nation states to control and, as such, impose considerable constraints on the policy options of national governments. However, responses to economic globalisation are by no means universal. For example, Japan and the so-called Asian Tiger countries retain considerably more control over their financial systems and trading arrangements than does Australia, suggesting that national responses may be conditioned as much by ideological and political factors as by any 'determining' imperatives of globalisation.

Questions of the extent of political globalisation require us to consider the character of the nation state and its historical origins. The nation state as we know it was the creation *par excellence* of the modernist project and grew into its mature form throughout the nineteenth and twentieth centuries. The result was a sophisticated political and administrative structure which was responsible for the welfare and security of the people within its national borders, as well as for a national economy, which was often protected from international competition through tariff barriers for imported goods. Central to this project was the creation of political citizenship linked to nation and the invention of national identity amongst disparate ethnic groups. Seen this way, nations are, as Benedict Anderson (1983) puts it, 'imagined communities' which seek to bring diverse groups of people together under a common set of beliefs and values. Geographical communities do exist, but as socially constructed entities around which notions of citizenships are ascribed.

Globalisation is placing pressures upon these features of the nation state. One dimension of this is seen in the domain of international relations. Increasingly since the Second World War there has been a recognition that many political problems to do with, say, the environment, disease, economic growth, maintaining peace and containing conflict are beyond the capacity of single nations to address. Hence the establishment of large intergovernmental organisations such as the United Nations system, military alliances such as the North Atlantic Treaty Organisation or the South East Asian Treaty Organisation and, especially since the 1960s, a rapidly increasing number and variety of international non-governmental organisations, for example Greenpeace, Amnesty International, the International Teachers' Federation. These latter, Waters suggests, collectively constitute 'a complex and ungovernable web of relationships that extends beyond the nation-state' (1995: 113). Further, there is evidence now of the emergence of supranational organisations, for example the European Parliament whose membership and decisions transcend nation states. Overall then, and especially with the attenuation of the superpower system in the post-Cold War period, international relations have become more fluid and multicentric in nature.

There have also been other ideological and economic pressures upon the organisation and administration of the nation state flowing from globalisation. In a recent report, the OECD (1995) has argued that new public sector management structures in OECD countries are linked to a more open international economy which demands increased competitiveness and forces a more intimate interrelationship between private and public sectors. Harvey puts it this way:

> The state is now in a more problematic position. It is called upon to regulate the activities of corporate capital in the national interest at the same time as it is forced, also in the national interest, to create a 'good business climate' to act as an inducement to trans-national and global finance capital.
>
> (Harvey 1989: 170)

Yeatman (1990), in speaking about attempts by federal Labour governments in Australia to restructure or 'internationalise' the economy, to use the parlance of contemporary political debate, suggests that economic restructuring has taken on meta-policy status. By this she means that policy options in other domains are framed and constrained by these new economic imperatives. The aptly titled report *Asian Languages and Australia's Economic Future* is one such example, arguing for the legitimacy of an Asian languages strategy as part of the creation of an 'Asia literate' Australian 'export culture' in the context of 'the internationalisation of the Australian economy' and 'Australia's international competitiveness' (Rudd 1994: ii). Pusey has observed that the attempt by governments to 'globalise' national economies 'presupposes a closer functional incorporation of the "political administrative" system (the state, and with it the obligatory conditions of elected governments) into an augmented economic system' (1991: 210–11). Thus what we have seen in many of the OECD countries are new public sector management practices and a restructuring of relations between the policy generating 'centre' of public bureaucracies and the policy implementing 'periphery'. We will take up these matters more explicitly in relation to education policy in the following chapter.

Earlier, mention was made of a growing awareness of the global dimensions of problems facing individual nations and their citizens. Alongside this awareness has come an increased scepticism about the capacity for governments at the national level to solve many intractable problems, along with an emergent notion of a global citizenship. Increasingly, then, social movements and pressure groups within nations are taking their causes to international jurisdictions in order to make political claims based on universal human rights or global imperatives for change within their nations. Giddens (1994: 4) speaks about the 'manufactured uncertainty' which national governments must deal with, uncertainties which have their source in earlier human interventions in both the natural and social worlds. As a consequence, he argues, governments are often as much involved in 'damage control' as anything else. There is thus a way in which an awareness of the global character of problems contributes to this scepticism about the political potential of national governments.

What this seems to be demonstrating is a new politics which illustrates twin elements of globalisation, notably global integration and national fragmentation. New politics associated with social movements such as feminism, green politics and the peace movement operating transnationally have destabilised traditional political organisation within nation states. This has broadened the arena for political organisation beyond the nation state or political units within it.

Additionally, alongside the emergence of supranational political units has been the disintegration of some nations into what Horsman and Marshall (1995) refer to as 'ethnic tribalism', seen, for example, in the break up of the Soviet Union and the former Yugoslavia. Similar trends can be seen in an increasing impetus towards Scottish and Welsh nationalism in the United Kingdom and the Quebecois separatist movement in Canada. In various ways, then, the links between ethnicity and the nation, which form the artifice of 'the nation', are being challenged and rearranged through these contrary pressures for integration and disintegration.

This challenge works at both the political and the cultural level, given that the destabilising of relationships between ethnicity and nationhood has also seen some fragmentation of national, group and individual identities. Giddens (1994: 253) has nicely encapsulated these simultaneous processes of global integration and national disintegration in his observation that today there are 'no others' and 'many others'. The ethnic diaspora, reconstituted by globalisation, has witnessed the emergence of hybrid 'new identities' (Hall 1992) within nation states, for example Greek-Australians or African-Americans. In this context, Stuart Hall speaks of post national identity, arguing that accelerating globalisation has destabilised ethnicity and that the dual processes of deterritorialisation and greater transnational 'connectedness' have profound implications for our understanding of the nation state. This cultural fragmentation carries significant implications for political organisation, particularly in view of the concentration of economic power which seems to accompany globalisation (Torres 1995).

Set against these fragmenting pressures, the increasing global distribution of images through concentrated media and technology ownership, for example the empires of Rupert Murdoch and Bill Gates, has potential for homogenising cultural differences, captured in talk of the 'McDonaldisation' of culture. In global media constructions of desire and taste we have seen the development of something of 'a common global lifestyle' (Waters 1995: 136). In the face of these processes, nations are attempting to hold on to the idiosyncratically national. French attempts to control the 'bastardization' of their language in the face of the import of English are a case in point. Similarly, in Australia the Keating government's *Creative Nation* (Commonwealth of Australia 1994) policy statement and initiatives represented both an assertion of the virtues of an open cultural community and an attempt to insert an explicitly Australian presence into that community.

EDUCATION POLICY AND PROCESSES OF GLOBALISATION

How, then, does all of this relate to education policy and policy development? In Chapter Two we noted one conceptualisation of policy as 'the authoritative allocation of values'. Leaving aside for the moment the question of values, we might ask, 'Where does this authority come from?' The most obvious answer to such a question would appear to be the nation state or a sub-national political unit within the nation state. It is at these levels that educational policy is made and funded for implementation, so not surprisingly educational policy analysis has taken the nation state or sub-national political units as the basis of analysis. This is true even of some comparative education policy studies which acknowledge the fact that educational reform proposals across nations bear remarkable similarity. Halpin, for example, has suggested the need for educational policy research to consider the extent and character of educational policy 'borrowing', 'modelling', 'transfer', 'diffusion', 'appropriation' and 'copying' which occur across the boundaries of nation states and 'which lead to universalising tendencies in educational reform' (1994: 204). But such an approach remains trapped within a traditional view of comparative research, which does not make the notion of nation state itself problematic. For example, in introducing their study of policy borrowing in education and training between England and the USA, Finegold *et al.* (1993) draw on the comparative education tradition; as such, they focus on borrowing across nations and tend to underplay the processes of globalisation.

However, and following our previous discussion, viewing the nation state as an unstable entity has implications for education policy analysis. For if educational policy analysis describes how nation states arrange and deliver their educational priorities, then such analysis must be informed by a recognition of the global factors now impacting upon the constitution of the nation state and its policy preferences. That is, a consideration of globalisation factors needs to be incorporated into any policy analysis of national developments. Some of the relevant issues to consider then, might include the way and extent to which:

- globalisation processes are taken into account in the policy priorities at nation-state level;
- ideological discourses which frame education policies at the national level might already be globalised;
- political structures operating beyond nations are framing national policy options;
- a global policy community may be emerging; and
- globalisation processes are affecting the cultural field within which education operates.

There is little published research in the education policy field which extends the analytical focus in this way, although some of these issues are being addressed in more recent studies in education policy. We will draw on three such studies with which we have been involved in recent years to illustrate how, in different ways and in different countries, some of these considerations are informing both the conceptualisation and analysis of policy research.

The case of Papua New Guinea

The first example we will look at, the case of Papua New Guinea (PNG), begins with Kulwaum's (1995) research on devolution in PNG which focussed in particular on problems that have been encountered in implementing devolution policies in educational administration. This study suggested that many of these problems are related to the nation's colonial legacy, no longer expressed in its traditional form but in more hegemonic and ideological forms. Kulwaum argued that, as a nation, PNG is a Western artefact, constructed as a fragile unity through the processes of colonialism. This unity is severely tested by PNG's cultural and linguistic diversity. While local communities wish their traditions to be protected, the centralised bureaucratic state dances to another tune dictated not only by those Bigmen (a mostly Western educated elite) in Port Moresby who have become assimilated into the Western bureaucratic culture, but also by overseas agencies which wish to see a particular form of educational development in PNG.

What is particularly pertinent from the point of view of our interest in globalisation is the question of the extent to which PNG's educational policy options are constrained by factors external to the nation. Kulwaum's thesis suggests that, as a poor country, PNG's dependency on overseas aid and loans may have already limited the way PNG is able to construct its own definition of educational development. PNG needs overseas aid not only to sustain its increasingly Western economic system, but also to meet the needs of the country's new requirements in education, health and so on. The cultural tastes and aspirations of the nation's elite, the Bigmen, have already become Westernised – there is no turning back to the traditional modes of social living. Here enter the aid agencies such as the World Bank, the International Monetary Fund, the Asian Development Bank and AusAid, who readily agree to provide aid in different forms such as capital, human resources, technology and equipment and, of course, consultancies. The aid given to PNG is no longer untied, however, but linked increasingly to tight conditions which emphasise efficient and effective management of projects ahead of any traditional cultural values of social interaction. This has led in PNG to devolution being defined in a very narrow way, consistent with a corporate instrumentalism rather than those traditional approaches which place greater emphasis on the values of sharing and caring.

It is clear that globalisation has impacted in a variety of ways on how educational policy is now developed in PNG. The nation's educational priorities are becoming rearticulated with certain economic, political and cultural global trends, as its policy options become limited and as it is forced to contemplate its survival and its sovereignty in a world in which national boundaries lose their earlier significance.

Like Kulwaum, Nick Faraclas (1993) has examined the ways in which globalisation has impacted on PNG's capacity to develop its own educational policies, especially in relation to programmes in critical literacy. According to Faraclas, the impact of global economic and cultural intervention into national lives is both alienating for individuals and exploitative of national cultures and indigenous social movements, making oppositional politics difficult to achieve. Faraclas maintains that while recent changes in the way global capitalism operates might open up new opportunities for those living in the wealthy 'First World' nations, to the people of the 'Third World' it appears simply as another form of colonisation. This is so because it is the West that has captured globalisation processes, constructing, in its own image, the cultural economies that affect us all. And since education is a central component of a nation's cultural economy, it is inevitably implicated in the processes of globalisation.

For a country like PNG, globalisation effectively represents yet another way in which the power of international capitalism serves to make its people dependent on commodities produced elsewhere. But globalisation also constitutes what Faraclas refers to as a set of 'New Enclosures', through which the cultural and political autonomy of Papua New Guineans is diminished. Faraclas is highly suspicious of the 'gleaming ideals of globalism', preferring to view its impact on PNG as a 'global wave of recolonisation'; though this time, he maintains, it is not any one nation that is seeking to subjugate the people of PNG, but a conglomeration of international organisations, such as the World Bank and the International Monetary Fund. These organisations are seeking to expropriate the rights of the indigenous people by insisting upon a set of conditions which define the policy parameters within which the government of PNG must define any programme of reform in education. Thus the critical literacy programmes which radical educators have attempted to establish in PNG have simply floundered for lack of resources and government support.

Faraclas argues that the problems that PNG currently confronts can be traced back to the 'big project' loans the PNG government accepted in the late 1970s from the international monetary organisations. These loans now have to be repaid in a climate of ever increasing interest rates and collapsing commodity prices. Unable to service the loans, in 1989 PNG was forced to renegotiate its debts which involved, amongst other things, accepting a Structural Adjustment Programme. The Programme not only meant slashing expenditure on welfare, health and educational programmes, but it also created a more regulative state which has had to pass legislation designed to create social conditions more conducive to overseas investment in the country. As part of the Structural Adjustment Programme, a Land Mobilisation Programme was introduced, which had the impact of overturning many of the traditional customs that defined the way people related to the land. There has now emerged a new discourse of land ownership, mobilisation and use that is linked to a capitalist notion of development, to what critical literacy workers in PNG call 'the Cargo discourse on development'. The Cargo discourse suggests that Papua New Guineans are not capable of defining what development might mean. As Faraclas puts it, the assumption underlying both the Structural Adjustment Programme and the Land Mobilisation Programme is that Papua New Guineans need to be 'saved from themselves and their traditions'. Thus, for the World Bank and the International Monetary Fund, the explanation of PNG's current economic difficulties lies in the cultural pathologies that are assumed to characterise PNG society.

To argue that the New Enclosures that diminish national sovereignty have a global character is not to suggest, however, that they work in the same way everywhere. Faraclas maintains that in order to understand the ways in which the New Enclosures function in Papua New Guinea, it is necessary to consider the relationship between the global and the local – the universal and the particular. It is much too easy to represent globalisation as a monolithic project. As Kulwaum (1995) noted, the activities of the international banks cannot succeed without the complicity of the new PNG elite which plays a significant role in the nation's public life and enjoys considerable prestige and power. This power articulates with global capitalism in a range of historically specific ways which clearly need to be taken into account in thinking about the manner in which globalisation constrains educational possibilities in PNG. The way the work of teachers and students in PNG schools is subjected to the New Enclosures is thus mediated by the country's political and administrative structures, formed historically around a Western concept of development, but now also implicated in the complex politics of overseas aid. To explore PNG's educational policies in the context of globalisation is therefore to understand the ways in which globalisation articulates with a whole range of local factors associated with the constitution of PNG's politics, the organisation of its bureaucracy and its attempts to keep the nation together as a single unified entity.

Malaysia and international education

Globalisation is an idea that is also helpful in explaining recent changes to educational policies in Malaysia, explored by Alexander and Rizvi (1993) in a study of the internationalisation of education. Alexander and Rizvi were interested in examining the nature of the relationship between Australian and Malaysian higher education policies, and in particular questions concerning the cultural politics of Malaysian education which lead to such a large number of Malaysian students going overseas to study.

In Malaysia there is great demand for higher education, reflecting not only the country's rapid economic growth but also the importance that most Malaysians attach to higher education. But places available for higher education in Malaysia do not match this demand, so that over 50 per cent of higher education students study abroad. However, for most Malaysians, overseas options are becoming too expensive, a problem also for the Australian universities which have become increasingly reliant on the funds generated through international education. One way in which Australian universities have been able to keep the costs down for Malaysian students has been to enter into 'twinning' arrangements with a number of colleges in Malaysia, some of which have been established

specifically for this purpose. Most of these are private colleges se
Malaysian entrepreneurs in order to take advantage of the oppor
that exist in the business of tertiary education. Twinning arrangemenω
have a variety of forms, but most arrangements with Australian universities involve students taking the first year of their courses within a twinning college in Malaysia and then completing the remainder of their
course in Australia, thereby obtaining Australian qualifications in the
end.

There is little doubt that twinning arrangements have been enormously successful in a number of ways. They have been an important mechanism for lowering the cost of an international education, providing many
Malaysian students educational opportunities they could not otherwise
afford – despite the fact that many take out substantial loans, as much as
$Aus100,000 in some instances. The emergence of private twinning col-
leges has also meant that the Malaysian government has not had to
invest in the development of its own public higher education system,
while still being able to meet the requirements of its fast growing and
diversified economy. As far as Australian universities are concerned, the
twinning arrangements have enabled them to expand their educational
markets, ensuring greater predictability in the numbers of international
students they can expect from a particular source.

However, the arrangements have also given rise to a number of complex issues, both in Malaysia and in Australia. For example, surveys carried out as part of the study suggested that the ethnic composition of the
twinning colleges, about 70 per cent from Chinese-speaking backgrounds, does not reflect Malaysia's population which is only 35 per cent
Chinese. The reason for this disparity is linked to Malaysia's ethnic politics, where educational opportunities for the Chinese are in part defined
by the government's affirmative action policies which favour the
Bumiputras, the term used to describe Muslim and indigenous people of
Malaysia.

Although many of the students surveyed in the study indicated that
they felt excluded from the country's public universities, most were
pleased to be studying for a degree from an English-speaking overseas
university. Paradoxically, their exclusion has brought them unexpected
personal benefits, in terms of their prospects of obtaining a better job in
the private sector. This is because while Bahasa Malay, the language of
instruction in local public universities, may be useful to those who find
employment in the public sector, by and large the private sector where
most of the new attractive jobs are emerging prefers graduates who are
able to speak English fluently, and who have had an exposure to a
Western education. Most students surveyed maintained that one of the
main reasons for wanting to study overseas was their perception that a
Western degree is worth more in the emerging labour market, both

within Malaysia and internationally. For this reason, more than three quarters of the students were enrolled in courses in commerce, economics and business management, that is in areas where most of the new jobs are to be found. With Malaysia's economy becoming increasingly globalised, international education is clearly attractive, especially for those students who have a very utilitarian view of education.

Now, a number of questions are raised by these arrangements. Some of these are technical, relating to financial and administrative matters; and indeed much of the dialogue between Australian universities and the Malaysian colleges has been at this level. But there are also more far-reaching cultural and educational questions which have received less attention, questions in which globalisation factors are intricately involved. Why has Malaysia been so reluctant to invest in the development of its own higher education system, given a rapidly growing economy? Given Malaysia's reputation as a highly regulated state, why has it allowed the development of a relatively unconstrained private education system within which the marketing activities of Australian universities are located? How is the Malaysian politics of nation building, particularly in relation to ethnic politics, affected by the rapid development of a large private education system? How do the educational and cultural experiences that Malaysian students have in Australian universities affect the ways they construct their identity – and also the way they think about Malaysia in relation to global cultural economies?

Some of the answers to these questions may usefully be explored in terms of the globalisation thesis. The accelerating pace of the globalisation of economy has been at the base of Malaysia's economic growth over the past two decades. Like Singapore and other newly industrialising countries, Malaysia has attracted massive amounts of investment from international corporations, so much so that its continued economic success has become inextricably tied to its ability to remain a key player in the global economy. This has required an increasingly educated workforce which can confidently engage on the international economic stage. Indeed, most of the new jobs in Malaysia are now either in the service sector or in private sector management, and in particular with those transnational corporations which are engaged in the business of exports and imports. This has required particular kinds of skills which the corporations feel that overseas universities are better able to provide. In the Malaysian job market these overseas graduates have a distinct advantage over the graduates from local universities. The transnational corporations feel that overseas graduates are not only more confident in the emerging global language of commerce – English – but, having been exposed to Western cultures, they are better able to deal with clients from Europe and North America. Alexander and Rizvi's research indicates that this perception is at least partly responsible for Malaysian students preferring an overseas education to the local one.

This argument is further supported by the fact that a large majority of Malaysian students in Australian universities were enrolled in faculties of management, commerce or economics. In these faculties students are taught a new, seemingly universal organisational ideology based on some of the principles of Japanese business practices and their American extensions – for example, ideas about strategic management, just-in-time, total quality management, teamwork, managerial decentralisation and flexibility which, Waters suggests, appear to have become central tenets of a 'single idealisation of appropriate organisational behaviour' (1995: 81). Malaysian students find it easier to obtain such an education in Western rather than in local Malaysian universities and, as a result, a large number prefer to go overseas, even at the cost of the huge financial sacrifices made by their parents.

In the context of such a clear cultural preference for Western universities, the Malaysian state finds itself on the horns of a dilemma. Its economic interests lie in supporting the trends towards international private education, but its interests in nation building suggest that it should attempt to expand its public education sector. Its labour market needs lie in a workforce confident on the global economic stage, but the government recognises that it cannot allow its national traditions to be subsumed by a clear preference for things Western that an international education encourages. At the same time, the current Malaysian government is ideologically committed to reducing its public sector, and has sought therefore to support the development of a relatively unconstrained private education system within Malaysia. What is clear from Alexander and Rizvi's research, however, is that Malaysia's higher education policies are being constructed in reference to the processes of globalisation. The five new Education Acts passed by the Malaysian parliament in January 1996 may then be viewed as its response to the dilemmas created for it by globalisation.

The policies encapsulated by these Acts have two main focusses: human resource development for Malaysia's integration into the global economy, and liberalisation of post-secondary education providing new opportunities for the private sector in education. A range of policy initiatives has followed, but a significant aspect of these reforms has been a shift away from the insistence upon public institutions to use Bahasa Malay as the medium of instruction in earlier educational policies to the abolition of this requirement. Public education institutions are now free to consider English as their medium of instruction both in order to compete more equally with the private sector and also to provide a 'globally-oriented' workforce for the Malaysian economy (Samuel 1996). In making this concession, the Malaysian government has in effect acknowledged a global imperative which makes a national priority secondary.

Australia and the Organisation for Economic Co-operation and Development

The third piece of research, conducted by ourselves, was concerned with exploring the relationship between the OECD and education policy in Australia (Rizvi *et al.* 1995–7). It sought amongst other things to examine the extent and manner in which the OECD has been able to steer education policy agendas towards certain ideological preferences over the past decade or so, and the way in which the Australian government has been able to use OECD reports to support its construction of a national framework in education. At a more theoretical level, it also sought to explore the extent to which the policy agendas of an international organisation such as the OECD were themselves being rearticulated through globalisation processes, and the implications of this for policy making at the national level.

Unlike, say, the World Bank, the OECD has no prescriptive mandate over its member countries. Rather, it describes itself as a place for reflection and discussion, research and analysis – a kind of international think tank – 'that may often help governments shape policy', exerting influence through processes of 'mutual examination by governments, multilateral surveillance and peer pressure to conform or reform' (OECD undated: 10). Of interest to this study, then, were questions about the nature of the research and analysis which helped governments to 'shape policy', in other words, about the influences shaping the organisation's policy agenda and way of operating.

The OECD's policy agenda in education is framed by its formal charter of a 'commitment to a market economy and a pluralistic democracy' (OECD undated: 1) and its priority of fostering a 'post-industrial age in which . . . OECD economies [can be woven] into a yet more prosperous and increasingly service-oriented world economy' (OECD undated: 6). Within this context, education as an activity within the OECD has been broadly legitimated on the basis of its contribution to economic growth, though such a role has not necessarily been narrowly interpreted. Indeed, the range of policy interests and stances in relation to education have been broader and more contested than the OECD's economic mission might indicate. They span pedagogic, administrative, resourcing and policy concerns on issues as diverse as the quality of teaching, performance indicators, curriculum innovation, educational inequality, educational restructuring, school effectiveness and the use of school buildings.

By the mid-1980s, however, the economic imperative was certainly taking centre stage in OECD thinking about education, prompted by the impact of globalisation pressures on national economies. These pressures were acknowledged in the first OECD education ministers' conference in 1978, *Future Educational Policies in the Changing Social and Economic Context* (OECD 1979) notable, Papadopoulos observes, 'for the force and urgency with which educational change was *politically* advocated to respond to the new economic imperative, marked by growing country interdependence and competition in the global economy' (1995: 171). In such a context, the conference noted, education policy was being framed by factors '*largely outside the ambit or control of education*' (OECD 1979: 12, original emphasis). At the same time, the social purposes of education continued to be strongly asserted, albeit largely framed in economic terms, for example in terms of labour market disadvantage for particular social groups. A decade later, in 1988, an intergovernmental conference, *Education and the Economy in a Changing Society*, saw the relationship between economic and social purposes of education as quite explicitly interlinked. The conference took as its theme the convergence of education and economic functions in the new global context, arguing the centrality of the 'human factor' as an element in production: 'the skills and qualifications of workers are coming to be viewed as critical determinants of effective performance of enterprises and economies' (OECD 1989a: 18). While the Secretary-General insisted that the conference would discuss 'much more than conditions of economic efficiency' (p. 8), matters of social equity in fact became framed by a dominant concern with economic efficiency. In the words of the conference chairperson, John Dawkins (then Minister for Employment, Education and Training in Australia):

> A society which does not respond to the needs of its disadvantaged groups will incur the heavy social and economic costs of under-developed and under-utilised human resources. From this viewpoint . . . I see the goals of equity and efficiency in our education and labour market arrangements as fundamentally compatible rather than conflicting.
>
> (OECD 1989a: 13)

According to Apple, the significance of the conference lay not so much in the details of the discussion as in 'the overall orientation of its analysis and its linguistic strategies in creating a rhetoric of justification for a tighter connection between educational systems and the world economy' (1992: 127). While some attention was paid to more general purposes of education, they were, Apple suggests, 'almost always seen against the backdrop of a crisis in productivity and competition'. From then on, the OECD's general stance on education policy, strongly conditioned by the organisation's ideological commitment to globalisation, served to further reinforce that commitment in its conceptualisation of the relationship between education and the economy.

Under Dawkins, Australia played an active part in both shaping and refracting the OECD's policy agenda in education. Within OECD forums, Australian policies in educational and public sector restructuring were seen as innovative in achieving goals of 'efficiency with equity'. (We will say more about this in Chapter Five.) At the same time, Dawkins used OECD analyses somewhat selectively to create and legitimate his own *national* policy agenda in education within Australia. For example, commenting on his performance in Paris, Vickers observes that: 'Upon returning home, Dawkins implemented the most extensive programme of reconstruction that has ever been imposed on Australia's higher education sector' (1994: 26). More generally, Vickers argues, the Commonwealth 'participated most actively in those projects that connect education to the economy, [showing] least interest in projects concerned with teaching, curriculum and learning' (p. 36) – thus depriving teachers of a valuable body of innovative research and analysis.

The study was also interested in how an international organisation such as the OECD constructs 'its own' agenda given its diverse membership, in other words, how the processes of 'mutual examination by governments' alluded to earlier actually work. In exploring this issue, questions surfaced about the OECD's constituency, the changing nature of the nation state and the implications of this for the organisation's education policy stances. Formally, the OECD is an intergovernmental organisation, but it connects to member countries at two, not necessarily congruent, levels – government and research communities. To some extent, then, it can be described as partially non-governmental in nature, embracing alternative networks of influence which form part of that 'complex web of ungovernable relationships' referred to by Waters (1995: 113). The question then arises as to the relationship between these two policy making arenas, governmental and non-governmental.

While governments see the OECD as their instrument, the organisation can also be viewed to some extent as an independent policy actor (Archer 1994), steered by its secretariat which fulfils both research and administrative functions. Thus at one level the secretariat is simply the administrative arm of an organisation which is the instrument of its member countries, a function becoming more complex in the context of the 'new world order'. On the one hand, the OECD appeared to be strengthening its links with newly emerging nations of the former Eastern Block eager for the organisation to undertake reviews of their education policies. At the same time, in the face of common problems facing many countries, there was an increasing awareness of the inadequacy of the nation state as an analytical unit, and hence a move towards more holistic or thematic analyses, for example on issues such as mass higher education, vocational education and training, and the development and use of performance indicators in education. Thematic analyses tended to promote links with sub-national units rather than national governments, with a consequent potential to undermine national control over the policy agenda.

This tendency was reinforced by two other factors. First, in its research capacity, the secretariat is linked into its own pool of consultants and experts as well as governmental forums, often using the former for policy research and advice. How governments choose to use that advice is a moot point, but paradoxically the OECD's influence and cachet stem to a significant degree from its perceived independence from the vested interests of governments. This tension provides secretariat staff with some 'freedom to manoeuvre' beyond the constraints of government-set agendas, seen for example in the wide-ranging and sophisticated analyses emerging from the vocational education and training project (Vickers 1994).

Second, the OECD is itself part of another sphere of influence, the network of international organisations, for example UNESCO, the World Bank, the International Labour Organisation, the Commonwealth Secretariat and the European Union (EU), all with an interest in education policy. The inclusion of a representative from the EU, a supranational organisation, on the governing Council and other forums of the OECD is symbolic of this trend, as is the proclivity for former OECD staffers to take consultancies with the EU and other tendering agencies in Europe. While these organisations have different constituencies and purposes, the congruence of policy positions on educational issues is notable, in particular around the recurring rhetoric of quality, diversity, flexibility, accountability and equity. What this suggests is the possibility of both a more competitive educational ideas market (with implications for the OECD's reflective think tank role), and a global policy community, constituted by an overlapping membership of senior public servants, policy makers and advisers, serving to possibly further restrict the parameters of debate around education policy making.

Discussion

Reflecting, then, on the three studies we have just discussed, a more general question to emerge is the extent to which such policy positions are mediated by local circumstances, or the extent to which they are seen as 'supra' to the particularities of nations. The studies suggest a variety of responses, illustrating the complex and contradictory ways globalisation pressures impact on national policy agendas.

In the case of PNG, from Kulwaum and Faraclas' point of view the ideology of globalisation, articulated by external agencies such as the

World Bank or the International Monetary Fund and rearticulated by the national government, has helped to construct an education policy agenda with disadvantaging effects, serving to consolidate PNG's (post) colonial status. Alexander and Rizvi's study suggested that Malaysia, on the other hand, from an economically and politically more independent position, was attempting to construct its position in the global community as a consumer not a pawn, purchasing products from the educational commodity market for its own ends. The OECD study pointed to the organisation's ideological role in constructing a particular view of globalisation processes and concomitant strategies for positioning member countries as winners in the global economy – strategies in which education was centrally important. The study also showed how Australia, as one member country, both contributed to and utilised OECD ideology to legitimate its own education policy agenda.

However, as we have indicated, there is no essential determinancy to the ways in which globalisation processes work, since for various globalisation pressures there are also sites of resistance and counter movements. Thus, for example, the PNG government has attempted to resist some World Bank-mandated reforms. The extent to which Malaysia can, in practice, remain immune from the globalisation forces with which it engages remains a moot point. Australia's capacity to exercise national options, including more equitable educational outcomes, is problematic given its insecure trading base and the extent to which it has surrendered political control to financial markets. And the OECD itself is bumping up against the contradictory tendencies of globalisation, with its reflective analytical role somewhat threatened by the pressures to engage in the 'real world' issues of its member countries which are no longer insulated from problems confronting the rest of the world.

Globalisation and the changing cultural field of educational policy

Returning now to education policy matters more generally, one important issue mentioned earlier remains unaddressed: the extent to which globalisation processes may affect the cultural field within which education operates. It is becoming clear that this field is changing markedly and quite rapidly, a process facilitated by the boundary-eroding imperatives of the new technologies as well as the imperatives of economic globalisation. For policy makers and analysts, the issues here have to do with the effects of these technologies – the compression of time and space – on the way education is thought about, practised and managed. Matters of pedagogy and curriculum, certification, decision-making and governance, the student body itself as well as, of course, policy making arenas are all implicated here.

Quite a deal has been written about the implications for teaching and learning of the new global technologies – the Internet and World Wide Web, CD-ROMs, Satellite Television and so on – and the potential for broader access to computers and the information superhighway to create alternative and parallel education systems to those run by various arms of state structures. Kenway, for example, points to the growing popularity of 'edu-tainment' science and technology parks, theme parks and the 'technologised educational arms of art galleries, libraries and museums' (1995: 22), while Luke (1996) suggests that within this supra-national education domain, a new breed of teachers is emerging to create the computer software for the global education market.

Another manifestation of the changing cultural field of education has been an unprecedented movement of students and the related reconstituting of education programmes (Neave 1991). Once students studied overseas mostly for reasons of 'cultural exchange' or as part of aid programmes which in fact were predicated on notions of geographic and even cultural separateness. Now, student exchange occurs within the logic of human resource development for national or even regional ends. Thus accompanying the global labour market has been the emergence of a more open education market enabling greater mobility across national borders – seen for example in the popular and ambitious European tertiary student exchange programme ERASMUS.

In this context, boundaries around how, where and under whose authority education is carried out and certified are becoming less clear as universities, technical and further education colleges and even schools internationalise their campuses, their curriculum and their teaching staff. For example, ERASMUS was a decision of the supranational European Parliament. What implications does this have for decision making at national, let alone local university level? In 1995, the Queensland Education Department sold its entire year ten curriculum to a province in China. What does this say about questions of cultural relevance? Western Australia's Curtin University of Technology has formed an arrangement with the Perth-based Australian Institute for University Studies (AIUS), an arrangement enabling students unable to meet Curtin's entrance quotas to pay private fees to enrol with the AIUS as a precursor to obtaining a Curtin qualification. AIUS is in turn backed by Excel Education Pty Ltd, a subsidiary of MUI Berhad, one of the corporate giants of the Malaysian stock exchange (Storey 1996). What pressures does this mix of private commercial interests – international education now exceeds wheat as an export earner – and public educational interests place on educational delivery and certification?

Where all this will lead is not predictable, for as we have already indicated, nations participate in this new educational field in different and contradictory ways. As we observed at the outset, there is considerable hype, or 'globalony' as one writer puts it, about the global imperatives driving these shifts. Nevertheless, there are undoubtedly real issues here. How can governments define their educational purposes and keep track of what is happening in their systems, given the tangle of institutional links now being created across regions and countries, and given the problems of regulating the borderless frontiers of cyberspace? How do governments defend the traditional nation-building purposes of education when the very notion of nation is being reconstituted? Policy analysis needs not only to document these trends but also to consider the policy dilemmas and practical implications that such rejigging entails.

Finally, there is the point that education policy analysis needs to take account of the fact that these days education policy is made elsewhere than in departments of education. While in Australia the creation of the mega Department of Employment, Education and Training made explicit the merging of education and training policy, it remains less recognised that policies about art teaching may be made in ministries of the arts, that policies about computer education may be announced in communications or technology policy forums, that prime ministers might be concerned with civics education and that environment policy may embrace environmental education. So, for example, the *National Asian Languages and Cultures Strategy* came from the Council of Australian Governments, not the Department of Employment, Education and Training, *Creative Nation* came from the Department of Prime Minister and Cabinet, *Whereas the People: Civics and Citizenship Education* came from a civics expert group appointed by then Prime Minister Keating, and *Networking Australia's Future* from a consultancy group on broadbanding – and all these reports had important implications for education.

Put more generally, while links between education and economic policy domains have long been recognised – and criticised – what is perhaps less evident is that education is equally becoming an arm of cultural policy, a phenomenon that may provide the potential for a new politics of education policy making within a global context. This is the subject of the concluding section of this chapter.

THE POLITICS OF THE GLOBAL CONTEXT: IMPLICATIONS FOR EDUCATION POLICY

The starting point for this discussion is a reminder that globalisation is not something that occurs outside the realm of human activity and political organisation. Like all social phenomena, globalisation processes are intrinsically political – that is, fought over and settled at particular times. This point is most obviously true in relation to the political options open to national governments and their citizens.

Perhaps we can start by noting the points made by Torres (1995) and

Falk (1993) who refer respectively to 'upper and lower circuits
ization' and 'globalization from above and below'. Here
attempting to distinguish on the one hand between the powerfu
capital and culture which seem to be having a homogenising ar
mining impact on nations from above, and on the other hand a ... emergent democratic grass roots politics based on notions of global
communities and proactive citizenship.

Globalisation from above, according to Falk, reflects:

> the collaboration between leading states and the main agents of capi-
> tal formation. This type of globalization disseminates a consumerist
> ethos and draws into its domain transnational business and political
> elites. It is the New World Order, whether depicted as a geopolitical
> project of the US government or as a technological and marketing pro-
> ject of large-scale capital, epitomised by Disney theme parks and fran-
> chised capitalism (McDonalds, Hilton, Hertz . . .).
>
> (Falk 1993: 39)

It is this New World Order which results in the redistribution of rich and
poor within and between nations (Harvey 1989, Sivanandan 1989,
Chomsky 1993). Third world societies can now be found within the
metropoles of first world nations, while an elite new middle class from
former third world societies constitute global networks of culture and
capital. In other words, globalisation has made problematic notions of
first, second, third and fourth world economies or of developed and
developing societies, with new configurations resulting in first–third
world divisions within, as well as between, countries.

By contrast, according to Falk, the politics of 'globalization from
below':

> consists of an array of transnational social forces animated by environ-
> mental concerns, human rights, hostility to patriarchy, and a vision of
> a human community based on the unity of diverse cultures seeking an
> end to poverty, oppression, humiliation, and collective violence.
>
> (Falk 1993: 39)

Such a politics seeks to construct a global civil society or democracy
without boundaries. David Held (1995a, 1995b) has argued the need for
the creation of 'cosmopolitan democracy' as a response to the weakened
capacities of nation states in the face of a globalised economy. He has
demonstrated how today there are several disjunctions between our conception of the nation state as being able to control its destiny, and global
pressures from a world economy, international organisations, regional
and global institutions, international law and military alliances (1995b:
99). Hobsbawm, too, points to the weakened position of the nation state
'against a world economy it could not control [and] against the

institutions it had constructed to remedy its own international weakness, such as the European Union' (1994: 576).

For all that, as both Held and Hobsbawm acknowledge, the nation state still remains a critical site for playing out global politics. Castles (1994: 2) too, a sceptic of the globalisation 'litany of the OECD', points to ways Singapore and Sweden have been able to arrange social security mechanisms with fundamentally similar goals despite their differing ideologies and despite the so-called pressure of international capital. However, while the globalisation thesis may well have been overstated, there seems to be little doubt that economic globalisation is contributing to intensified inequalities between its beneficiaries and victims. In such a context, as Hobsbawm argues, 'the state or some other form of public authority representing the public interest [would be] more indispensable than ever if the social and environmental inequities of the market economy were to be countered' (1994: 577).

This underside of globalisation sometimes tends to be ignored in the light of its somewhat beguiling cultural face, with its hi-tech glitz and joys of cybertravel. In relation to this discussion we would simply note that the new technologies have the capacity to facilitate both circuits of globalisation. At one level, they constitute a major (male-dominated) capital-generating source and a means of propagating consumerist culture. At another level, they could be viewed as inherently democratic in their 'ungovernability' and potential for mobilising individuals in a world-wide communications system – despite observations that so far the net remains another male colony (Spender 1995).

What, then, are the implications of all this for education policy making and analysis? The first thing to reiterate is that globalisation is a complex set of processes in which all the social, economic and cultural inequalities of nation states are refigured and in some ways intensified. This may seem self evident, but it is important because globalisation factors are often either oversimplified or ignored in policy formulation and analysis. For example, the promises of training programmes for unemployed youth, these days almost routinely gesturing towards the 'global context', may turn out to be empty if complementary labour market programmes are not also put in place to offset the impact of globalisation pressures on domestic labour markets. Or to take a more micro example: although the document *Whereas the People*, referred to earlier, made mention of international developments in citizenship education, its curriculum principles ignored the global context in which questions of citizenship are now embedded – a significant omission in our view.

Secondly, an understanding of the complexity and ambiguity of global processes may provide some strategic leverage against their seeming determinacy. So far, education policy appears to have articulated largely with the 'upper circuit' of globalisation through a predominantly economic framing. The result has been an intensified commodification of education and a kind of cultural cynicism. That is, as we will elaborate further in the next chapter, education systems have been made objects of micro-economic reform with educational activities being turned into saleable or corporatised market products as part of a national efficiency drive. In this context, questions of cultural appropriateness of educational offerings – to overseas students who take our courses, to the countries who purchase our curriculum packages, or to ourselves as we access Americanised computer software – have been made to seem oddly old-fashioned given the existence of a global market place where consumers presumably are free to purchase whatever messages they choose.

Nevertheless, in our view these are questions which should be posed by policy analysts, questions which may be more satisfactorily addressed if education is conceptualised as part of the cultural rather than the economic domain. While we would not want to dismiss the importance of making education relevant to employment – a point developed further in Chapter Six – we would agree with critics such as Apple (1994) who point to the potentially dehumanising effects of the economic ascendancy in education, especially when the economy is so closely identified with market liberalism. While the cultural field itself, as we have seen, is also increasingly framed in economic terms, an articulation of education policy with cultural policy may offer better possibilities, we believe, for a more humanistic interpretation of the role of education in what Eva Cox (1995) calls 'a truly civil society'. In other words, framing education policy culturally may enable connections with the 'lower circuits' of globalisation in ways which enable more critical questions to be raised – often ignored in the romanticised globalisation hype – for example, about citizenship and identity and about the 'winners and losers' in this brave new globalised world.

We will return to some of these questions in the final chapter of the book when considering issues of social change. In the next chapter, we concentrate upon documenting the changes to the structure and operations of the state which have resulted from the impact of globalisation processes, and the consequent implications of this for the production of education policy.

Chapter 5

Educational restructuring

[S]ince the 1970s, reality has been turned upside down and society has been recast as the object of politics (rather than, at least in the norms of the earlier discourses, as the subject of politics). Further, society has been represented as some sort of stubbornly resisting sludge, as a 'generic externality' and even as an idealised opponent of 'the economy'. The tail that is the economy wags the dog that is society.

(Michael Pusey 1991: 10)

INTRODUCTION

In Chapter Two we argued that it was necessary to take account of the state for understanding policy processes. But what is the state? Previously we have noted that the state refers to practices, processes and structures of governments at each of the political, legislative, judicial and administrative levels. It frames the relationship between the various activities of the government as it seeks to manage society and the conduct of its institutions and its citizens. In recent years, the practices, processes and structures of the state have undergone major changes everywhere, affecting various aspects of policy making and practice. No nation state has escaped these pressures to change. Collectively, these changes are often referred as the 'restructuring of the state'. It is this restructuring and its implications for educational policy that are discussed in this chapter.

Why have there been such great pressures for restructuring? Part of the answer has already been suggested in our discussion of globalisation in Chapter Four. The globalisation of the economy has, to some extent, reduced the capacity of individual states to consider their own distinctive policy options. All nation states are today encouraged to 'internationalise' their economies, with profound implications for the restructuring of the state. Market activities are now considered the core building blocks of the very formation of the state itself. The state is thus no longer expected to mediate the excesses of the market, but rather provide conditions that support its operations. In recent years this mode of thinking has become the dominant way of conceptualising the state. Some politicians have gone so far as to suggest that we have no option but to accept the imperatives of globalisation in thinking about state activities. In this sense, globalisation has become an ideology, proselytised by international organisations such as the OECD and the World Bank in assertions of the need for less interventionist and leaner government and for freer forms of economic competition between nations.

This demand for smaller government is based on the assumption that the older bureaucratic structures and practices of the state were inefficient and expensive, that they inhibited market competition and were incapable of responding quickly to rapid change which had become endemic. For example, an OECD (1995: 7) study of public sector reforms observed that old style bureaucratic structures which were 'highly centralised, rule-bound, and inflexible' and which emphasised 'process rather than results' inhibited efficiency and effectiveness and were not able to respond rapidly enough to the demands of change. Such pressures resulted in the reform of public administration and organisational features of the public sector. These new practices and structures, borrowed from the private sector, are usually referred to under the generic name of 'corporate managerialism'.

It has to be admitted that there is an element of truth in the OECD's assessment of older style bureaucracies: they were indeed inflexible and rule-bound, and, significantly from our point of view, also somewhat undemocratic. Additionally, it needs to be recognised that following the events surrounding the 1974 OPEC oil crisis, most Western states were in crisis, finding it increasingly difficult to meet the greater expectations of their populations while at the same time satisfactorily managing their economies. This destabilised the Keynesian settlement which had been in place in most Western countries for the thirty years after the Second World War. Keynesianism was based on the moral idea that the state had a responsibility to intervene to manage demand in the economy in order to produce a just society with full employment and improving standards of living for all. In the past two decades, such assumptions have been rejected by a whole range of economists, and more particularly by governments throughout the Western world, led in the first instance by Margaret Thatcher and Ronald Reagan. Many analysts (for example, Freeland 1986, Beilharz et al. 1992) speak of the search for a 'post-Keynesian' settlement which has sought to redefine the economic behaviour of states in ways that are fundamental to an understanding of 'restructuring'.

At the same time, societies have increasingly become fragmented along a variety of dimensions, as many writers about postmodernism have indicated (for example, Harvey 1989, Jameson 1991). These dimensions include complex patterns of communication between people and nations, the impact of new information technologies upon civic life, the emergence of a robust consumer culture, the doubts about old epistemological certainties, the almost universal worshipping of the idea of flexibility in all social practices and the rise of new social movements. These movements have asserted their distinctive claims upon the state, highlighting the need for more complex ways in which they wish to see the state respond to their interests. As such, these movements have rejected a singular class politics in favour of the multiple elements of identity politics. The state cannot, therefore, expect its relationship with its political constituencies to be as straight-forward as it might once have been and has to somehow manage this complex politics of difference and shifting identities.

It is these various pressures – the impact of globalisation, crises of the state, the search for a post-Keynesian settlement, fragmentary impulses in society and the contradictions of identity politics – which serve to explain the widespread calls for the restructuring of the state. Of course, the form restructuring takes is not the same in all nations, but varies according to the specific political strategies, structures, cultures and histories of particular nations. For example, it could be argued that restructuring in Sweden has taken a different form from that in the US because the commitment to Keynesianism was more institutionalised in Sweden than in the US. In the UK, restructuring has taken place under a Tory government with a vigorous commitment to a deregulated labour market and an attack upon the organised trade union movement, whereas in Australia restructuring has been achieved at the national level by Labor governments more sympathetic to organised labour. Thus, the restructuring of the state has to be viewed against historical specificities. In short, national politics do matter.

Yet everywhere the objective of restructuring has been the delivery of more efficient and effective services across the board. In Australia this has been achieved through a variety of ways. First, there has been an attempt to narrow the state's policy agendas, subsuming social and cultural policies under the rubric of economic concerns. Thus, for example, Yeatman (1990) has noted how the national Labor governments in Australia from 1983 to 1996 granted 'meta-policy' status to economic restructuring which framed other policy domains, including education. Not only have government policies been aimed at workplace reforms throughout all sectors of the economy to ensure greater productivity and international competitiveness, but the agencies and practices of the state have themselves been the focus of 'micro-economic' reforms, that is, they have been asked to become more productive at lower costs, mimicking practices in the private sector. As part of this reform, central administrations have been devolved to ensure greater efficiency and effectiveness of policy delivery. However, and perhaps paradoxically, while local sites have been made responsible for policy implementation, and have been given some freedom to manage devolved resources, policy generation has become more centralised and politicised. That is, political leadership has taken a greater role in the making of policy than has probably been the case in the past, resulting in a reconstituted relationship between ministers and their public service bureaucracies. Also restructured has been the relationship between the two levels of government in Australia's federal system – the Commonwealth and the States – as part of the process of creating a national economic infrastructure and single economic market.

The restructuring of the Australian state has impacted substantially upon the character of educational policy, as well as upon the structures of policy production and practice. To begin with, whereas economic outcomes were once considered to be only one aspect of educational policy, they have now become central. The goals of education are thus in danger of becoming reconstituted. For example, the Labour period (1983–96) saw the emergence of a new form of human capital theory in national educational policy development across the three educational sectors of schools, technical and further education (TAFE) and higher education (Marginson 1993). Furthermore, the manner in which educational policy is now produced has become implicated in general public sector reforms. Thus, as we have said, each of the State educational bureaucracies in Australia has been restructured by corporate managerialism, a concept used to describe the ways in which the state and its agencies are now expected to manage change and deliver policy outcomes more cheaply.

Corporate managerialism, devolution, the role of markets in education, the new federalism and the development of human capital theory, then, are some of the key elements of the restructuring of the Australian state. In what follows, these elements will be discussed in greater detail in order to provide a better understanding of the ways in which restructuring has reframed the content of education policy, as well as the processes of policy making and practice.

CORPORATE MANAGERIALISM

So what do we mean by this rather awkward term corporate managerialism? Corporate managerialism has been defined by Sinclair as a 'rational, output-oriented, plan-based and management-led view of organisational reform' (1989: 389), while Weller and Lewis claim that 'managing for results' best encapsulates the essence of such reforms (1989: 1). Yeatman suggests that corporate managerialism is about 'doing more with less' (efficiency), 'focussing on outcomes and results' (effectiveness) and 'managing change better' (1987: 341). Unlike older style bureaucratic arrangements where the emphasis was on correct processes and rule orientation, with corporate managerialism the stress is on outputs and outcomes. Complementing the stress upon outcomes and performance are strategic mission statements and objectives, with the achievement of these objectives – effectiveness – measured through performance indicators. The central arms of government departments thus now attempt to steer practice more firmly through linking strategic statements and performance outcome measures. In speaking about a new paradigm for public management, the OECD (1995: 8) has noted that the goal has been the creation of a 'performance-oriented' and 'less centralised' public sector with the following characteristics: a focus on results and efficiency and effectiveness, decentralised management environments, flexibility to explore alternatives to public provision of services, establishment of productivity targets and a competitive environment between public sector organisations, along with the strengthening of strategic capacities at the centre of the organisation. This characterisation of corporate managerialism implies an imperative to privatise as many government services as possible, provided the costs to the state are lower. Here efficiency is often measured as reduced costs. Another way that costs are reduced is through the 'user pays' principle, that is, the view that only those using the service should be required to pay, thus rejecting the older idea that some services should be provided universally by the state on the basis of need rather than ability to pay.

Considine (1988) argues that the implementation of corporate managerialism involves a narrowing of policy goals which are set at a higher level within the organisation, with responsibility for the achievement of such goals devolved to lower levels within the organisation. Accompanying those changes are a number of other features, including corporate planning, programme budgeting, programme goals, performance indicators, some performance-based employment contracts for senior managers, appointment of generic managers expert in management but not in a specific professional domain, a more flexible 'hiring and firing' regime (beyond the career public service) and the introduction of efficiency audits and the like. Also, as noted above, these central office activities are accompanied by the devolution of some administrative tasks and budgeting. These changes have resulted in the creation of what Cerny (1990) has called the new 'competition state'. The idea of a 'competition state' highlights the dominance of market ideologies which imply the need for smaller and more efficient government and a less state directed market economy.

In Australia a key intellectual architect of corporate managerialism, Peter Wilenski (1986, 1988), some time senior public servant and management theorist, formulated a Labourite version of public sector restructuring aimed at achieving greater efficiency and effectiveness of government

policy delivery, while at the same time retaining Labour's commi
social justice and democratic participation. Such an approach cc
with that in the US or the UK where social justice agendas did no
so prominently in policy debates or initiatives. Certainly Labour governments embraced corporate managerialist restructurings with some
enthusiasm, first in New South Wales in the late 1970s, then in Western
Australia in the 1980s, where a key document, *Managing Change in the
Public Sector*, was produced. In general terms, though, public sector
restructuring using the principles of corporate management has been a
feature of governments from both sides of politics.

Corporate managerialist approaches were also adopted in education,
seen for example in the Western Australian report *Better Schools* (1987) or
the later Queensland Department of Education report *Focus on Schools*
(1990). Such reports provide a good example of the changes which have
been implemented in educational systems profoundly affecting schools
throughout Australia as part of overall public sector restructuring. Some
of the central characteristics of the restructuring of State educational systems could be described as follows:

- There is a mandatory development plan in each school. That is,
  schools have to create their own objectives, but within the framework provided by the overall goals of the Department.
- Schools must work from 'single-line' budgets. That is, where previously they were given funds ear-marked for particular purposes,
  they are now provided with a lump sum on which they have to
  operate for the year. They must do their own financial planning and
  decide how and on what they will use the funds.
- There are formally constituted school decision-making groups consisting of staff, students, parents and community representatives
  which endorse and in some cases help to formulate development
  plans and authorise budgets.
- Schools will be 'audited' by the central administration for both
  financial and educational purposes. That is, they are held accountable for how they use their money and for their educational 'outcomes'.
- The central office is now more focussed on defining policy and formulating strategic plans than in the day-to-day administration of
  schools.
- Rather than being centrally organised and provided, support services for schools (often called school support centres) are decentralised, being based either in schools or regions.

(Lingard, Knight and Porter 1995: 83)

Something of the dualistic centralising/decentralising characteristics of
managerialism in education are picked up in this listing, with the School

Development Plan being an important link between central office statements of mission and objectives and the school. School principals sit at
the nexus between the two sites. These reforms have been accompanied
by talk of self-governing, self-managing or self-determining schools, but
all within centrally determined policy frameworks and accountability
requirements, as well as reduced resources. Such a situation possibly
leaves central bureaucrats with power without responsibility and school
'managers' with responsibility without power. Stephen Kemmis has
commented somewhat acerbically on this situation:

> Regrettably the rhetoric of corporate management now widely
> adopted in public administration in Australia (including the adminis-
> tration of education) has come to be seen only as 'corporate' for man-
> agers – for others in departmental bureaucracies (and for people in
> schools), it is not seen as expressing authentic local commitment to
> corporate identity.
>
> (Kemmis 1990a: 22)

Kemmis goes on to add that corporate managerialism in education
involves 'the muscular imposition of systemic objectives' at the school
site. In outlining the 'steering at a distance' model of public administration implemented in higher education in the Netherlands, Kickert (1991)
describes how the usual hierarchical forms of control, such as regulations
and legal prescriptions, are rejected in favour of some institutional
autonomy and self-steering with 'ex-post corrections' made on the basis
of 'quality of outcomes'. In contrast, the new managerialism in
Australian schooling has often retained many of the top-down, hierarchical forms of control within a rhetoric of self-managing schools – with
self-management having more to do with managing reduced funding at
the school site than with anything else. As Ball notes, this is about asking
'those being cut to cut themselves' (1993: 77).

Across the 1980s and into the 1990s, as the economic circumstances
worsened, the progressive aspects of Labour's new managerialism – the
retention of social justice concerns – were weakened with the focus moving to efficiency and effectiveness or outcome measures. The latter has
the potential to emphasise the easily quantifiable at the expense of the
significant, a real danger in education systems. Despite this danger, most
State systems of education introduced standardised testing for accountability purposes across the period in question, yet another manifestation
of performance indicators characteristic of corporate managerialism. In a
field as complex and as contested as education, this focus on performance indicators runs the risk of reducing the range of curricula and
pedagogies that are valued.

A number of authors have pointed to a gendered dimension to these
overall restructurings. Lingard and Limerick (1995: 5), for example, have

suggested that educational restructuring has installed a more masculine policy regime within the state, while relations in schools have been re-gendered through (largely) male managers and a more heavily feminised teaching profession. Blackmore (1995) notes that it is very often women middle managers in schools – heads of department in particular – who are called upon to deal with the emotional labour necessary as a result of the disruptive effects of restructuring. To state the situation somewhat crudely, then, following restructuring males are making educational poli-cy and females are implementing it in schools.

CHANGING PRACTICES OF DEVOLUTION

As indicated in the previous section, corporate managerialism in educa-tion has seen new relationships emerge between the head offices of State departments of education and schools. Head offices have become more policy focussed and their relationship with schools has been reconstitut-ed through policy and performance measures. This rejigging has had both centralising and decentralising characteristics, reflected in the con-ceptualisation of 'managed decentralisation' (Curtain 1992). The ideas of decentralisation and devolution have been quite central to the processes of the restructuring of the state. Devolution has been seen as a possible response to the fragmentation of social life in most Western countries. It has been seen as a way of bringing about greater rationality and coher-ence to policy practices in the face of this fragmentation. It has also been viewed as a way of reducing duplication and costs, and achieving more predictable and effective outcomes.

Rizvi (1994) has traced three contrasting perspectives on devolution which have been manifest in education in Australia during the last twen-ty years, indicating the socially constructed and political character of the concept whose meaning is continually contested. These perspectives are the social democratic, the corporate managerialist and the market views; while one has tended to supersede the other, at present they probably sit in a residual, dominant and emergent relationship with each other (Williams 1981). Although the focus in this section will be on Australia, these contrasting accounts of devolution have also been played out in other comparable countries in a variety of ways during the last two decades.

Until the 1970s, Australia probably had the most centralised State sys-tems of schooling in the Western world, with the possible exception of France. They were classical examples of bureaucracy with hierarchical patterns of authority stretching from the minister to the director-general down through deputies, regional directors to principals and teachers in classrooms, with inspectors surveilling what went on in schools. When the Whitlam Labour government won office in 1972, it appointed the

Interim Committee of the Schools Commission which produced the Karmel Report (1973); this resulted in full systematisation of federal involvement in schooling geared to achieving more equal outcomes for all social groups. In addition, the Karmel Report highlighted the principles of devolution and participation, and as such challenged the long-standing centralist bureaucratic tradition in Australian schooling. The report articulated a socially democratic agenda, insisting that both teachers and parents be granted the resources to manage their own affairs in education to a greater extent. This was deemed necessary to recognise teacher professionalism and to ensure better educational outcomes for all students, particularly those from disadvantaged backgrounds. The Karmel Report thus provided a Commonwealth 'beachhead' into the bureaucratic State systems of education in its direct support for schools and teachers (Johnston 1993). The report was wary of top-down approaches, supporting instead bottom-up approaches and the devolution of decision making. Specifically, the Karmel Report asserted that 'responsibility should be devolved as far as possible upon the people involved in the actual task of schooling, in consultation with the parents of pupils they teach and, at a senior level, with students themselves' (Schools Commission 1973: 41).

Rizvi (1994) notes that Raymond Williams' *The Long Revolution* (1961) established the social principles to which the report aspired. Williams rejected both market capitalism and centralised bureaucratic socialism, and argued that 'self management and devolution' are important mechanisms for releasing 'a tremendous reservoir of social energy, now locked in resentment of bureaucratic and hierarchical organisation' (1961: 334), and for creating caring and participative communities. He emphasised the need for the establishment of an educated and participative citizenry which he justified in terms of democratic principles, as well as efficiency.

The social democratic conception of devolution articulated in the Karmel Report has continued to be influential despite changed economic and political circumstances. Its principles have survived in the decision-making mechanisms of the Disadvantaged Schools Programme, a Karmel creation, despite managerialist pressures upon it (Johnston 1993). Such values also underpinned some innovations of the 1980s, notably the Commonwealth's Participation and Equity Programme (1984–6) and the Victorian Cain Labour government's *Ministerial Papers* (1983), which articulated a social democratic version of devolution. This tradition appealed to teachers with its promise of greater professional autonomy and has become almost institutionalised within the teaching profession. It also appealed to parent activists with its commitment to democratic involvement of communities in schools.

The emergence of the corporate managerialist rearticulation of devolution may be seen as a response to pressures for a smaller and more competitive state. The language of devolution has played a significant role in corporate managerialist restructurings pursued by Labour governments at State and federal levels in Australia during the late eighties and early nineties. While equity and social justice remained on their agendas, the emphasis was upon efficiency and effectiveness, with concerns for democratic community participation somewhat dissipated. Considine (1988) has shown how the efficiency focus of corporate managerialism has encouraged a stress upon policy integration and the eradication of putative policy duplication, resulting in a narrowing of policy goals set at a higher level. Generic managers set these goals and attempt to ensure the integration of across-government policy. Here, democracy is reinterpreted to mean participation of the relevant interest groups in the policy process at the central level. Federal Labour took a corporatist approach in involving representatives from peak bodies in policy development. However, such involvement was often only symbolic, given that the authority for controlling policy development and implementation resides with the corporate management group in central office.

Corporate managerialism has involved the dual processes of centralisation and decentralisation with the aim of giving governments greater policy flexibility and achieving efficiencies in policy delivery. This rearticulation of devolution is nicely encapsulated by the observation of Max Angus, a former senior official with the Western Australian Department of Education:

> In the education context, the government was not intent upon devolving to schools the authority to determine what the ends should be. Quite the opposite. Underpinning the paradigm is the belief that better performance will result from sharper focusing on systemic priorities. What is being devolved to schools is the authority (and the capacity) to determine the way in which the school will achieve the agreed outcomes.
>
> (Angus 1990: 5)

What is also very relevant here is that the school's authority to determine the way in which it will achieve centrally determined goals is limited by cuts in overall educational expenditure and the devolution of a range of administrative and budgetary tasks from head offices to schools, thus intensifying the work of school administrators and teachers in the process. Lawrie Angus (1993) has suggested that such a managerialist construction of devolution is more about 'efficient site management' in schools than about democratic participation for educative ends. For teachers this has meant implementing centrally determined curricula and working as technicians to implement standardised testing for accountability purposes. For principals it has meant a more managerial character to their work.

The corporate managerialist view of devolution more recently has been ambiguously linked with what Rizvi (1994) calls the market conception. The market view in Australia has been pursued by Liberal governments in New South Wales and in Victoria and stems from new right opposition to the bureaucratisation of education and the desire to enhance parental choice in education – or at least utilise an ideology of parental choice. In England and Wales this ideology has been linked to a concern to break so-called 'producer capture', that is, the view that educational systems are dominated by teacher interests – run for the benefit of teachers rather than students. The market conception of devolution is just one element of a broader philosophy of market individualism which is about the enhancement of consumer choice within a less restrained market. This idea of devolution, then, has been rearticulated away from a social democratic construction to an individualistic one of self-interest and the right to make choices. The philosophical justification of such a view derives from the work of theorists such as Adam Smith, who argued that the collective well-being or common good is more likely to be realised when all individuals pursue their own goals with minimal interference from the state. This model reconstitutes citizens as consumers and supports a weakened role for the state as simply enforcing general rules to protect the rights of individuals to choose.

In education, such a model has potentially dire consequences for equality. For example, local control of schooling in the US results in very unequal provision, and while the older style bureaucratic Australian systems might have encouraged uniformity, they at least ensured a minimal level of equality of provision. Gewirtz et al. (1995) have also demonstrated the negative impact upon equality of the marketisation of schooling in England. Clearly, not all parents have the same capacities to make choices; choices are constrained by a complex range of material, cultural and social factors. In contrast, the market view assumes that choice is simply a matter of individual preference, unaffected by cultural learning and social and material conditions. A large body of research within the sociology of education has demonstrated how the culture of schooling works to the advantage of students from particular backgrounds. The implementation of a market definition of devolution will only intensify this situation and exacerbate the gap between the educational opportunities of the better-off and those of the poor. As Watt (1989) has argued, the differential curricular and pedagogical experiences which will result from a market conception of devolution will inescapably disadvantage poor students. In the English context this has led Ball (1994a) to observe that markets in education work as a class strategy mobilised by the middle classes to reassert their advantages in schooling in a political climate conducive to such mobilisation. In this context, policy making at the school site is concerned to ensure the school's competitive advantage rather than involve parents for educative purposes.

The corporate managerialist and market constructions of devolution both reconstitute the principal as a manager in which self-management becomes 'a mechanism for delivering reform' rather than one which provides 'a vehicle for institutional initiative and innovation' (Ball 1994a: 78). Here principals do 'the work of the state in imposing financial limits and disciplines in the practices of colleagues' (Ball 1994a: 74) and thus furnish a situation in which the state retains 'power without responsibility'. It is no coincidence, then, in such circumstances as in England and Wales, and as in Victoria under the *Schools of the Future* 'reforms', that a wedge has been driven between principals and teachers with negative consequences for collegiality. Little wonder, then, at the sales success of so many books on self-management in schools, which, as Ball (1994a) caustically remarks, usually bowdlerise self-managing schools as Mary Poppins places free of conflict, cuts in expenditure and emergent tensions between principals focussed on managing with less and teachers concentrating on educational effectiveness. What distinguishes the managerialist and market conceptions of devolution is that, with the latter, school principals are taken to be individually responsible for the fortunes of their schools. Further, Labour implementation of corporate managerialism has been accompanied by attempts to centrally mandate social justice policies, while under markets such matters are left to individual schools and can be ignored depending on market demands. As well as these market conceptions of devolution in schooling, a broader marketisation of education has occurred, which is discussed in the following section.

MARKETISATION OF EDUCATION

In educational policy, the idea of marketisation takes two distinct forms. One of these may involve attempts by educational institutions to market their academic wares in the commercial world, while the other form implies the restructuring of educational institutions so that business principles are applied to its administration. Buchbinder and Newson (1990) call these two aspects of marketisation 'inside-out' and 'outside-in'. In relation to higher education, they argue that university workers have been asked to become entrepreneurial and to convert their research into marketable products. These aspects of marketisation do not sit easily with many of the traditional cultural concerns of education.

The marketisation of education is of course part of the broader processes of restructuring taking place around the globe which have impacted upon the state. In the process, clear-cut public–private divisions between state activities and those of the market have been blurred.

Indeed, a number of private sector practices have been incorporated within state practices. For example, some state services have been privatised, some state monopolies have been subjected to competition, user-pays principles have been introduced for some government services and there has been a residualisation of the universal provision of many state services. The major aim of these changes has been the creation of smaller government. This has in a sense reconstituted the relationship of people to the state from one of citizens to that of consumers of state services.

In Australia it is perhaps the higher education sector that has been most affected by marketisation. Indeed, one of the central motivations for the creation of a unified national system of higher education in Australia has been the desire to create conditions necessary for mass participation. Since the state could not fully fund such a move, it could only be supported by attracting funds from elsewhere. Thus on top of a mixture of public funding and student fees, the universities were asked to find other sources of funding from a variety of activities within the private sector. Universities have responded by seeking alternative private sources of funding through a number of strategies, including the selling of university consultancy services, research capacities and research findings, and the introduction of some full fee-paying short courses, as well as degrees, particularly at the postgraduate level. Institutions also have to compete with each other for publicly funded research with limited success rates for applications.

Full fee-paying overseas students have also become important in this new scenario, with some institutions becoming very heavily dependent upon this funding source. In a deregulatory climate, most universities have viewed the 'export of educational services' as an important way of overcoming some of the fiscal problems they confront. Their entrepreneurial efforts in the selling of education in South-east Asia in particular have been extensive; so much so that the total number of full fee-paying overseas students has increased from around one thousand in 1987 to thirty thousand in 1993 (Alexander and Rizvi 1993). It is estimated that overseas students now bring some two billion dollars into the Australian economy annually.

Australian universities now provide education for a much larger percentage of the age cohort than in the past – almost 30 per cent. At the same time each institution has been placed in a more competitive relationship with other institutions within the system in terms of competition for both funding and students. Universities have thus been forced into elaborate advertising campaigns (Symes and Hopkins 1994), with a much higher percentage of university budgets now consumed by marketing activity than was the case in the past. According to Marginson (1993), a mixed economy now operates in relation to universities. As a result, the role of vice-chancellors has been partially reconstituted as that of a chief executive officer responsible to a board of directors – the senate or university council. There has also been pressure to reduce the size and representative character of governing bodies, resulting in a reduced emphasis upon the 'collective and democratic aspects' of university education and research and an enhanced stress on 'competitive forms of education' linked to individual advantage and competition between institutions (Marginson 1993: 175).

As a result of these changes, the language in which educational policies is now expressed is premised on market considerations and borrowed from the commercial world. As Kenway *et al.* observes:

> the market metaphor heads up a new policy and administration lexicon in education which includes such terms as *educational property, educational enterprise, entrepreneurial approaches to education, educational services, products, packages, sponsors, commodities and consumers, value-added education, user-pays, choice, competition* and so on. These and other terms both reflect and are helping to bring into effect, a relatively new and different era in public education in Australia, one in which educational purposes, languages and practices are being subsumed by marketing purposes, languages and practices.
>
> (Kenway *et al.* 1993: 4)

What we may now be witnessing is a major cultural change, with education conceptualised as simply another commodity for sale in the market place. This redefinition is complemented by developments taking place in various media and information technologies. Increasingly as education takes advantage of new broadcasting, publishing, computing and telecommunication possibilities in distance and electronic forms of education, it does so on the tacit terms of markets. The feasibility of particular initiatives in this area is judged more in terms of market reach and financial viability than educational or cultural benefits. As Hinkson (1991) has argued, there is now emerging a new nexus between the discourses of marketing, information technology and education.

Marketisation has also occurred in other sectors of education. The technical and further education sector has been encouraged to create mixed public/private provision of training and the use of a number of fee-for-service activities. The community access courses which the TAFE colleges used to provide as part of their civic responsibility have now been replaced with fee-paying lifestyle courses for those who can afford them. School systems in Australia have also been subject to pressures of marketisation, although schooling's intrinsic social purposes, however weakened, impose limits on the development of a pure market in this arena. Market effects have been seen in Victoria, where the *Schools of the Future* programme has sought to mimic corporate sector practices. Elements of marketisation have been introduced in the other State systems as well – particularly through internal markets whereby departments and sections pay for services provided by other arms of the state.

It is perhaps the schooling systems of England and Wales which have been subjected to the most thoroughgoing marketisation, following the Education Reform Act of 1988 and subsequent legislation. Gewirtz *et al.* demonstrate how this marketisation of schooling has been presented as a solution to the ' "problems" of cost, control and performance in the public sector' and that such a solution is linked to new right ideologies of smaller government, competitive individualism and self-interest as the basis for the 'good society' (1995: 2). They show how ideas of parental choice of schools, open enrolment practices, devolved budgets and 'self-managing' schools in which head teachers become managers responsible for the viability of their schools, have become important structural elements of the marketisation of schooling. Also central is the publication of test results or league tables for schools across the country, as well as school prospectuses which seek to 'impression manage' for desired clients – parents and students who will enhance rather than detract from the school's marketability.

Conceptually, then, the ideas of self-interest and choice are central to the changes taking place in the UK. Self-interest operates in two ways: in parents pursuing the best education possible for their children, and in head teachers ensuring the continuing viability of their schools in the market place. Gewirtz *et al.* sum up the findings of their research into the marketisation of schooling in England by noting that the outcome is the 'decomprehensivisation of schooling' as it becomes increasingly oriented 'to meeting the perceived demands of middle class parents' (1995: 181). In the process some government schools enter into competition with private schools, attendance at which is assumed to provide positional advantage in terms of access to higher education and to life chances.

This emphasis on choice and self-interest illustrates the extent to which market ideologies saturate the educational policy vocabulary. The ideology of choice is linked to the consumerist notion of 'the right of individuals to be able to choose in an unconstrained market'. However, the ideology of choice, as it relates to its professed commitment to improvement, is deeply contradictory, and certainly does not function *by itself* to produce the social benefits it frequently claims. Glenn (1993) has shown, for example, how the choice programme in Boston, USA, has in fact served to reduce the resources available to improve schools that most poor and minority children attend. The theoretical notion of 'choice' itself has not been problematised. The view of choice that is celebrated is derived from the notion of preference in neo-classical economics and a pluralist politics. But this view of choice is highly individualistic, overlooking its essential *social* character. It obscures the fact that choices are culturally constructed, and that institutions such as

schools have a major role in fostering those capacities that enab'
to choose intelligently and thereby secure some measure of cor
their lives. This view also fails to acknowledge that people's capacity
make certain choices is often dependent upon their cultural and material
resources and their social locations, which are frequently defined in class,
race and gender terms.

What these developments have done is to change the very focus of
educational practices away from social and cultural concerns to those of
individuals and the economies in which they participate. Central to this
shift has been the re-emergence of human capital theory, in terms of
which educational policy deliberations now take place. Whereas such
deliberations once took place at the State level, they now also occur in
the context of a changing Australian federalism. It is a discussion of these
matters to which we now turn.

CHANGING FEDERALISMS AND HUMAN CAPITAL THEORY

The pressures to restructure the state dealt with in this chapter, along
with the character of restructuring, have also had important implications
for the working of federalism generally and specifically in education.
Within Australia's federal political structure, roles and responsibilities
are divided between the two tiers of government, Commonwealth and
State, with Section 51 of the constitution outlining the powers of the
Commonwealth and those not listed remaining as the residual powers of
the States. Section 51 (xxiiiA), added to the constitution in the 1946 refer-
endum which justified the creation of the postwar Keynesian welfare
state, mentions 'benefits to students', but this is usually regarded as simply legitimating Commonwealth provision of scholarships and
allowances for students. However, it has been argued that this gives the
federal government considerable 'latent power' in education (Tannock
and Birch 1976), though education is not mentioned in the constitution
apart from this reference to 'benefits to students'. It is Section 96 which
allows the Commonwealth to make financial assistance grants to the
States, and which has been the basis for increased Commonwealth
involvement in education during the postwar period. Since the
Commonwealth took over income tax raising powers from the States in
1942, it has had a much greater revenue raising capacity than the States.
Indeed, the Commonwealth raises more revenue than it expends on its
own services, while the States raise less than they require to provide their
services. Consequently, the States remain heavily dependent upon the
transfer of Commonwealth payments. This situation – referred to as ver-
tical fiscal imbalance – when combined with the use of Section 96 grants,
has meant a considerably augmented federal involvement in all levels of
educational policy.

The result of all this has been an exceedingly complex picture of the working of federalism in Australian education which operates as much in political and financial terms as in legal or constitutional ways (Lingard 1993a, Borgeest 1994). Furthermore, the relationships between the States and Commonwealth are not constant but change over time. At times there has been co-operation between the two tiers of government, for example, when Whitlam took over full funding control of the higher education sector from the States in the 1970s. At other times there have been lengthy negotiations to achieve national policies, for example with the *National Policy for the Education of Girls in Australian Schools* (1987), discussed in Chapter Three. In relation to the TAFE sector, dealt with in more detail in Chapter Six, there have also been complex negotiations to establish the national education and training reform agenda. The political complexions of Commonwealth and State governments at any time are also compounding factors.

What we have seen, then, since the 1970s is the working of different federalisms in the three sectors of education (Lingard, Porter, Bartlett and Knight 1995). Differing Commonwealth/State funding arrangements in each of these sectors have been important determinants of the way in which federalism has worked in each case. Thus the surrendering by the States of control of higher education funding to the Commonwealth basically gives *de facto* control of higher education policy to the Commonwealth. Yet universities are still established under State legislation. In TAFE there is a very complex interplay of Commonwealth and State policy and financial initiatives, but at least since the early 1990s there has been some apparent agreement on the need for a national approach, given the perceived link between TAFE and the economy. It is the schools domain which is most jealously protected by the States as their responsibility. The figure of about 12 per cent is usually used to describe the Commonwealth's direct contribution to the funding of State systems of schooling. However, Marginson *et al.* (1995: 25–6) argue for a figure of 22 per cent for 1993–4 and add that, if one also considers the contribution of untied general purpose Commonwealth grants to the States, the Commonwealth's overall contribution to schooling is much higher again. Nevertheless, despite the Commonwealth's limited direct financial leverage, even in this policy domain there was some move towards national policy frameworks in the late 1980s and early 1990s when Labour governments dominated at both State and Commonwealth levels. Before looking at these developments further, however, something needs to be said about the new human capital theory which underpinned the attempted restructuring of federalism in education.

The expansion of education in the 1960s and early 1970s was predicated upon a generalised human capital theory which argued that education contributed to those elements of economic growth which could not be accounted for by other factors. This argument about the economic contribution of education was used as a justification of expanded provision and expenditure in the face of increased demand for education, and underpinned by the commitment of the Keynesian welfare state to equality of opportunity for all. Hence both individuals and society were seen to benefit from this increased provision. Following the economic recession of the mid-1970s, however, support for a human capital perspective on education went into a 'period of eclipse', though the theory itself appeared to underpin the scapegoating of education as the cause of high levels of youth unemployment and recession (Marginson 1993: 43). None the less, a reframed human capital theory was to come back into vogue in the vastly different political and economic context of the 1980s. Marginson (1993) traces the emergence of a new market version of human capital theory which regarded higher levels of education as necessary for the workforce to cope with rapid technological change. Workplace restructuring, referred to as micro-economic reform, was deemed to be essential to greater productivity, while better trained workers – usually referred to as multi-skilled and flexible – were thought necessary to such reform. There was another element which distinguished this human capital theory from earlier versions, notably the idea that because individuals benefited from prolonged educational participation in terms of better jobs, better career prospects and higher pay, they should contribute to the costs of their education through user-pays approaches. Marginson documents the significance across the 1980s of the OECD in proselytising this micro-economic version of human capital theory, and shows how it dovetailed nicely with the policy requirements of the time for a cheaper state and a restructured economy.

As Marginson (1993: 50) demonstrates, this new version of human capital theory, coupled with 'market reforms and higher private costs', underpinned many of the educational changes in OECD countries throughout the 1980s. Certainly, John Dawkins utilised such a theory to justify the restructuring of Australian higher education:

An expansion of the higher education system is important for several reasons. A better educated and more highly skilled population will be able to deal more effectively with change. A major function of education is, after all, to increase individuals' capacity to learn, to provide them with a framework with which to analyse problems and to increase their capacity to deal with new information. At the same time, education facilitates adaptability, making it easier for individuals to learn skills related to their intended profession and improve their ability to learn while pursuing their profession.

(Dawkins 1987: 1)

Because the Commonwealth funded higher education, Dawkins was able to utilise such human capital theory to create the unified national system of higher education which abolished the earlier binary system of universities and colleges of advanced education. Because of the different federalisms in TAFE and schooling, alternative political strategies and compromises were required to achieve national policies. None the less, human capital theory was one important underpinning of such attempts.

It is in this context that the Australian Education Council (AEC), the intergovernmental council in education consisting of Commonwealth, State and Territory ministers for education, became a more important site for the development of a range of national school policies. John Dawkins as federal minister (1987–91) utilised the AEC to pursue this agenda, particularly across the period in which Labour dominated State governments around the country. This was assisted by Labour's historical propensity to greater centralism than non-Labour governments, which have tended to be more federalist with greater support for so-called 'States' rights'. The enhanced policy significance of the AEC during this period is an indication of the politicisation of policy making which occurred in education as a result of the new corporate managerialism. Here the Commonwealth had more of a strategic role, while the States were involved in the running of the large government school systems. Despite this complex situation, the AEC endorsed the *National Policy for the Education of Girls in Australian Schools* (1987), approved *National Goals for Schools* (1989) and a *National Equity Strategy*. Subsequently, the AEC went some way towards accepting national curriculum statements and profiles and a set of competencies for schools, as well as approving a system for equating the different tertiary entrance scores from the various schooling systems around the country. There was also a range of other national policies, including the *National Aboriginal and Torres Strait Islander Education Policy*. This range of national policy developments built on a mixture of human capital, managerialist and equity assumptions, another manifestation of Labour's attempted conjoining in policy terms of economic rationalism with social justice concerns (Lingard *et al.* 1993).

The importance of the confluence of a large number of State Labour governments with a federal Labour government to the achievement of these national policies in schooling became very clear at the July 1993 AEC meeting in Perth. At that meeting, the conservative parties utilised their new majority to halt or at least slow down such national moves (Bartlett *et al.* 1994). Following acrimonious debate, the AEC agreed that subsequently the national curriculum statements and profiles, along with the competencies, would be pursued by the States in their own ways. The result has been a somewhat uneasy agreement on what has been called a 'minimalist national agenda' in schooling (Bartlett *et al.* 1994). Until its defeat in March 1996, the federal Labour government

continued to pursue its national schooling agenda. It did this by substantial financial support for teacher professional development through
the National Professional Development Programme (NPDP) and
through an accord between the Australian Education Union and the
federal government signed before the 1993 federal election. The national
agenda in respect of vocational education and training appeared to continue in a stronger fashion, probably because of greater consensus
across party lines that there was a need for a national approach in this
policy domain.

In March 1996 the federal Labour government lost an election amid
considerable community anxiety over more than ten years of restructuring. Yet the new conservative government under Prime Minister John
Howard is no less committed to the principles of corporate managerialism and internationalising the Australian economy. Indeed, it seeks to
reassert in more fundamental ways some of the Thatcherite principles of
market liberalism, including further deregulation of the labour market.
Also, it is committed to reducing federal government outlays by eight
billion dollars in the 1996 and 1997 budgets in an attempt to make the
government even 'leaner and meaner'. The Howard government is also
not as supportive of social justice principles which it feels are best deliv-
ered by economic growth and market activity. Additionally and in contrast to Labour, it supports more federalist views. In the late 1980s and
1990s federal Labour governments reduced grants to the States as part of
their budgetary strategy, rather than reducing Commonwealth outlays. It
would appear that the Howard government will probably cut both, with
considerable consequences for all sectors of education. The election of
the Howard coalition government has thus witnessed a new stage in the
working of federalism which is likely to result in yet another move to
reduce the supposed duplication of funding, policy and bureaucracy in
schooling. However, this will probably be achieved through the reduction of Commonwealth involvement in schooling, rather then via the
pursuit of national policies as attempted by Labour. What is certain is the
continued commitment by this government to micro-economic reform,
more efficiencies and even smaller government. This scenario does not
augur well for government schooling in Australia, nor for universities,
given their heavy dependence upon federal funding.

CONCLUSION

The restructuring documented throughout this chapter has meant a
number of things for educational policy. Educational policy has become
one element of broader economic policy as a new human capital view of
education has taken hold. A number of national educational policies
have thus emerged, even in schooling which, while drawing upon both

direct and indirect financial support from the Commonwealth, remains a State responsibility in Australia.

State education departments have been affected by the corporate managerialist restructuring of the entire public sector. They have put in place new head office relationships with schools, often within the rhetoric of devolution. However, as this chapter has been at pains to demonstrate, this has been managed decentralisation which has seen head offices develop a tighter and narrower policy focus and an emphasis upon strategic planning. What has been devolved to schools is the capacity to manage reduced budgets and 'self-manage' within the frameworks set by head office. The restructuring has been predicated on 'a clear separation between those who conceptualise policy (elite policy makers and interest groups) and those who execute or implement policy (operatives i.e. teachers)' (Smyth 1993: 3). The more recent move within Australian schooling under non-Labour governments to market approaches has seen further cuts in expenditure, the creation of competition between schools and weakened commitment to education as a public good to which all have a right. This has multiplied the demands upon 'self-managing' school principals, particularly to be efficient financial managers, that is, manage with less, and has adversely affected collegiality within schools.

Teachers' voices have been largely marginalised within this new structural framework for policy development. Thus new policy frameworks have been imposed on teachers who have been increasingly perceived as the implementers of policies constructed elsewhere and by other people. As Stephen Ball has put it in the English context: 'The teacher is increasingly an absent presence in the discourses of education policy, an object rather than a subject of discourse' (1994a: 50).

It is this situation, together with increased expectations and more centrally framed curriculum and accountability testing, which has changed the work of teachers. Australian Teaching Council (ATC) (1994) research found that teachers believed that the many recent changes at both State and national levels had reduced their scope for professional discretion and judgement, while at the same time they recognised that teaching and education were in a 'state of profound flux and change'. As an indication of the silencing of teachers' voices within the new structural framework for policy generation, including the politicisation of policy production and the incorporation of education policy as part of economic policy, the ATC research observed, regarding the perceptions of teachers:

> For them, the concern is that they do not feel that they are contributing as forcefully or effectively as they would like to the debates and policy changes which are so dramatically reshaping the world they live and work in.

(ATC 1994: 12)

We would note here, however, the lessons which can be learned from implementation research which starkly demonstrate the capacity of principals and teachers to resist the impact of imposed top-down policy frameworks. This is even more particularly the case when the policy is a national one derived from considerable negotiation at the intergovernmental council level and with various sites for potential refraction of original policy intentions in the stages of implementation.

This chapter has concentrated largely on the impact of state restructuring upon school systems and to a lesser extent within higher education. A national training reform agenda, including the role of technical and further education, has been another important element of restructuring; it is dealt with in the next chapter.

Chapter 6

Putting education to work

There'll be a convergence of work and learning, and the convergence of the workplace into both a work and learning place will have developed to such a degree that academic witchcraft will finally disappear.

(Laurie Carmichael, *The Australian* 2 June 1992)

THE VOCATIONALIST DISCOURSE IN EDUCATION

This chapter takes its name from the title of a report *Putting General Education to Work* (the 'Mayer Report', Australian Education Council/Ministers of Vocational Education, Employment and Training 1992), one of a series which appeared in Australia in the early 1990s advocating better linkages between education and the world of work. Collectively, these reports reflect an ascendant vocationalist discourse in education which began to take effect in the late 1980s, the context for which was signalled in the foreword to the Mayer Report.

> The changes currently occurring in Australian industry to enable Australia to compete in international markets depend on developing a workforce capable of participating effectively in new forms of work and work organisation. This requires a renewed emphasis on the role of general education in providing the foundation for a multi-skilled, flexible and adaptable workforce and a greater emphasis on broader employment-related competencies in vocational education and training.
>
> (Australian Education Council/Ministers of Vocational Education,
> Employment and Training 1992: foreword)

Of course, the vocationalist emphasis in education extends further back into Australian educational history – indeed, Marginson (1993: 147) argues that Australian education has always been utilitarian – and the recent interest in vocationalism is not confined to Australia. Vocational education and training policy is high on the political agenda of most OECD countries (OECD 1994a), and the World Bank (1991) has published a policy statement on vocational education and training with respect to developing countries. The new developments highlight the general point made in earlier chapters that education is no longer – if ever this were true – the province solely of education policy making. At the same time, it should be stressed that education cannot be depicted solely within vocationalist terms, no matter how dominant the current trends.

Educational purposes historically have always been ambiguous and controversial, meeting diverse and sometimes contradictory demands. In Western societies these could be broadly categorised as: social or nation building, aimed at producing an informed citizenry integral to the modern liberal or social democratic state; economic, relating to the production of a range of appropriately skilled workers for the labour market; and meeting individual needs for employment and/or personal development. How these at times conflicting demands have been reconciled, and which purposes have received policy priority at any given time, are reflected in 'policy settlements' (see Chapter Two) reflecting prevailing economic, political and social circumstances. In relation to the broad sweep of education policy making in Australia, Seddon refers to the dominant liberal-meritocratic settlement of the early twentieth century, 'imbued with liberal democratic commitments to public service and the public good', reframed more recently by an 'economic reductionist context' in which 'public policy objectives [are] couched in terms of economic goods' (1992/3: 8).

The focus of this chapter will be on how the vocationalist agenda in education is being played out in this new context. But to understand why the shift occurred, the compromises and conflicting interests involved, and the difficulties involved in moving to a new policy agenda, we need at least a brief overview of prior educational arrangements.

POLICY ANTECEDENTS

Broadly speaking, the liberal-meritocratic settlement involved reconciling competing claims between political imperatives for equality in democratic societies and the structured inequalities of capitalist economies. The meritocratic solution lay in the translation of the principle of 'equality' into provision of 'equality of opportunity' for all individuals on the basis of talent and effort; that is, regardless of the ascriptions of birth, individuals were seen to have an equal opportunity to climb the social ladder. Education became a pivotal mechanism in this process through the establishment of a variety of sifting and sorting mechanisms (the most evident of which were external examinations and other forms of standardised tests) which filtered and stratified students ostensibly on the basis of merit.

A key element of educational stratification was the creation of a dual approach which distinguished 'academic education' and 'vocational training', both in the structure of education systems and in the curriculum. General education was viewed primarily as academic knowledge, with an emphasis on abstract subjects such as maths, the sciences, literature and traditional languages such as French, German or even Latin. In Australia, the 'competitive academic curriculum' (Connell *et al.* 1982) dominated in the elite private schools and in the academic streams of comprehensive state and Catholic schools (which educated a goodly proportion of Australian youth). The predominantly middle- or ruling-class students who completed such an education and generally proceeded to university were destined – or at least aiming – for well-paid professions or senior administrative posts. Vocational training, by contrast, tended to be seen as an alternative for those 'without brains' waiting until such time as they were free to leave school and get a job. Vocational streams were found in most state schools and some private schools (particularly in the poorer parish Catholic schools). A vocational (mostly male) elite went on to gain trades qualifications at technical and further education institutions.

While these two strands were sociologically class (and gender and race) based, they were rarely presented as such but rather as options for students to take according to aspirations and ability – reflecting, in other words, meritocratic assumptions. In this, Australia was hardly alone, for similarly stratified educational arrangements, though with considerable variations in detail, were found in all Western societies. In some cases, like Germany, technical, vocational and academic education streams were structurally separated, with the former being well-funded and valued. In many European countries, as in Australia, vocational and academic streams within comprehensive schools were separated more by curriculum than by structure (OECD 1989b).

Critical accounts of education challenged the meritocratic ideal, arguing in effect that a schooling system divided along 'practical' and 'academic' lines served to lock individuals into class strata rather than to promote social mobility. Seddon, for example, commenting on the history of the separation of education and training in Australia into two distinct streams during the 1920s, points to its social effects:

> Liberal democracy's enclaves of 'education' and 'training' served academic and labour elites well, through higher education – the closed shop of the professions – and apprenticeships – the closed shop of skilled work. It did a disservice to those beyond the frames of the 'intellectually able' (and culturally privileged) and the skilled male worker. Those who did not belong to the 'education' and 'training' hierarchies were 'disadvantaged'.

> (Seddon 1992/3: 7)

Similarly, in relation to the UK, Young (1993: 213) points to ↑
vocabulary of a deeply divided system' – for example, 'technical', 'aca.
mic' and 'vocational' education, 'knowledge' and 'skills' – reflected and
helped shape underlying class contours and labour market inequalities.

Although meritocracy was embedded in liberal notions of a public
good, its critics argued that, in practice, education was overly beholden
to economic imperatives flowing from the organisation of industrial production processes. In the early twentieth century, these were influenced
by the principles of Frederick Taylor, an American time and motion
expert who advocated a strict division of labour, including separation of
mental and manual work and total management control over the labour
process (Braverman 1974). Taylorist organisation was exemplified in one
of the early showcases of industrial capitalism, the mass production lines
of the Ford motor company, hence the term 'fordism' to denote this particular form of organisation.

Bowles and Gintis (1976) elaborated on this thesis in *Schooling in
Capitalist America*, arguing that schooling served to produce a suitably
differentiated workforce for an unequal and class-based labour market.
They suggested that this process occurred not so much through curriculum content as through the hidden curriculum of values and relationships, in particular through a correspondence between the hierarchical
social relations of schooling and work. In similar vein and also in relation
to the United States, Jean Anyon (1980) observed how pedagogical
processes conditioned future workers for their position in the workforce,
with children attending elite private schools (potential executive material) receiving a challenging and liberal education emphasising qualities of
independence, problem-solving and abstract thinking, while their
working-class counterparts were taught passivity and obedience through
an emphasis on rote learning and basic skills. Similar observations were
made of British and Australian education (e.g. Dale *et al*. 1976, Connell *et
al*. 1982, Shilling 1989).

As we have indicated, these broad developments seem to have been
endemic to Western education, though most countries in various ways
have over time tried to find ways of realising the meritocratic ideal, for
example through an expansion of comprehensive secondary education
(extended in the US to a form of mass tertiary education in pre-vocation-
al colleges offering a broad liberal curriculum), or through special programmes for disadvantaged students (for example British and US
programmes in compensatory education). In Australia, the most sus-
tained attempts to do this came from the Commonwealth Schools
Commission which argued that, in order to achieve more equitable outcomes of schooling, more inclusive and participative approaches to education needed to be developed. Under its auspices until its abolition in
1987, a wide array of policies and practices emerged which many

would argue significantly contributed to making Australian education more humanistic and equitable (Connell *et al.* 1991, Dudley and Vidovich 1995).

By the mid-1980s in Australia, as elsewhere, the dual system was becoming significantly eroded by a changing economic and labour market context with consequent devastating effects on employment, especially for young people. Seddon (1992/3: 8) refers to this as the context of economic reductionist modernisation, the main effect of which, she argues, was to position education more centrally within a market rather than a public sector setting, thus transforming individual students (or their parents) into market players – consumers – rather than citizens. A related effect, we would add, is that the new context also framed education more explicitly in terms of national interest, defined in terms of the role of human capital formation in economic competitiveness.

This theme had been heavily promoted by the OECD, arguing, as we saw in Chapter Four, that 'the skills and qualifications of workers are coming to be viewed as critical determinants of effective performance of enterprises and economies' (OECD 1989a: 18). In Australia, this argument was reiterated by the Commonwealth on many occasions as the basis for its 'national interest' in education across all sectors, even schooling, a particularly sacrosanct State preserve:

> The lesson we have learnt is the need for a more balanced industrial structure and increased flexibility and responsiveness in the economy. Adjustment of our society and economy is inevitable and necessary if we and our children are to have meaningful and fulfilling lives . . . schools are the starting point of an integrated education and training structure in the economy. . . . They also form the basis of a more highly skilled, adaptive and productive workforce.
>
> (Dawkins 1988b: 1, *Strengthening Australia's Schools*)

The focus on investment in human capital, as we saw in the previous chapter, was hardly new; funding for the development and expansion of mass secondary education in the 1950s and 1960s had been justified on essentially just such grounds. What was new, however, about the 'new vocationalism' was its location in economic rather than education policy, and the greater direct involvement of business and industry and, in some instances, unions in vocational education and training (OECD 1994a). In Australia, the trend was exemplified in the very formation of the Department of Employment, Education and Training (DEET) in 1987 and in the constitution of the committees making education policy. For example, the key reports in vocational education and training, which we will look at shortly, were produced by committees chaired by business executives (Brian Finn and Eric Mayer) and a former assistant secretary of the Australian Council of Trade Unions (Laurie Carmichael).

The argument of the new vocationalists was that changes in the nature and organisation of work demanded changes to existing educational arrangements and curricula. The general argument went something like this. In the post-industrial and technologically sophisticated global economy, fordist mass production methods have been replaced by flexible specialisation techniques. In this context, the competitive edge will be gained through the quality of the workforce in a changed workplace culture, rather than through the efficient standardisation of production design. Hence the requirement now was for multi-skilled workers, able to respond quickly and intelligently to the ever-shifting demands of niche marketing. The rigid hierarchical Taylorist division of labour and mental–manual divide, characteristic of old fordist production methods, had to give way to more flexible, team-oriented and holistic approaches to work (Henry and Franzway 1993: 128).

Against this backdrop, arguments were made for new approaches to education and training: a convergence of general and vocational education; more flexibility and better articulation between previously segregated sectors; and encouragement for young people to stay in the education and training system much longer. The end result, it was argued, would serve both national interests in the form of value-added human capital, and personal interests in the form of improved employment options, especially for young people excluded from the traditional academic pathways between school and university.

These trends aroused considerable controversy, especially among the educational establishment (and particularly in the older universities) which had been largely excluded from the committees writing the reports and who saw in the new proposals a dangerous potential for a narrow instrumentalism. In the words of one vice-chancellor: 'Universities are not about preparing for economic consequences and to look after microeconomic reform. They are not about training people for jobs. A university education is about training people to think' (*The Australian*, 23 September 1992). Debates raged around questions such as the more general purposes that education should serve, how to define employment-related education and in whose interests this might be, how and where such education should be conducted, how it should be resourced and, of course, about who it was that should decide such matters.

These developments, then, form the background to the policy questions addressed in this chapter, of the 'what, how, why and why now' kind suggested in Chapter Three. We want to discuss what the policies are saying (their content), their underlying assumptions (how they are framed), why they emerged at this particular time and how they have been received and implemented. In doing this, we are interested in looking at the various interests involved, the compromises reached and the issues which were ignored or put in the 'too hard' basket. And of course, we want to consider how the policies actually worked, that is, how they were resourced and administered, which aspects were taken up and in whose interests.

These issues are explored further in the remainder of this chapter in the form of a case study, which looks at the evolution and early implementation in Australia of a series of education and training initiatives forming part of a broader national training reform agenda – in Maguire and Ball's (1994) terms, as we noted in Chapter Three, a trajectory study. While the context is Australian, the policy implications, which we discuss towards the end of the chapter, have wider application given, as we have indicated, the pervasiveness of these policy trends world-wide.

AUSTRALIAN POLICY INITIATIVES AND THEIR CONTEXT

The opening few pages of policy documents often give a glimpse of their main concerns and underlying assumptions, as we just saw in the case of *Strengthening Australia's Schools*. Here are two more:

> Australia will remain part of an international economy in which change is continuous. A highly trained and flexible labour force makes possible sustained improvements in living standards through the capacity to adapt to major changes in the economic environment. . . . The world's most successful economies have typically given high priority to basic education and to the skills which determine competence at work. They have shaped their skills development policies accordingly. Australia has not seen this relationship so clearly; the time has come to do so.
>
> (Dawkins and Holding 1987: 3–5)

> Enhancing the skills of the workforce improves Australia's international competitiveness. It also improves general productivity and the quality of goods and services; it increases flexibility; and it increases the capacity of workers to adapt to change and improve their career opportunities.
>
> (Australian National Training Authority 1994a: 2)

Key words and phrases clearly signal the new vocationalist agenda: international competitiveness, flexibility, productivity, competence, skills. Had we gone beyond the opening pages, we would have encountered another discourse, relating to equity and disadvantage, for example: 'The AVC [Australian Vocational Certificate] system cannot directly change the underlying causes of inequality in society, or the existing patterns of social disadvantage. But it can help by improving access to training' (Employment and Skills Formation Council 1992: 14). We will say more about the juxtaposition of these two discourses later, but first let us look at how some of these ideas were developed in three key reports, generally referred to in Australia as the Finn, Carmichael and Mayer reports.

Finn, Carmichael and Mayer reports

Young People's Participation in Post-Compulsory Education and Training (Australian Education Council Review Committee 1991), more generally known as the Finn Report, emphasised the need for a convergence of general and vocational education and of work and training, underpinned by a number of 'key competencies' necessary for all young people to learn in their preparation for employment. The report stressed the need for a variety of pathways for students through the education system, with improved articulation between the schooling, technical and further education and higher education sectors, as well as with workplaces and training providers. In addition, it paid some attention to strategies required for the successful participation of young people from socially and economically disadvantaged groups.

The Carmichael Report, the *Australian Vocational Certificate Training System* (Employment and Skills Formation Council (ESFC) 1992) set out the broad parameters for a new training system, the Australian Vocational Certificate training system (later the Australian Vocational Training System – the AVTS). The AVTS effectively extended schooling to the end of year twelve by offering various education and training 'pathways', and various combinations of work and schooling. It also embraced a competency-based approach taking account of 'what a person can do, rather than how long they spend in training. With competency based training, what the student already knows (their "prior learning") is assessed and built on' (ESFC 1992: 8). The AVTS was seen to contribute to equity by improving access to training, providing training opportunities for a wider range of occupations and through the emphasis on flexible pathways (p. 14).

The final report in this triad, *Putting General Education to Work: The Key Competencies Report* (Australian Education Council/Ministers of Vocational Education, Employment and Training 1992), otherwise known as the Mayer Report, fleshed out the key competencies initially flagged in the Finn Report. These were seen as generic in nature, that is, applying to work generally as well as to further education and adult life. The Mayer competencies were identified as: collecting, analysing and organising information; communicating ideas and information; planning and organising activities; working with others and in teams; using mathematical ideas and techniques; solving problems; using technology. An eighth competency, cultural understanding, mentioned in the Finn Report, was approved only after several years of debate (Scott 1995).

As indicated, a secondary theme running through these reports was the concern with equity, and in this, unlike the UK for example, Australia adopted the social democratic tradition viewing social equity and economic efficiency as complementary rather than antithetical goals. In the reports, equity was conceptualised in two ways: specifically in relation to the needs of identified disadvantaged (or equity target) groups; and more broadly in terms of the argument that the policies would lead to more generally equitable outcomes because of their more inclusive education and training provisions. As Laurie Carmichael (1992), one of the chief architects of training reform put it: 'If we get the basics right, equity will follow' – a sentiment reaching its apotheosis on the frontispiece of yet another document proclaiming: 'The issue of vocational education and training transcends all other loyalties . . . it is in the first place, a national issue of equity' (Australian National Training Authority 1995).

These documents laid the basis for a good deal of subsequent policy development and associated restructuring of education and training arrangements, some of which we will mention shortly. We have already alluded in a general way to some of the reasons for these developments. These are elaborated in more detail now in relation to the Australian context.

Why the new policies, and why now?

Three factors are important in explaining the emergence of the new policies in vocational education and training in Australia: changes in the labour market and impact on employment patterns; developments in progressive education policy aimed at promoting more equitable educational outcomes; and links with older socialist worker education agendas.

Labour market changes were initially signalled in the collapse of the youth labour market, a process which began in the sixties but only became apparent a decade later, as evidence mounted as to the limited job prospects available to young people without educational or vocational credentials. In the past, employment for early school leavers without such credentials was not problematic, so the fact that secondary schools remained to a significant extent elitist, as we indicated earlier, was not a major concern to politicians or policy makers. What to do with reluctant school stayers, whose job prospects were increasingly likely to depend on educational qualifications, was thus one major factor driving the new policies.

By the 1980s, it was becoming evident that labour market changes were likely to impact significantly on employment patterns more broadly. The educational implications of these were foreshadowed in a key document, *Australia Reconstructed* (Australian Council of Trade

Unions/Trade Development Commission 1987), a blueprint for union and workplace reform published following a joint mission by the ACTU and the TDC (an Australian government instrumentality) in 1987 to Scandinavian and northern European countries to see how those countries were restructuring their economies. Out of *Australia Reconstructed* came proposals for workplace changes which formed such an important part of Labour's micro-economic reform agenda, including an ambitious programme of training reform, referred to as the National Training Reform Agenda (NTRA).

The NTRA embraced a number of developments. Chief among these were the establishment of a National Training Board to develop a national framework for competency-based training across all industries; the restructuring of the TAFE sector and creation of an open training market; the endorsement of the Australian Vocational Training System and other policies flowing from the Finn and Mayer reports; and the establishment of the Australian National Training Authority to oversee and coordinate vocational education and training provision nationally.

As well as these developments relating to the changing labour market, the policies also built on progressive educational thought as seen in various blueprints for socialist education. For example, linking education with work was basic to Marxist theories of education which advocated a high level of education for everyone, overcoming the division between manual and mental work; removal of the distinction between working and learning, and between school and work; and a democratic society where everybody is involved in planning and decision making (Castles and Wustenberg 1979: 7). For this reason, although the new policies were opposed by some progressive educators who regarded them as excessively instrumental, they were also supported by others for their potential to break down the class effects in education.

Additionally, the new policy agenda also built on earlier attempts at overcoming educational inequalities which began in the 1960s with the development of comprehensive coeducational secondary schooling to the end of year ten, that is, over the compulsory years. In Australia, these reached their most elaborated form, as we saw, during the Whitlam years and the initial phase of the Commonwealth Schools Commission in the early seventies. As the effects of youth unemployment started to appear in the mid-seventies, efforts were made to increase participation in years eleven and twelve (Ruby 1992). Although the reason for youth unemployment had to do with structural changes in the labour market, initially the phenomenon was interpreted as a failure of education to prepare young people for work. In 1979 the influential Williams Report on the relationship between employment, education and training (Williams 1979), commissioned by the then Liberal Prime Minister, Malcolm Fraser, recommended tighter links between education and employment and more relevant vocational education in schools. Consequently, an emphasis on 'transition education' (incorporating features such as work experience programmes) became prevalent, premised on the assumption that lack of skills was the cause of teenage unemployment. In this context, although the goal was comprehensive education with better retention rates for all students, vocational education continued to be viewed as an alternative for so-called non-academic students.

With the election of the Hawke Labour government in 1983, this dual approach was again challenged, though from two rather different policy directions. During Susan Ryan's term as Minister for Education (1983–7), the Schools Commission again exerted a considerable humanistic and egalitarian influence, though within more straightened economic circumstances. Significant amongst its work was the establishment of the Participation and Equity Programme, which placed on the policy agenda the total reform of the secondary school curriculum in order to cater for the needs of a broader group of students. John Freeland argues that the Participation and Equity Programme (Commonwealth Schools Commission 1984) represented the capturing of the 'vocational relevance' argument by progressive educators, with 'the instrumentalist conservative push for vocational and attitudinal training [being] hijacked by the liberal progressives and converted into an agenda more consistent with comprehensive post-compulsory education reform' (1992: 73). In 1987 the policy approach shifted, though the reform agenda remained. As we saw in previous chapters, John Dawkins, as Minister for Employment, Education and Training, set a new economic rationalist (or economic reductionist, in Seddon's terms) context for educational policy aimed at achieving efficiency with equity.

At the level of rhetoric, then, the new policies in vocational education and training were not cast simply in an economic mould. Furthermore, as we have indicated, they linked with earlier traditions of educational reform, including attempts to address the 'culture of failure' which the liberal meritocratic settlement had produced. Essentially, then, the 1980s new vocationalist policy agenda in Australia, as in many other countries, reflected a complex set of policy goals which attempted to bring together 'the concern with education and equality in the 1970s, and with education and the economy in the 1980s' (OECD 1989b: 15). As McFarland and Vickers suggest in more general terms, vocational education and training held out 'a promise that [it] can meet the international economic challenge of building a skilled workforce while at the same time responding to the social challenge of expanding educational access and opportunity' (1994: 16).

An agenda 'stitched together'? Competing interests and discourses

As we can see, then, the themes embraced in the new policy agenda were sufficiently ambiguous to mobilise diverse interests. As Freeland put it, there was 'a peculiar coincidence of interests between progressive democratic educators, those seeking greater equity in labour market access, participation and returns, and those seeking a fundamental restructuring of the economy based on the principles of cooperative tripartite planning' (1992: 86). However, not all industry groups were sympathetic, and many progressive educators joined with educational conservatives in dismissing the agenda as overly instrumental and centralist. In Fulcher's (1989) terms, the agenda was riddled with competing interests and discourses, a point we will return to later in the discussion on implementation issues. But let us take just one example, the issue of competencies, in order to illustrate some of the complexities involved in this rather 'stitched up' agenda.

At least three strands of competence were identified in the documents: developments in competency-based training, assessment and certification associated with the work of the National Training Board; the more specific employment-related competencies associated with the AVTS; and the generic or key competencies of the Finn and Mayer reports which, Eric Mayer stressed, should be seen as distinct from specific employment contexts: 'There is a fear that the key competencies will be linked to the proposed Australian Vocational Certificate and end up being driven by industrial relations issues. I do not believe industrial relations concerns should determine what people learn for work' (*The Australian*, 14 October 1992). Given the discursive range, however, proponents were able to read their own – and at times quite different – version of competence into the policies. For example, a leading industrialist argued at the time that business should be entering the debate 'as to how education might best respond to the growing need for tightly focussed, employment-related skills for students entering the workforce' (*The Australian*, 3 June 1992). At the same time, the Union of the Australian Council of Academics was able to assert that:

> narrow, simplistic and behaviouristic definitions of competencies must, of course, be rejected. [However], it is possible to embrace the ideas of competencies, broadly defined, and of competency-based training. If we do not we run the risk of isolating higher education, rendering it an elite and largely obsolete structure.
>
> (Nicholls 1992: 4)

Equally, opponents were able simply to conflate the competency strands, dismissing the whole 'competency movement' as technicist, centralist and simply uneducational. One vice-chancellor, for example, criticised 'the seemingly inexorable thrust for the application of competency-based standards in education', arguing that 'the presumption that all education was work-related embodied an embarrassingly materialistic approach' (*The Australian*, 23 July 1992). David Penington, then Vice-Chancellor of Melbourne University and staunch critic of Labor's centralist policy approaches generally, charged that 'the competencies movement' sought to 'control all education and training in terms of "work-related competencies" and to bring all within a seamless web of control . . . through a network of tripartite committees of union, industry and government representatives' (*The Australian*, 18 November 1992).

Other key notions of equity, pathways and convergence were similarly ambiguous and contentious, as we will see later. Also relevant, though, was the tangle of interests involved in Australia's federal structure, further complicated, in the case of vocational education and training, because of the multiple policy fields involved: employment, labour market, youth affairs and vocational education within schools and TAFE institutions.

The context for the training reform agenda, as we saw, was inexorably national. At the same time, TAFE and schooling – the chief providers of vocational education and training – were historically and jealously guarded State preserves, highly resistant to 'the clammy hands of Canberra' (South Australian Minister for Further Education, *The Australian*, 16 October 1991). Commonwealth moves to restructure TAFE nationally and establish an open training market provoked intense opposition from the States who initially rejected an offer of two billion dollars from the Commonwealth for their stake in TAFE. After considerable wrangling, agreement was reached between Commonwealth and State governments over the establishment of the Australian National Training Authority (ANTA) in 1992, with the Commonwealth's financial muscle being offset by the States' voting rights. The States would take responsibility for their own training systems, but within ANTA guidelines. ANTA would coordinate and disperse funding for vocational education and training across the States via a network of consultative arrangements with State training authorities and State and national Industry Training Advisory Boards.

However, schools are also involved in vocational education and training, particularly at the senior secondary level where links with TAFE institutions and workplaces have become more common. As we saw in the previous chapter, bringing State schooling systems within a national framework has been a politically fraught process, a factor of some significance in promoting a national approach to vocational education and training. Hence, as we will see, negotiating around States' interests remained a key feature of the policies as they were taken up.

HOW HAVE THE POLICIES BEEN TAKEN UP?

So far, in terms of the context-text-consequences framework for policy analysis outlined in Chapter Three, we have been looking mostly at the relationship between context and text. What this showed were some continuities and points of difference with previous policy agendas, and also the compromises and competing interests embedded in the new policies. These contextual factors have implications for policy outcomes, that is, for the way in which policies are taken up in practice – the focus of our discussion in this section where we are looking at the relationship between text and consequences. Our concern here is on how, and in what ways, the key elements of the new policies have been adopted, for certainly it would be true to say that developments moved very rapidly during the 1990s. In all States there were moves to broaden the academic curriculum and to create better linkages between schools, TAFE colleges and workplaces. State education systems set up committees to examine ways of implementing the Mayer competencies. Universities developed policies on cross credit transfer, including in the area of recognition of prior learning (that is, giving credit for previously acquired competencies obtained in informal settings, for example organisational skills acquired through childrearing). TAFE institutions embarked on a comprehensive programme of rewriting curriculum in competency-based modules and developing 'flexible delivery' strategies. Even universities began to examine ways of adopting competency-based approaches and convergence strategies in some subjects or areas of study. Pathways between TAFE and university education have become well established, and while TAFE generally remains a stepping stone to a university degree, a significant number of students has reversed that direction.

What interested us in all of this was the question of which interests and which meanings came to dominate in these developments. This was the focus of our own research on the Australian Vocational Training System (Henry and Taylor 1995a, 1995b) and other developments in the training reform agenda (Taylor and Henry 1994, 1996). We were particularly interested in early developments because of their likely impact on how the agenda would consolidate over time. By and large we restricted our interest to the educational rather than the industrial aspects of the agenda, though it is not always easy to separate the two. For example, there are educational issues in industry-based training, and there are industrial issues in competency-based curriculum development in schools.

The research focussed on two aspects of the training reform agenda seen as particularly significant, given the educational problems and associated 'culture of failure' the policies were attempting to address: the extent to which the academic–vocational divide was being broken down, and the extent to which the needs of groups traditionally disadvantaged in education and training were being picked up. Of the various target groups identified in the documents (women, Aborigines and Torres Strait Islanders, people from non-English speaking backgrounds, people with a disability, people in rural or remote areas, the unemployed, particularly the long-term unemployed, and people with low literacy levels) we chose to look in particular at how the new policies were impacting on women and girls. But our more general analysis was concerned with evaluating the claim: 'If we get the basics right, equity will follow,' a claim referring essentially to the class effects of traditional educational arrangements.

The Australian Vocational Training System was formally adopted in 1995 when it became part of ANTA's general responsibility for vocational education and training. Initially, though, the AVTS was trialled via a number of pilot projects administered and funded through the Department of Employment, Education and Training and the State education departments. Pilots were classified as either institution-based or work-based, with trainees in the latter being paid and subject to industrial agreements. We examined the documentation surrounding the pilot projects – at the Commonwealth, State and local levels – in order to trace the implementation and monitoring procedures which were emerging, as well as emergent patterns of participation. In follow-up research and as part of our overall aim to follow a policy initiative through from inception to its implementation phase, we also looked at early ANTA documentation in order to see how ANTA was framing its approach to implementation and conceptualising equity within that framework.

Our policy 'texts', then, included policy statements and implementation guidelines, submissions, minutes of meetings, statistical compilations and project evaluations. Additionally, we interviewed a number of key players from State and Commonwealth bureaucracies and other institutions involved in education and training, from ANTA and from the trade unions, in order to gather their impressions of emerging trends. To gather more detailed information about how the new policies were being taken up in practice, we studied in some depth four institution-based pilots in Queensland: a teacher training project, a retail project, a trades project and a senior studies curriculum project.

Developments 'on the ground'

In general terms, the research suggested that the progressive (from our point of view) potential of the new policies was not realised in the early implementation stages. While the pilots certainly embraced the new rhetoric of convergence, pathways and competencies, there seemed to be little evidence that traditional arrangements – in particular, the vocational–academic divide – were radically disturbed. Gender patterns remained almost totally unchanged! What happened, and why?

Part of 'what happened' had to do with slippages between different levels of involvement with the policy processes, for example between Commonwealth- and State-based procedures and between these official processes and the conduct of the projects themselves. Commonwealth procedures for dealing with the projects were set out in a set of guidelines in 1992, followed a year later by a national evaluation strategy. More particular strategies for addressing equity concerns were distributed by DEET in two documents, *Access and Equity: Explanatory Notes for AVC Pilot Proposals* (1993b) and a *Draft Equity Strategy* (undated) – the first as addenda almost six months after the guidelines had been released, and the second almost a year after the pilot phase had commenced!

Nevertheless, in this documentation the rhetoric in relation to equity goals was reasonably strong. Amongst other things, the strategy indicated that 'a matrix of pilot projects will be developed and maintained . . . to identify gaps in the pilot coverage of equity issues in relation to the identified groups' (DEET undated: 4). In order to carry out this task, a question on equity had been included in the application forms used to determine pilot project status, asking applicants to: 'Describe features of the pilot project designed to facilitate access and equity'.

However, the emergence of potential loopholes was evident from the outset. For example, DEET's monitoring procedures required that collection of equity-related data take place across the suite of pilots in a State, rather than in relation to any individual project, thus putting a heavy (unfulfilled) monitoring onus on the States themselves; in addition, a concern to get things 'up and running' took priority. As the National Evaluation Strategy noted: 'The "bottom line" for the evaluation is to identify those things that work, those that do not, and the reasons why' (DEET 1993a: 6) – a bottom line that ultimately translated into a concern with the many practicalities of implementation rather than the more complex and long-term issues of equity.

This pragmatic approach was reinforced rather than challenged at the State level where the approval and administration of the projects occurred. Priorities lay more with the intricacies of industrial agreements than with educational concerns, and on equity matters the approach was decidedly desultory. For example, examination of responses to the compulsory question on approaches to equity (DEET 1994) revealed that in all States the blandest of statements passed scrutiny. For example, one pilot suggested that 'Access will be open to any person who has completed compulsory education' while another laconically indicated: 'Access and equity to be determined as part of the project'. Yet another simply stated that it had 'an Equity Statement and Equitable Recruitment and Selection Policy and Procedures'.

How, then, were the policies taken up in the conduct of the projects themselves? Only one of the pilot projects investigated in detail seemed to be really engaging with the reform agenda in the sense of challenging fundamental education arrangements and curricula. This pilot, initiated in a middle-class state school with a strong academic tradition, aimed to develop credentialled pathways between school, work and further education, and to provide options for students wishing to bridge the academic divide. A flexible two year Senior Applied Studies Curriculum was developed providing a core of general education subjects plus vocational electives covering a wide span of industries. Credentialling arrangements enabled students to obtain university entrance, entrance to TAFE or a combination of both. TAFE and local enterprises were involved in the delivery of modules, and competency based approaches were being incorporated into all subjects. The principal of the school, with a strong background in TAFE reform, was an enthusiastic advocate of the new policy directions and had pioneered some of the policy principles well in advance of the key reports. Indeed, this school had been visited by both Finn and Carmichael during their investigations. For the principal, 'Finn validated what we were on about, Mayer and Carmichael gave us some structure'.

The other three projects were more narrowly conceived and pragmatic in their approach. The trades-based pilot, initiated in a working-class high school feeling the pressure of reluctant school stayers, claimed to provide 'a convergent model of general and vocational education and training using accredited TAFE curriculum and on the job training'. However, what really seemed to be happening was the offering of a more viable alternative to an academic curriculum in which a sprinkling of 'general subjects' was added to the vocational mix. Ironically, the pilot was highly selective in its intake, requiring prerequisites of English, Maths, Shop A and Shop B – catering in fact for a vocational, and male, elite. The retail pilot also embraced the new rhetoric. It aimed to identify pathways between local enterprises and TAFE, leading to a new competency-based Certificate of Retailing. While initiated in a large comprehensive state school, an elite private girls' school was also involved in the project. The teacher training pilot was initiated by an independent schools lobby in conjunction with a large hotel chain. It aimed to develop a model for teacher in-service training in the hospitality industry, with a view to increasing teacher awareness of concepts such as pathways, competency-based training and recognition of prior learning, in order to improve the quality of vocational training in schools for the hospitality industry.

Research on the more specific issue of women's participation in the

AVTS pilot projects showed a continuing reflection of traditional labour market patterns. In the work-based pilots, women trained as pharmacy assistants and care workers with only a very small number in the trades; men were spread more evenly though they were more dominant in electrical, metals and transport projects. In the institution-based pilot projects, women fared slightly better, but remained concentrated in the traditional areas of retail, tourism and hospitality and office studies, with men dominating in the trades area. In other words, the participation patterns in the pilot projects reflected the gender segmentation of existing training arrangements and the labour market, a pattern reinforced by resistance from some (mostly male) employers, unions and trainees themselves to the dismantling of apprenticeships and the extension of the new system to cover areas traditionally defined as 'women's work'.

Discussion of developments

By and large, then, there was little evidence that the needs of groups specifically disadvantaged by existing arrangements were being addressed. As we have just seen, patterns for women and girls remained unchanged. Although the retail pilot stated that its selection procedures would be 'based on equity principles', this was aimed at getting boys into a female dominated industry! The trades-based pilot referred to the need to provide access 'for females, students with disabilities, Aborigines and Torres Strait Islanders and adults', but in fact, no students from these target groups appeared to be involved in the pilot – certainly no girls – and indeed some staff at the school were openly hostile to what one referred to as 'the equity industry'.

On the other hand, the projects were concerned with challenging the academic–vocational divide, interpreted as 'broadening the curriculum' and 'catering for the needs of all students' – a point made by a key player from the retailing pilot:

> Perhaps pilots like this will eventually force the Department of Education to look at their curriculum because they are going to have to adapt. . . . [The Department is] finally waking up to the fact that school success rate cannot just be measured by [achievements in the Senior School Certificate.] What they are realising is important is how many students get jobs.

> (Henry and Taylor 1995a: 94)

However, although serious attention was given to so-called non-academic students, the absence of a holistic approach in all but one of the projects foreshadowed a danger that what was on offer might be simply another version of traditional divisions, glossed with the rhetoric of pathways, convergence and competencies. This tendency manifested itself in two rather contradictory ways.

On the one hand, the tendency for bringing TAFE modules into schools unreconstructed, except perhaps for being rewritten in competency mode, potentially served to reinforce the vocational–academic divide at an even earlier stage in students' educational careers. Similarly, the tendency for pathways to be constituted as uncredentialled cobblings of school and (often industry-driven) TAFE modules supplemented by work experience components, signalled a possible new version of streaming continuing to lock students into narrow vocational tracks. In many respects, then, the pilot projects appeared to demonstrate little more than a pragmatic response to the urgent problem of what to do with reluctant school stayers unable to find jobs, reflecting much older and somewhat discredited versions of school-to-work transition programmes which had singularly failed in their aim, given the broader employment context.

On the other hand, the pathways logic also pointed to the upgrading of the status of vocational education and training, and that strategy was clearly succeeding to some extent. One outcome of this was the emergence of a new form of territoriality: the development and jealous preservation of particular links between schools (often the private schools) and enterprises, as well as the arrangements some schools were making with private training providers for their 'brightest' students. Ironically, then, there were signs that the new agenda was becoming a channelling device whose benefits were being coopted by the private schools for a vocational elite. Even the one project that exemplified what could be called a 'best practice' version of the new policies was problematic. It was heavily reliant on the almost crusading spirit of its well-informed and well-connected initiator; and its industry placement component – the hours students needed to spend in workplaces – was highly resource-intensive. In other words, as is often the case with showcase initiatives, replicating the project across the system as a whole would have been almost impossible.

What seems clear, then, is that achievement of equity goals, whether characterised in their broad or more targeted sense, was problematic in the early implementation phases despite the ready adoption of the rhetoric of convergence, pathways and competencies. Why did this occur and what are the implications? As we saw, part of the reason had to do with the conduct and administration of the projects. But there were more fundamental issues involved, relating to the nature of the policy making process and the broader context of the policy agenda.

POLICY ISSUES

Our discussion of the broader policy issues is framed in terms of the two aspects of policy consequences identified by Ball (1994a): the policy objectives themselves and the broader goals of social justice. A number of factors are involved here: processes of policy refraction, problematic underlying assumptions and the unravelling of competing discourses, deeper tensions in the policy agenda and tensions between long-term and short-term imperatives. While at one level the discussion relates to the particularities of the Australian case study, at another level many of the points made here have broader applicability given, as we indicated at the outset, the pervasiveness of vocationalist trends in all Western societies.

Policy refraction

As indicated earlier, the inherent tension between 'States' rights' and 'the national interest' in the Australian federal context creates a major barrier for cooperative and coordinated policy making. Commonwealth–State tensions, however, are but one element of the broader policy problem of negotiating tensions between top-down decision making and actions or practices at the 'grass roots' (Ham and Hill 1993). In essence, this was a top-down and nationally driven policy agenda involving all levels of government as well as multiple interest groups, with the research on the AVTS showing wide discrepancies between the view from the top – the vanguard, as they were referred to on a number of occasions – defined by a small group of influential key players, and practices 'on the ground' defined by different players with different interests.

The notion of 'policy refraction' is useful to describe processes of distortion which result from this complex layering of policy interests. This was seen, for example, in the way strongly stated equity objectives at the Commonwealth level were progressively weakened in the face of buck-passing along the 'policy chain'. Hence the minimal efforts by individual pilot projects to comply with the formal equity requirements were consolidated by the lack of effort at the State level to gather or monitor data because this was seen as 'DEET's responsibility'. But DEET's main concern appeared to be with the practicalities of getting the agenda 'up and running' – that is, with logistics rather than more complex educational objectives.

These refractive processes resulted in, from our point of view, a conservative implementation impulse, a tendency reinforced by what one observer referred to as a 'bucket of money' mentality: a tendency for using project money to build on already existing initiatives, certainly true of all four pilots studied above. While this may have served a useful purpose in consolidating progressive innovations, it also served, as we observed in our research, to reinforce existing channelling practices which the policy agenda aimed at overcoming.

Some of these problems were acknowledged by ANTA. In its review of progress in implementing the training reform agenda, it noted that there was 'little evidence to suggest that [mechanisms to reduce social bias] have had any major impact on access and equity within the national vocational education and training system' (1994b: 29). For ANTA, this failure was part of a broader failure to engage local interests in national policy goals, a problem identified by Knox and Pickersgill in their discussion of the failure of training reforms to deliver more equitable outcomes: 'Access and equity needs to begin at the workplace where (enterprise) training decisions are made. An imposed national training structure may give formal equity without advancing substantive equity' (1993: 27). ANTA similarly concluded that, amongst other things, the approach was 'too top down' (1994b: 4), there was a 'need to make the system more relevant and accessible to small business' (p. 2) and that the system 'needs to serve more effectively the short term demands of employers, industries, students, employees and the broader community. It also needs to ensure that longer term social and industry goals are met' (p. 5).

ANTA attempted to resolve this policy problem by resorting to the tools of corporate management through which, as we saw in the previous chapter, central authorities attempt to achieve their policy goals in devolved systems. Key elements of ANTA's implementation procedures were State training profiles and industry training plans which, amongst other things, were required to show how the needs of equity target groups would be addressed. In particular, they were required to identify priorities 'for improving the outcomes for and/or increasing the participation of individuals from target groups in accredited training' (ANTA 1995: 6). While such approaches have been supported by proponents as delivering real gains, for example in relation to improving outcomes for girls in schooling, others have expressed reservations. Burton, for example, former Commissioner for Equal Employment Opportunity in the New South Wales and then the Queensland public service, argues that the seeming rationality of corporate management techniques acts as a smokescreen obscuring the underlying politics of organisations: 'A reputation for managerial efficiency makes it difficult for anyone to challenge a corporate plan' (1993: 161).

The notion of an 'underlying politics' usefully points to the fact that the outcomes reflected more than technical problems of coordination; they also related to the broader contextual and conceptual factors noted at the beginning of the chapter.

Competing discourses and problematic underlying assumptions

As we saw earlier, the Finn, Carmichael and Mayer reports attempted to open up a new vocationalist discourse, with key words such as 'convergence', 'pathways', 'flexibility' and 'equity' acting, in a sense, as linguistic parking stations for a variety of interpretations. The research showed how, in the politics of policy implementation, older and more powerful meanings came to dominate. So, for example, the trades pilot was able to use the language of 'convergence' to significantly increase its stakes in what seemed to be a fairly traditional and masculine version of vocational education. The teacher training project was able to gesture towards the new vocationalist acronyms – RPL, CBT – to legitimate what appeared to be an otherwise quite conventional and narrowly conceived set of vocationally oriented modules.

To some extent, this kind of 'playing the agenda' may simply have reflected the unravelling of competing discourses in the rough and tumble of implementation. But more fundamentally, we would argue, assumptions underlying notions of convergence, pathways and equity were flawed, given the sociological complexities of the social divide that vocational education and training reforms were attempting to address. Two somewhat contrary tendencies emerged as a result. On the one hand, attempts to converge or link general and vocational education in fact served to highlight their essentially different and unequal terrains – seen, for example, in the vehemence of the university voice in the debates over the policies as they emerged, or seen in the continuing preoccupation with league tables of 'excellent' schools (determined by results in year twelve external examinations or their equivalent), despite some tampering at the edges of the traditional academic curriculum.

Simultaneously and ironically, though, because of the continuing high retention rates – as well as perhaps the policy emphases and funding – vocational education has become a positional good colonised, as some of the pilots revealed, by some of the most privileged schools for their own vocational elite, with TAFE increasingly serving as a back door into university. Symptomatic of this tendency, as Raffe (1994) has pointed out in relation to UK trends, has been a creeping 'conservative credentialism' – the tendency for employers to pick the 'best' candidates, often those with traditional academic qualifications, from a greater pool of trained talent. Either way, and exemplifying what Raffe refers to as the 'zero-sum' problem accompanying attempts to redistribute educational opportunity within a fixed hierarchy of opportunity, the most disadvantaged retain their relative position at the bottom of the education and training, and labour market, hierarchy.

Similarly with the gender divide. Assumptions about more equitable outcomes for women to be gained from the new policies failed to take account of the strength of patriarchal practices and attitudes underlying existing gendered education and training tracks and the sex-segmented labour market – a phenomenon hardly confined to Australia (Pocock 1992, OECD 1994b). The pilots showed little evidence of tackling the cultural bases of gender discrimination, either through neglect – for example, an absence of will to alter patterns of recruitment – or through more subtle means. For example, wanting 'a good kid' (in the trades) or 'someone with the right attitude' hardly sounds sexist, but as informal selection criteria in appraising competence such sentiments served to cement traditional gender divisions (Australian Centre for Industrial Relations Research and Teaching 1994: 26). Again, the end result was that women continued to retain their relatively disadvantaged position in vocational education and training.

Equally problematic, and shifting to another aspect, was the fundamental assumption of a partnership between goals of social equity and economic efficiency in a market context. The complicated and interrelated tensions here between equity and efficiency, regulation and deregulation, have been particularly noted by feminist critiques of economic rationalism (Henry and Taylor 1993) – aptly captured in Sawer's sardonic observation that: 'Giving responsibility for equity programs to those whose faith is in the market has been compared to putting mice in charge of the cheese shop' (1989: 150). The balancing act, and the tensions, are exemplified in much of ANTA's documentation. For example, its statement of corporate directions (undated, circa 1995, unpaged) suggests a need for 'more freedom and support for providers to respond flexibly to the needs of their clients' and 'an access and equity planning model accepted by States and Territories'. Its guidelines for state training profiles referred to the need for 'planning within an *agreed framework of national priorities* while ensuring diversity and choice at the State and Territory level' in the context of 'the *concept of a competitive training market*' (ANTA 1994c: 2, original emphasis). Key themes of its national strategy included 'accessibility, so that all Australians who want and need training can get it' and 'efficiency, so that value for money and accountability are emphasised' (ANTA 1994a: 1).

Critics, however, saw the logics of equity and efficiency pulling in different directions, making a balance unsustainable in practice. For example, Taylor and Henry's (1996) study of ANTA's documentation pointed to the way in which the market context had contributed to a discursive conjuring act, transforming original notions of equity as 'social disadvantage' into individualistic notions of 'client choice'. Given the material context of the linguistic shifts – greater autonomy for industry in an open training market – Taylor and Henry argued that equity was likely to emerge as a poor partner in the relationship, especially given the proclivity for enterprises to see 'efficiency oriented provisions treating equity as a cost, an unwanted cost, rather than a desirable outcome' (Barnett and Wilson 1995: xi).

How to maintain an effective policy presence against deregulatory pressures returns us to the top-down–bottom-up conundrum referred to earlier. It also points to a central feature of policy processes in general: their essentially *political* nature and the unpredictability therefore of policy outcomes.

There are some complex theoretical issues here about the relationship between education and the broader social structure which we will not enter into in any detail. But pertinent is the critique of schooling we referred to earlier which suggested a correspondence between the structure and curriculum of schooling and the imperatives of fordist production processes. More recent critics, though they do not use the terminology, point to a similar correspondence between postfordist modes of production and the new vocationalist rhetoric (Gee and Lankshear 1995, Symes 1995), showing how terms such as 'teaming', 'quality circles', 'collaboration' and 'problem solving' may appear as readily in a modern management manual as in an education policy document. At issue here is the validity of underlying assumptions about a 'new compact' between capital and labour in the so-called postfordist context, and, related, the transformative potential of the new policy agenda seen by enthusiasts such as John Mathews (1989). Given the persistence of class and gender patterns in developments to date, and given the strengthened social divisions accompanying the international restructuring of capital and labour alluded to in Chapter Four, such assumptions remain, in our view, problematic.

CONCLUDING COMMENTS

We conclude, however, on a more pragmatic note, and point to a further complicating factor, that of electoral politics and associated problems of juggling long-term policy objectives and short-term political pressures. Electoral pressures to some extent explained the urgency of getting the new policies up and running in Australia, and the consequent emphasis on technicalities rather than principles. Electoral pressures were also evident in the way the agenda was undermined by other policy initiatives. For example, in 1994, responding to the political flak from rising unemployment among older men, a new policy statement, *Working Nation* (Commonwealth of Australia 1994b), announced another set of employment and training initiatives. *Working Nation* not only drew resources away from ongoing training reform initiatives, but its 'fast-track' implementation procedures, aimed at gaining employer support quickly, to some extent put pressure on ANTA's more measured accountability processes.

Meanwhile, things have moved on. In 1996, a new Liberal–National Party coalition government was elected, a government with a strong agenda of States' rights, smaller government and reduced public sector spending, encouragement of private sector entrepreneurialism and the reduction of union power. In this new political climate, criticisms of the 'over-engineered, bureaucratic structure' of the NTRA have surfaced again (Sloan 1996). There is now some doubt about ANTA's future altogether, and some signs that 'putting education to work' may take a more explicitly instrumentalist form. Questions then remain about which aspects of the training reform agenda have been sufficiently embedded, or institutionalised, to become permanent features of the educational landscape, which features will vanish altogether, and which features would have occurred regardless of this sprawling set of policy initiatives. Such questions of the relationship between policy and social change are taken up again in the final chapter of the book.

By way of conclusion, though, we will cite portions of a letter to Australia's national newspaper from a frustrated former DEET official (head of the Vocational Education and Training Division and responsible for the initial development and negotiation of the training reform agenda), responding to criticisms of the way training reform had been implemented. Pointing to the difficulties of dealing with a federal system, the mire of industrial relations and the 'small-minded vested interests that frustrate progress at every turn', the letter continued:

The ACTU hierarchy wanted some changes to training arrangements but could never let go sufficient of the old shibboleths. Time and again they demonstrated their capacity for more bureaucracy than the bureaucrats . . . [Workers] pursued the training agenda mainly for the potential windfall wage gains it promised. In the traditional blue collar areas there was enormous resistance to changes to an apprenticeship system that all acknowledged was outdated. . . . The Business Council of Australia . . . was prepared to go along with some of the reform provided BCA companies could be entirely self-regulating, completely exempted from national accreditation and registration arrangements. . . . The Australian Chamber of Commerce and Industry . . . was inclined to see training as a cost, not as an investment, and therefore always tended to seek solutions that minimised the costs to employers regardless of educational considerations.

And then there were the shenanigans of the States and Territories and their officials. They were fond of little coalitions: big States v small States; Labour States v Liberal States etc. but at the end of the day, as one senior State official once confided . . . 'the thing that will always bind us together is our common hatred of the Commonwealth'. The States' major objective was to organise things so that the Commonwealth officials did all the work, the Commonwealth met all the costs, and the States maintained a power of veto which they would exercise frequently.

Lastly but not least were the special interest groups who circled like a pack of hyenas, ready to dash in at the first sniff of a new policy to ensure that their particular clientele got special treatment. By the time all the special things that had to be done for disadvantaged groups were written into program guidelines, together with all the things that could not be done for IR [industrial relations] reasons, the guidelines became the mass of red tape about which industry so rightly complained.

(Fooks 1996: 12)

What could we possibly add to this list of policy issues, except to note the position of the analyst. Others, no doubt, would tell different stories!

Chapter 7

Difference, social justice and educational policy

> There have always been young persons in our classrooms that most teachers did not, could not, see or hear. In recent years, however, invisibility has been refused on many sides. Old silences have been shattered; long repressed voices are making themselves heard.
>
> (Maxine Green 1995: 155)

INTRODUCTION

Questions of justice and education have been a part of educational thinking as long as there has been a formal schooling system. The introduction of mass schooling itself arose in the broader context of a struggle for social improvement and transformation, to provide opportunities for the 'poorer classes'. This is not to deny that the introduction of mass schooling was also motivated by a number of other purposes, including the need to supply a more educated workforce for the newly mechanised industries and the desire of the authorities to contain social disorder among the propertyless masses. But mass schooling also had a moral purpose: it was an extension of the ideas of social transformation and enlightenment. In the nineteenth century, social reformers argued that a society that did not provide educational opportunities to all its citizens could not claim to be fair and just. They thus viewed the expansion of school systems under compulsory education laws as a great achievement because such laws reflected an overriding concern for social justice. With mass schooling, so it was thought, everyone was given an opportunity for social improvement, and for access to power and privilege which only a few in society had hitherto enjoyed. For most of this century, then, governments assumed that their role in ensuring educational justice could not extend beyond the provision of universal access. After all, if every child had an opportunity to attend schooling, then governments had done as much as they could.

In the 1960s, this assumption was challenged by teachers, educational researchers, social activists and many government officials alike. With the rise of popular social movements like the civil rights movement in the US and the feminist movement world-wide, governments were increasingly forced to acknowledge that they had an important role to play in devising policies and programmes which went beyond access, addressing some of the basic causes of educational disadvantage. It was argued that children from different backgrounds related to schools differently, and that they therefore secured differential benefits from schools. Not only did schools in richer areas tend to be better resourced but also the whole structure of school knowledge was linked to middle-class male values of the dominant culture, so that girls, working-class children and children from a different culture could not get the same benefits. Mass schooling was based on the hope that educational institutions could make an impact on the reproductive cycle of poverty and privilege, but numerous studies in the 1960s demonstrated how marginal the effect of schooling really was in bringing about greater equality of social outcomes. Clearly, educational policy needed to do more than simply provide access. But what and how?

This question has become a consistent theme in much of the policy work in education since the 1960s. The relationship between social justice and education has been one of the most hotly debated topics in education. In this chapter we will look at some of the ways in which Australian governments have responded to the calls for greater equality of educational opportunity. We will also examine the various ways in which the idea of equity has been interpreted in policies and programmes – how it has challenged existing power relations in fundamental ways, and has, in turn, been rearticulated by the state to contain radical demands for social transformation. We will also look at some of the enduring dilemmas that confront policy makers in this area, particularly those relating to the difficulties associated with reconciling notions of equity and difference. This discussion will seek to bring many of the aspects of policy processes which we have discussed in earlier chapters into sharp focus. In particular, we want to show that in order to analyse the development of educational policies, we need to understand them *historically*, that is, in the contexts in which they appear as temporary settlements between competing views about social order and reform. We also suggest that while social justice policies in education may appear inherently progressive they can be framed in a variety of different ways, only some of which serve purposes that are progressive. It is possible, for example, for social justice to be framed in such ways as to contain problems and defuse democratic demands.

ΗΕ IDEA OF SOCIAL JUSTICE

An immediate difficulty one confronts when examining the idea of social justice, as it has been used in educational policies, is that it does not appear to have a single common meaning across all its uses. Thus the assumptions underlying a particular usage often have to be inferred from the justificatory arguments presented and the policy prescriptions proposed.

What this suggests is that the idea of social justice is historically constituted and that it is a site of conflicting and divergent political endeavours. Justice does not refer to a single set of primary or basic goods, conceivable across all moral and material domains. Its social meaning, as Walzer (1983) has pointed out, is historical in character. Having said this, however, it needs to be acknowledged that injustice does have a material reality that is readily recognised by those who are subjected to it. Those who are hungry or poor or homeless do not need abstract definitions in order to be able to recognise injustice. In policy discourses, then, the idea of justice relates to something real. Policy prescriptions thus have practical consequences, reflecting particular values about how society ought to be organised and how education should contribute to individual and social improvement.

In the Australian context, MacIntyre has provided ample evidence to show how the political ideal of justice – an essentially contested notion – has expressed itself in different forms at different times over the past two hundred years, arguing that the search for social justice 'arises from the meeting of a particular kind of authority with particular aspirations that are located in particular historical circumstances' (1985: 112). Tracing its Australian genealogy, MacIntyre has demonstrated how, since the Second World War, the idea of justice has been struggled over by various social movements determined to achieve a better deal for the constituencies they represent. Governments, in turn, have had to manage popular demands for justice, though they have seldom been able to deliver on the social justice promises they make at election times. In Australia, governments cannot afford to be seen to be not promoting some form of a justice agenda. This is so because the idea of social justice has always played an important role in the myths that Australia has constructed for its sense of nationhood.

Yet the form in which the idea of justice has been expressed has varied greatly, often reflecting changing social and economic conditions. Now while the idea of social justice does not have an essential meaning, it is possible to identify a number of traditions of thinking that have characterised policy debates over the concept. The three main traditions of thinking about social justice may be identified as 'liberal-individualism', 'market-individualism' and 'social-democratic'. Before discussing these traditions, it is worth noting that in policy discourses the terms 'social justice', 'equality' and 'equity' often appear as synonymous. This in itself is a point of contention because it is possible to view 'social justice' as a broader moral concept than the narrowly framed idea 'equity'. As Young (1990) has pointed out, to view social justice in terms of equity alone is to stress already a particular construction of justice, which is linked more to administrative considerations of how resources ought to be distributed than to cultural and moral concerns.

Let us turn then to the three traditions of thinking about social justice which have informed recent policy debates. The liberal-individualist view conceptualises social justice variously in terms of either *fairness* or what is *deserved*. In recent philosophical literature, perhaps the most outstanding contemporary advocate of the fairness view is John Rawls (1972). Rawls suggests two principles of social justice: that each person should have the most extensive basic liberty compatible with similar liberty for others; and there should be equal distribution of primary social goods – unless unequal distribution is to the advantage of the least favoured. The first principle implies individual freedom, while the second principle suggests that the state has a special responsibility to create policy initiatives and programmes directed towards 'removing barriers, arising from unequal power relations and preventing equity, access and participation'. Rawls' theory of social justice has been enormously influential in most Western countries. During the 1960s and 1970s, it led to the creation of various programmes of affirmative action, as well as some, though not as many as some imagine, redistributive policies.

In opposition to Rawls' view, Nozick (1976) has presented a different account of social justice based on a market-individualism that invokes the idea of what people deserve. Writing in the tradition of conservative philosophers like John Locke, Nozick argues that Rawls' theory is mistaken in focussing attention on the issue of distribution and thus ignoring the issue of people's entitlements to what they produce. Most theories of social justice, he maintains, focus only on the end distribution of holdings, and do not pay enough attention to the processes by which holdings are acquired. Nozick suggests that it is the justice of the competition – that is, the way competition is carried on and not its outcome – that counts. He argues for a minimal state, limited in its functions to the protection of its citizens from force, theft, fraud and so on – that is, to the protection of individuals to exercise their liberty without state interference. He thus rejects redistributive notions of social and economic justice, and by implication the idea of affirmative action, on the grounds that it is unjust for the state to transfer property which belongs to individuals who have worked for it.

Now while differences between Rawls and Nozick are considerable, they both assume that people always act in their own self-interest. They both consider individualistic liberty as a value prior to any consideration of social justice; in addition they both assume the idea of community to be simply a sum of the individuals who reside in it. These assumptions are questioned by those who belong to another tradition of thinking about social justice, namely the social democratic tradition. The social democratic tradition is derived from Marx and stresses the idea of *needs*. As Beilharz points out, this way of looking at social justice 'is qualitatively different to the preceding understandings, in that need is viewed as a primary rather than a residual category' (1989: 94). It is this interpretation of needs, Beilharz suggests, which sets the social democratic view of social justice apart from the charity-based arguments about the 'needy' which are compatible with either the 'desert' or the 'fairness' principles. The 'needs' tradition thus highlights a more collectivist and co-operative image of society.

It is important to note that market-individualist and social democratic traditions rest on very different understandings about the nature of the relationship between social justice and the market. The market-individualist regards the market as the most basic provider of social justice, of employment, services and welfare. The state is seen simply as a vehicle for promoting the activities of the market. It is assumed that the market, if left to operate freely, will be able to deliver the distributive fairness on its own accord. According to the social democratic view, on the other hand, as Agnes Heller (1987) has pointed out, the idea of social justice may not necessarily be incompatible with markets, but it is unlikely to be achieved unless the market is controlled in sufficiently rigorous ways. State activity is thus seen as 'market replacing' (Heller 1987), correcting its excesses, and minimising the costs of its arbitrary exercise.

In recent years the market-individualist view of social justice, and more particularly the view of social justice as 'desert', has become increasingly popular among policy makers. In Australia the conservative side of politics has always been attracted to it, but in recent years sections of the Australian Labour Party have also become 'converted' to market ideology. However, Labour's assumption that the 'economy itself can be steered in the direction of "social justice"' is, as Beilharz suggests,

> a non-sequitur outside the logic of markets, necessarily introducing residual welfare mechanisms in order to buoy up the human flotsam which cannot negotiate justice for itself through the market. To argue in this way is necessarily to introduce the logic of charity, and the language of the 'needy', for there are citizens, and there are those outside the city gates, who are deserving compassion.
>
> (Beilharz 1989: 92–3)

These assumptions necessarily introduce deficit considerations, with the markets accepting no special responsibility towards the disadvantaged members of the community, including many women, migrants, people with disabilities and the poor, and especially the unemployed. On the other hand, the state is given the responsibility of creating a policy climate in which the markets can deliver the economic circumstances conducive, eventually, to the welfare of the people, and perhaps assist, under extreme circumstances, those whom the market cannot help. Thus, as Beilharz notes, social justice understood in this way becomes not so much a universal ethical principle as an administrative principle, the practical symbol of which is the targeting of funds to ameliorate the most harmful consequences of market activity. Such a view of the relationship between the state and the market implies that the government's primary responsibility is that of 'good management' of the social and cultural conditions necessary for capital accumulation.

Now while market-individualism appears to have become the dominant view of social justice among policy makers in most Western countries, it is not without its critics. Michael Apple (1988), for example, argues that market-individualism is based on a sharp separation between the ideas of property rights and person rights. A property right, he suggests, vests in individuals the power to enter into social relationships on the basis and extent of their property, while person rights are based on simple membership in their social collectivity. Person rights involve equal treatment of citizens, freedom of expression and movement, equal access to participation in decision making in social institutions and reciprocity in relations of power and authority. The most worrying aspect of the market view of social justice is that it eliminates all transfer payments through the state, as Barry points out, leaving 'the sick, the old, the disabled, the mothers with young children and no breadwinner and so on, to the tender mercies of private charity, given at the whim and pleasure of the donors and on any terms they choose to impose' (1973: 88). In this way, the freedom it guarantees individuals benefits the privileged in a disproportionate way. Further, as Norman notes, market-individualism appears to ignore 'the possibility that what goes into the pot may be, from the start, socially produced and socially owned' (1988: 93).

What these arguments show is that, morally, market criteria are insufficient for determining public policy, which requires reference to the general welfare of the community; and that solely procedural criteria are insufficient for achieving social justice, because to use them is to privilege the economic – as well as to assume that they are somehow unconnected to the cultural and the social. It is the social in the notion of social justice that we need to stress. The moral idea of social suggests, above all, the need to develop a sense of co-operative community in which rewards are not determined simply on the basis of productive contribution, but also on broader considerations of need and the right everyone has to participate in social life to the best of her or his ability. We believe that a community that is not genuinely co-operative in this way cannot be just.

Debates about social justice over the past thirty years or so have revolved around the three traditions of thinking which we have outlined. These traditions have served to inform the theoretical frameworks within which various positions on educational policy are located. It is important to note, however, that policy positions do not emerge neatly from theoretical conceptions of social justice. The struggles over policies and programmes are historical in character and revolve around pragmatic considerations and the differing ways in which social movements mobilise public opinion in favour of particular initiatives. Of course, in promoting their position, both social movements and the state rely upon particular theoretical constructions, but these constructions never constitute a coherent set of ideas but rather a pragmatic expression of what appears feasible.

Not surprisingly, therefore, policy initiatives around different interests have their own historical trajectory. In the next four sections, we will look at how some of these interests have prevailed in just four arenas. We will explore how concerns of social-economic disadvantage, gender, ethnic inequalities and the inequalities faced by students with disabilities have been managed by policy makers in education, with a particular focus on the changing ways in which the policy issues have been *framed* or conceptualised in these areas over time.

POVERTY AND EDUCATIONAL DISADVANTAGE

Poverty did not become a significant issue on the educational policy agenda until the 1960s, and the question arises as to why it was not an issue until then. An answer to this question requires us to understand the history of the development of mass schooling. We suggest that poverty only became an educational issue with the consolidation of the idea of the welfare state in the 1960s, and that this historical conjunction impacted on the way in which the relationship between poverty and education was interpreted.

Until the 1960s, governments assumed that so long as there was universal access to the system of mass schooling, justice would inevitably prevail. Even with the expansion of mass schooling to include secondary education, access was considered sufficient to provide equality of educational opportunity. During the post-Second World War expansion in education, the main policy concern was 'how to keep afloat in the flood of numbers' (Connell *et al.* 1991: 22); how to resource the expanding system. Education was perceived as a long ladder which students climbed – how far students climbed the 'ladder of opportunity' (MacIntyre 1985) reflected their ability and their motivation to succeed. The responsibility of governments was simply to provide the schools.

In the mid-1960s, however, many educational researchers showed that the ladder analogy was fundamentally flawed. They questioned the myth of meritocracy upon which much of educational planning was based. Equality in education, they argued, was not simply a matter of formal access but about the ways schools related to students of different class, gender and ethnic backgrounds. It was not simply the input that was important but also the students' background and the treatment they received in schools. Educational success was as much a function of family background as it was of how intelligent students were and how hard they worked. Sociologists found that schools played a major role in maintaining social inequality by sifting and sorting students into ability rankings which reinforced the status the student had on entering the school.

At the same time, social researchers 'rediscovered' poverty as a political issue (Harrington 1963) which was subsequently taken up by the emerging social movements. The civil rights movements in the US, for example, demonstrated how schools in poorer inner-city districts were deteriorating badly – classes were oversized, buildings were run-down, books were scarce and teacher morale was low. The attempts by the state to suggest that the poor blacks were lacking either motivation or ability were soundly challenged by the civil rights movement. The increasing level of black militancy targeted economic and educational opportunities and racist political and cultural practices as the main concerns of their struggle. In response, in 1965, President Johnson launched Project Headstart, a comprehensive pre-school programme designed to break the 'cycle of poverty', based on the assumption that children from poor backgrounds needed compensatory treatment for their 'inadequate' home background. The project funded year round training for children from age three, and involved five components: health, nutrition, education, parental involvement and social and psychological services. Similar programmes were introduced in Britain, with the establishment of Educational Priority Areas (EPAs) in an attempt to 'break the vicious circle of deprivation'. However, an assumption fundamental to all such compensatory programmes was not that schools needed to change, but that change needed to be made to the children and their families so that they would fit better into the school culture.

It is important to note that the compensatory programmes of the 1960s would not have got off the ground if it had not been for the fact that the structure of the state in most Western countries was at the same time undergoing substantial change. Historically, the mid-1960s was a period during which the principles of the welfare state were consolidated not only in the UK but also in the US and Australia. In each of these countries the Fabian attitude, encapsulated in the political ideas of John Maynard Keynes, was fundamental to the development of the welfare state. Within the welfare state, equality of opportunity required more than simple access to the society's dominant institutions. The fundamental commitment of a welfare state was to the equalising of opportunities for all, to the creation of the conditions that enabled everyone to exercise autonomy. Equality was thus regarded as a fundamental condition for freedom. The welfare state had a duty to devote all its legislative and economic resources to combat the inequalities of the market system – to ensure that redistributive policies were implemented in order to bring about equitable outcomes. In a sense, then, programmes like Headstart and EPA expressed the Rawlsian 'liberal-individualistic' view of social justice in the broader context of the historical consolidation of the welfare state and the emergence of the new social movements.

Such programmes were, however, flawed in a number of ways. Their focus on concepts such as 'cultural deprivation', 'compensation' and 'linguistic disadvantage' distracted from the deficiencies of the educational processes and instead highlighted presumed deficiencies in the family, the community or the child. In this way, they blamed the very victims of poverty they were designed to help (Ryan 1971). They worked on a deficit model that was both patronising and insensitive to differences between communities. But most significantly, they did not critically examine the structure of the school, its programmes, its curriculum, pedagogy and organisation, and the resources of the schools in the poorest neighbourhoods.

By the time the Karmel Report was launched in Australia in 1973, these problems with the ideas of compensatory education were already well known. In recommending the Disadvantaged Schools Programme (DSP), the report enjoyed the benefit of the insights generated as part of the inequalities debate in the UK and US. It thus avoided many of the most obvious limitations of the compensatory logic. Conceived under a social democratic Labour government, the DSP was also framed within a language of needs rather than deficit, making it a very radical programme for the early 1970s. Indeed, its durability is due not only to the commitment of many teachers and parents across Australia but also to the sound analysis of the problems of educational disadvantage upon which it is based.

Established in 1974, the DSP is based on a concept of affirmative action, and benefits some 15 per cent of the school population. It provides extra resources to selected schools, encouraging parents and teachers at those schools to work together to develop school level projects to improve the learning outcomes of students. Over the years, schools have worked on a variety of programmes which have challenged the structures of inequality which persist in Australian schools and society. According to Johnston, the DSP 'was characterised by a ground-swell of popular movements, all seeking in various ways to redefine social and cultural boundaries' (1993: 107). As a result, the DSP has had a catalytic effect on teachers and schools, enlivening them 'through contact with a wider movement of egalitarian reform'. The programme has always assumed that its resources must work in concert with other reforms taking place in the school. At the same time, the programme has been continually reframed in the light of changing cultural and economic circumstances and the imperatives of new corporate managerialism.

Despite its successes, however, the DSP cannot claim to have had any significant impact on the structures of inequality that characterise Australian schools. To begin with, it has to contend with deteriorating economic conditions in Australia, and also with a sea change in support for the policies of the welfare state. Through the 1980s, market ideologies became increasingly dominant, leading to greater social inequalities. Indeed, there is now evidence to suggest that there is a growing disparity in income distribution between the rich and the poor in Australia. There is also evidence to suggest that poverty is the most reliable indicator of a person's life chances, with education becoming increasingly critical to the financial and career success of students as they pass into adulthood. However, the link between poverty and education is not only instrumental – poverty impacts on education in other more complex ways. For example, because of poverty, certain children are denied the less tangible social benefits of schooling.

Yet this way of looking at the issues seems to suggest that inequalities are a problem to do with only a section of the community – those who are poor – and not the whole of the community. Yet as Connell *et al.* (1991) have pointed out, poverty is not only a problem for individuals. It is not a welfare issue in the way that compensatory programmes so clearly assumed, but an *educational* issue – about how relations of social distribution are arranged and how curriculum and pedagogy serve the interests of some groups better than others. The problem is about the wider play of class relations:

> Poor people suffer most from this interplay; their educational problems are indeed the worst. They generally have little power to change educational institutions set up by others, or to make them function in their own interests. For equity reasons, if there are limited dollars or limited political will, it is right to focus action on the education of the poorest groups. But it should never be thought that this will work very well as an isolated enterprise. Many of the educational problems

of children in poverty arise from systemic effects which cannot be remedied by action at the school or even the regional level.

(Connell *et al.* 1991: 24)

Connell and his colleagues suggest that *all* educational policies should be framed in order to take into account the interplay between poverty and education.

The major problem with the welfare approach which has informed many educational policies is that poverty and education are somehow *external* to each other, related only in a contingent manner. This myth needs to be exploded. We need to recognise that the educational system not only reproduces inequality but also *generates* it. A recognition of this kind is helpful in breaking down the assumption that poverty is largely a welfare matter, in which schools play only a minor part. Rather, from the point of view of educational policy, it is helpful to think of poverty as a *curriculum* issue. We need to consider how curriculum and pedagogy contribute, over time, not only to the reproduction of poverty but also its production.

GIRLS AND GENDER EQUITY

In the case study of *The National Policy for the Education of Girls in Australian Schools* (Commonwealth Schools Commission 1987) in Chapter Three, we emphasised the historical development of this policy – particularly highlighting its national character and the way in which all the States were involved in its development. This state-centric approach is a significant feature of policy development in gender equity policy in Australia, and contrasts markedly with the situation in the UK and US where there have been no such policy developments at a national level. In that case study little attention was given to the way in which gender issues were framed within the policy – apart from a brief mention of the impact of developments in feminist theory.

We discussed above the ways in which governments have framed their approaches to addressing educational inequalities based on differing ideological assumptions, and differing conceptions of social justice. By and large, Liberal governments have tended to adopt 'weaker' equality of opportunity, liberal or market-individualistic approaches which focus on access, while Labour governments have been more prepared to adopt 'stronger' social democratic approaches which focus on participation and outcomes. These broad general differences in approach have also been reflected in developments in gender equity policy.

This brief discussion will focus on another aspect of framing the issues – namely how gender issues have been conceptualised in policy developments in this area. We will trace how major changes in the framing of the issues have reflected developments in theory – and in particular feminist theory – leading to more sophisticated explanations of the relationship between education and gender inequalities in society. At the same time as these understandings have informed policy developments, the complexities of the issues and the difficulties of making change in this area have become apparent. The discussion refers mainly to Australia, though similar trends have occurred in other parts of the world where gender equity policies have been developed (ten Dam and Volman 1995).

Changing trends have been reflected most obviously in the terminology which has been used in the policies over the years in Australia – from 'equality of opportunity', through to 'elimination of sexism', 'the education of girls' and 'gender equity' (Gilbert 1996). However, we need to remember that these terms have specific meanings in particular historical and cultural contexts, as we have explained, and may be used differently in other parts of the world.

In relation to conceptualisation of gender issues in Australian education policy, it is possible to identify three broad phases in educational reform: 'an initial struggle to achieve equity and access; . . . a concerted effort to value women's knowledge and experiences, and to integrate them into the curriculum; . . . and a recognition of the construction of "gender"' (Gilbert 1996: 11). These phases represented different stages in feminist understandings of the issues.

The initial struggle to achieve equity and access followed sex difference research in the late 1960s which documented sex differences in participation and achievement in education. Previously such inequalities were not seen as problematic, rather they were seen as natural – based on views about the biological basis of sex differences and of presumed future roles of boys and girls.

The education of girls first became a policy issue in Australia in the early 1970s, following pressure from the women's movement. The Schools Commission, which was set up by the Whitlam Labour government late in 1973 to advise the government on education policy issues, took up equality as a major theme and defined girls as a disadvantaged group needing special attention. At the same time the various State governments also developed policies in the area. The focus at this time was on increasing participation and retention rates, and improving outcomes for girls. Policies drew on liberal feminism and sex role theory, and were underpinned by an equality of opportunity approach. During this phase, sexism in education was documented in numerous research studies and many State policies reflected this approach in terminology. For example, Victoria's policy was entitled *Equal Opportunity and the Elimination of Sexism* (Victorian Ministry of Education 1980). A significant feature of this phase was that the existing structure of schooling was accepted as given – the main challenge was making sure that girls had equal access to educational opportunities. Policy documents from this phase often mentioned both sexes – for example, Queensland Department of Education's (1981) *Equality of Opportunity in Education for Girls and Boys* (see Lingard *et al.* 1987). Even where there was a stronger approach – focussing on equal participation and outcomes – the structure and experience of schooling tended not to be questioned. So a good deal of attention at this time was given to issues such as sex differences in subject choices – especially the unequal participation of girls in mathematics and science. Strategies aimed to raise girls' aspirations and to encourage girls to go into non-traditional areas, such as engineering and the trades. By and large these policies operated using a 'let's fix up the girls' approach – often referred to as a deficit approach. Retention and participation rates improved for girls, but this was as much the result of growing youth unemployment, which has had a particularly marked impact on teenage girls, as the result of policy initiatives. Some of the initiatives, for example encouraging girls to study mathematics and science, did help middle-class girls, but gradually feminist educators began to see the curriculum and school organisation as the problem – rather than the girls themselves.

It became apparent that the 'equity and access' approaches failed to challenge patriarchal power relations and that different strategies were needed. Thus followed the second stage of reform identified by Gilbert, influenced by radical feminism, where there was an attempt to value women's knowledge and experiences, and to integrate them into the curriculum. Schooling was seen as 'malestream' knowledge and one important policy focus was around the idea of the 'gender inclusive curriculum'. Policy initiatives during this stage, then, included the introduction of women's studies into the curriculum, with more attention being given to the use of resources which reflected women's experience. Gilbert suggests that: 'Terminology that sought deliberately to focus on "the education of girls" acknowledged this shift in conceptualising educational reform' (1996: 13), and notes that this focus made it possible to address issues such as sexual harassment. This issue is referred to in *The National Policy for the Education of Girls in Australian Schools* (Commonwealth Schools Commission 1987) and addressed through one of the policy's objectives – the provision of a supportive school environment.

In our view, socialist feminism was also a significant influence during this second phase – particularly socialist feminism's emphasis on gender relations as power relations. This in turn led to an emphasis on structural aspects of inequality, for example on the ways in which the relations of schooling replicated the gender inequalities of the labour market. The influence of socialist feminism formed a separate strand in policy development during the second phase identified by Gilbert. Socialist feminism was also influential in raising questions concerning the differences between girls – on the basis of class, race, ethnicity and disability – which we will discuss further shortly.

The third phase of reform identified by Gilbert built on the increasing concerns among feminists about sexual harassment and violence, and is related to theoretical developments around the idea of the 'construction of gender'. This phase was influenced by a number of different strands of feminism, including post-structuralist approaches. Feminists began to problematise masculinity and to argue that attempting to deal with the education of girls without also considering boys' issues was misguided and that a relational theoretical approach was necessary. These developments coincided with debates around the 'What about the boys?' issue which had emerged in response to the increasing educational success of some groups of girls. In this context, the idea that boys were now a disadvantaged group gained some currency. A general policy shift towards the use of the term 'gender equity' occurred, reflecting both the theoretical move to a construction of gender framework, as well as the more strategic move to 'hold the line' in the face of a challenge to the policy focus on the education of girls. This shift was reflected explicitly in policy content – for example, the *National Action Plan for the Education of Girls* (Australian Education Council 1993) included 'examining the construction of gender' as well as 'eliminating sex-based harassment' in its eight priority areas.

The shift from the education of girls to gender equity was also apparent in a later document released for discussion in 1996 – *Gender Equity: A Framework for Australian Schools* (Gender Equity Taskforce 1996). Leonie Daws comments on 'the Framework's consistent inclusion of "girls and boys" as a modifier for all claims made regarding the statements of strategic direction'. She adds that, 'the effect is to convey the impression that there is no systematic advantage or disadvantage to any group in any of these issues' (Daws 1996). The complete reframing of the issue which resulted is seen clearly in an example she cites from the document: 'Violence, including sex-based harassment, inhibits learning and impacts on the experiences and outcomes of schooling for girls and boys' (Gender Equity Taskforce 1996: 15).

Gilbert (1996) sees the three stages outlined as being broadly chronological and highlights the way each stage of policy development built on previous understandings:

It has only been possible for instance to move towards newer forms of understanding 'gender' because of earlier ground breaking work in areas of affirmative action and equity. It was only after forms of inequality between women and men had been documented in the seventies, that it was possible to critically reassess those forms, and to

)k towards more alternative (more women-centred) ways of operat-
; in the eighties. Similarly, it was only after inequality was documented, and alternative modes of practice were constructed, that it
became easier to see how relations between women and men in the
nineties needed changing, and how constructions of masculinity and
femininity were implicated in such change. The stages of reform built
on each other, and upon the understandings that each new phase had
made possible.

(Gilbert 1996: 11)

We agree with Gilbert's broad analysis, but would suggest that in no
sense has each phase replaced the previous one. Rather, vestiges of earlier phases can be found in recent policy developments. For example,
aspects of all the phases are evident in both *The National Policy for the
Education of Girls in Australian Schools* and in the *National Action Plan for
the Education of Girls*. Indeed, liberal feminist goals such as equal access
to resources can be important in current debates at the school level
over policies to ensure that girls have access to computer laboratories
or sporting equipment. And there is still a need for appropriate curriculum which takes account of girls' and women's knowledge and
experiences, as well as an examination of the construction of gender by
students.

Finally, there is the important issue of how differences between
groups of girls have been acknowledged and addressed in gender
equity policies. So far in this discussion we have referred to girls as if
they are a homogeneous group with common needs and problems to
be addressed in policies. Although initially policies often did in fact
deal with girls in this way, there has been a growing recognition of the
need to take account of difference – particularly as a result of the
influence of socialist feminism as mentioned above. There was a recognition of the impact of class in the Karmel Report's comment that:
'Being a girl is an educational disadvantage except when it is associated with high socio-economic status' (Schools Commission 1973: 19).
And *The National Policy for the Education of Girls* attempted to come to
grips with the varying needs of girls from different backgrounds 'taking account of their cultural, language and socio-economic diversity'
(Commonwealth Schools Commission 1987: 25). It is significant that
the National Aboriginal Education Committee's response to the policy,
included as an appendix to the report, suggests that for Aboriginal
and Torres Strait Islander children racial discrimination is a more
pressing problem than gender discrimination, and the point is made
that Aboriginal and Torres Strait Islander girls are 'doubly disadvantaged' in the education system. More recent theoretical work on difference – influenced by post-structuralism – highlights the complex ways

in which class, gender and ethnicity, for example, intersect in shaping girls' experience, and policies have attempted to address this complexity. For example, a recent Queensland Education Department project is attempting to develop policies to address gendered and racist violence in schools. This discussion highlights the growing realisation that girls cannot be assumed to belong to a homogeneous category and that girls from different cultural backgrounds may have different needs and experiences.

MULTICULTURALISM AS AN EDUCATIONAL POLICY

In most Western countries with culturally diverse populations, policies dealing with the inequalities faced by migrants and ethnic minorities fall under the rubric of 'multiculturalism'. The policy idea of multiculturalism did not emerge in Australia until the mid-1970s, but has now become entrenched in public discourse. It is important to note, however, that the emergence and the rapid rise of multiculturalism cannot be explained in terms of the organic growth of a popular social movement, like the feminist movement. Rather, it is best viewed as a construction of the state. As such it is framed in a particular way which is located very much within the mainstream political framework, and does not disturb current distribution of power. In this section, then, we examine some of the ways in which policies of multiculturalism have been framed in order to assess their potential for tackling issues of inequality, in particular, racism.

Multiculturalism was formulated by the state in response to what the state saw as a growing crisis in ethnic relations resulting from the widespread recognition that migrant groups, which made up some 25 per cent of the Australian population, were systematically disadvantaged. In the early 1970s many migrants, who had begrudgingly accepted the policy of assimilation a generation earlier, were no longer prepared to tolerate the injustices this represented. From their point of view, assimilation was morally unacceptable. From the point of view of the state, assimilation as a policy instrument was abandoned because it was no longer capable of either fulfilling the need of ethnic minorities or of containing migrant unrest.

In an influential paper, Jakubowicz (1981) argued that the policy of multiculturalism emerged in the 1970s as a compromise formation, designed to contain the political and economic demands of ethnic minorities on the one hand, and to restore their acquiescence to the existing structure of Australian society on the other. Indeed, one of the most important reports on multiculturalism in Australia, the Galbally Report (1978: 6), viewed multiculturalism as a solution to the critical problem of ethnic unrest and growing migrant militancy. It spoke of the

ble alternatives' the nation faced if the increasingly volatile
munities were not controlled.

lucational policy, the basic premise upon which multicultural-
d is that the experiences of ethnic minority students can no
longer be structured around a notion of linguistic or cultural deficit, and
that multicultural education must utilise the social context of children's
lives outside the classroom. Unless this is done, it is argued, schools will
produce a generation of students who are alienated, have low self esteem
and are unlikely to be able to contribute to the mainstream society.
However, the rationale for a multicultural education does not reside in
this defensive logic alone. It is based also on the political imperative that
all groups within society should enjoy equal access to power, status and
wealth, and that success should not depend on renouncing group values,
norms and lifestyles. Multiculturalism suggests, therefore, that major
changes are required to curriculum, teacher education and development,
and school organisation and administration, if Australian schools are to
be become truly multicultural.

The main focus of multiculturalism is thus on the notion of 'culture',
though unlike the educators of the sixties who had consistently advocated compensatory education as a means of overcoming 'cultural deprivation', the contemporary policies of multicultural education view culture
as something positive. They suggest that cultural differences should be
celebrated, and that every effort should be made to ensure that minority
students are able to maintain their cultural heritage. Multiculturalism
suggests that such an approach is essential if problems of racism –
understood as a broad notion describing the practices of racial, ethnic
and cultural exclusion, bias and discrimination – are to be adequately
tackled.

In more recent years, multiculturalism has undergone numerous modifications in light of changing social, political and economic circumstances. In 1989, for example, the Labour government launched *A
National Agenda for a Multicultural Australia,* responding to what Castles
(1987) has referred to as the 'maturing of the migratory process', including the existence of the second and third generation Australians of
minority ethnic backgrounds and the emergence of new forms of racism
in Australian society. The *National Agenda* rearticulated the principles of
multiculturalism to include economic benefits of cultural diversity. The
economic dimensions of multiculturalism, it insisted, 'means that
Australia should be able to make effective use of the nation's human
resources' (Office of Multicultural Affairs 1989: 6). More recently, the
Australian government has used the notion of productive diversity to
highlight the economic opportunities that migrants can provide for
Australian business in their countries of origin.

Now, while multiculturalism is clearly a dynamic policy linked to changing conditions, support for its main principles has not been extensive. Conservatives view it as socially divisive, while its radical critics dismiss it as an ideology, concerned more with maintaining social order than with transformation towards a more just society. Whatever the merits of these positions, it is clear that multiculturalism remains trapped within existing mainstream political structures. While it recognises that ethnic minorities are indeed systematically disadvantaged, the notion of equality with which it works is a minimalist one, concerned with equality of access of individuals to the dominant institutions which, paradoxically, symbolise inequalities for many ethnic people in the first place.

A fundamental conflict exists between its espousal of a commitment to equality and multiculturalism's other objective: the right of minorities to maintain their cultural identity. This permits the maintenance of only those minority cultural practices which do not challenge the dominant culture. Not surprisingly, then, it is the pluralist objective – rather than the equity one – that has become dominant in schools. This emphasis on 'spaghetti and dance' highlights issues of lifestyles, obscuring issues of disadvantage and structural inequalities which would seem to be much more crucial in any attempt to provide minorities access to power and to improve their life chances (Jayasuriya 1987).

Underpinning the celebratory focus on lifestyle is the problematic assumption of culture as the primary category of social analysis. While it has to be acknowledged that people do conceive of themselves as belonging to certain groups, do describe certain sorts of situations and relations as ethnically or racially defined, it does not follow from this that social analysis must therefore be restricted to these interpretative categories. Thus, for example, minority experiences are not confined to matters of lifestyle. They cannot therefore be entirely explicable in ethnic or racial terms. This is so because minorities also occupy a particular position in the class structure of society and play an important part in the production and reproduction of economic relations. By divorcing issues of ethnicity from issues of class and gender, the policy of multiculturalism thus reifies ethnic identity, and obscures its social construction.

Issues of identity, subjectivity, group formation and solidarity are relevant to an understanding of the policies developed to redress the disadvantages experienced by indigenous people in Australia. This discussion reveals the complexities inherent in theorising the relationship between ethnic identity and difference. As Stuart Hall (1991: 18) has argued, ethnicity and 'race' need to be understood in terms of a politics of location, positionality and enunciation – not so much as a process of discovery of lost 'roots' but of construction of a 'new' or 'emergent' culture, linked to contemporary social relations and to relations of power. While marginalised people clearly need to honour many of the aspects of their traditions and history, Hall suggests that they also need to 'understand the

es which they've been taught to not speak. They need to under-
...d revalue the traditions and inheritances of cultural expression
and creativity' (1991: 15). Hall thus presents a dynamic view of identity
and difference which appears undermined by policies such as multiculturalism.

A final point concerning multiculturalism's focus on culture relates to
the highly questionable assumption that the emphasis on the maintenance of cultural traditions is somehow sufficient for the elimination of
racism. Now, while any effort to remove prejudice should be welcomed,
programmes focussing only on the development of 'multicultural' or
conciliatory attitudes are unlikely to have any real impact on the life
chances of minorities. This is so because the major source of racism in
Australia, as elsewhere, lies not only in the existence of prejudiced attitudes but also in historical patterns of inequality and the economic conditions under which many migrants and indigenous people live. Thus,
anti-racism policies in education need to be predicated on the assumption that institutions such as schools are implicated in these patterns of
inequalities through the practices they privilege. In other words, it is not
only disadvantage that needs to be theorised or made problematic, but
also advantage. Anti-racism policies will therefore have to address
broader structural conditions of exclusion, discrimination and oppression, and investigate the elements of the dominant culture and its norms
to determine the biases they promote in education. Otherwise, educational policies designed to bring about greater social justice are unlikely
to be effective. This applies not only to multiculturalism but also to the
field of disability and education.

DISABILITY AND INTEGRATION

In this field, pressures from the professionals working with children with
disabilities have significantly shaped educational policies. These professionals include social and community workers, doctors and other health
care givers as well as educators. Historically, they have been able to exert
enormous influence in framing the problems and issues confronting children with disabilities and their parents. They have mobilised their interests in such a way as to make it difficult for governments to ignore them.
In this section, we will focus on the manner in which recent policies in
relation to disability and education have been framed in response to professional pressures.

Recent policy debates in relation to the education of students with disabilities have revolved around the idea of integration, or as it is sometimes called, mainstreaming. The policy of integration emerged in the
early 1970s in reaction to the practices of institutionalisation which
involved those assessed as disabled being segregated from the rest of

society. Babies who were viewed in some way as 'defective' by professionals in the field were routinely incarcerated in large institutions for the rest of their lives. In such institutions, conditions were inhumane, often worse than those found in jails. In the 1960s there was an avalanche of protests, critique and litigation that challenged the policies of institutionalisation. There was emerging public realisation of the gross injustice faced by people with disabilities. At the same time, the 1960s saw the introduction of a range of new equal opportunity legislation which enabled disability advocates to push for greater justice for students with disabilities. Indeed, international covenants like the United Nations Declaration of Rights and legislative frameworks have played a major part in the development of educational policies for students with disabilities.

The 1960s also witnessed the emergence of the field of special education, with one of its basic tenets being an implicit moral commitment to the welfare of students with disabilities. Yet for a field committed to social justice, special education is surprisingly devoid of an explicit examination of its moral premises. As Solity has observed:

> The fact that the earliest forms of special education were for those with physical and sensory difficulties, which were seen to be clearly identifiable medical conditions, gave the medical model (that is, that difficulties arise due to the characteristics of the child and that there is therefore something wrong with the child) considerable currency in special education.
>
> (Solity 1992: 4)

The medical model viewed disability as a problem with associated signs and symptoms which could either be remedied or whose impact could be minimised or managed with appropriate treatment. Such a view was, however, based on a range of normative assumptions about what constituted a 'normal' person. But those working with the medical model seldom questioned the moral constitution of such assumptions. Nor did they consider issues of educational treatment in ethical terms.

Special education thus developed as a *technical* field, located within a positivist framework, concerned with issues of diagnosis, assessment and causes of disability and appropriate forms of treatment. This technical emphasis enabled the field to constitute itself as a separate area of expertise, setting itself apart from other fields of education. It developed a distinctive language of its own to deal with issues and make its claims upon the state. So dominant has the medical model been that it initially resisted the idea that children with disabilities could be satisfactorily 'treated' in mainstream schools. It wished this responsibility to remain with the health departments and not with educational authorities. Indeed, in the US, despite many court cases aimed at obliging regular schools to admit children with disabilities, it was not until 1975 with the passage of the Education of all Handicapped Children's Act that the federal government recognised the rights of all students with disabilities to mainstream public education (Pijl 1994).

In Australia, the Karmel Report (1973) provided a new framework for the development of educational policies in relation to students with disabilities. This framework extended the idea of 'normalisation' first put forward by Wolf Wolfensberger in 1972. The idea of normalisation is captured in the phrase 'the right to as normal a life as possible'. Normalisation requires that people with disabilities should have the same rights and social resources as the rest of society. It has led to a range of intervention programmes, and the placement of students with disabilities within mainstream society – or in the least restrictive environment as is possible. In the early 1980s the idea of normalisation was developed into policies of integration. In Victoria, for example, integration was given a firm legislative authority in 1984 (Fulcher 1989).

The aim of integration policies is a simple one: children with disabilities are to be educated in regular schools provided certain conditions are met, and when in regular schools they are to engage in activities of the school alongside other students to the greatest extent possible. Thus the rationale for the policy of integration is both educational and moral, grounded in the idea that stresses equality of access and opportunity for all. However, the practices of integration have not quite lived up to their political aspirations. As Fulcher (1989) has pointed out, in Victoria the practices of integration have varied a great deal from school to school, and segregation and integration continue to exist alongside each other. There has been a great deal of professional resistance. Nor, as Slee (1993) argues, has the medical model in special education disappeared entirely. Rather, those working with positivist assumptions have simply appropriated the language of social justice to continue to pursue their policies and practices underpinned by the idea of individual deficit.

At the same time, the practices surrounding integration have given rise to a whole range of dilemmas, both theoretical and practical. As numerous educational advisers in the UK (see Adams 1986) have pointed out, while the policy of integration may be progressive and egalitarian, it contains a number of inherent dangers for students with disabilities – especially in times of reduced state resources for schools. The integration argument suggests that on the grounds of human and educational rights, everyone should have access to regular schools and classrooms. However, when this strategy is invoked to suggest that the needs of everyone could be catered for through the same generalised services, it simply becomes an instrument of the drive for efficiency rather than a moral idea designed to promote social justice. Moreover, access itself does not guarantee either full participation or more equal outcomes.

Without adequate levels of funding, access simply becomes an administrative rather than an ethical idea. In a system which does not have an adequate financial and support base, the needs of students with disabilities often become marginal, even with the best intentions of teachers. Not surprisingly, therefore, many professionals in the field are now demanding a return to the idea of special schools for students with disabilities.

Of course, this demand has support because the restructuring of the Australian state has had a number of implications for the provision of services to people labelled as disabled. The structure of many welfare services has changed as levels of funding have been reduced. There has been a greater reliance on user-pays principles, and new managerial practices have been developed which have made access to services difficult. But beyond these, more significant have been the ideological changes that have occurred which have altered the form in which the state now expresses its responsibility to people. The market logic has intervened to change citizens into clients, with social relations with the state now increasingly mediated by concerns about their productivity and contribution to the national economy. Nowhere are these cultural changes more significant than in education, as education impacts on the ways in which people view their sense of social worth.

We have argued that most policy initiatives in relation to the education of students with disabilities have been framed by a range of professional interests concerned with the issues of access. But what has become increasingly clear in recent years is that these concerns are not sufficient to account adequately for the various complex ways in which exclusion and discrimination are now practised, in both their individual and institutional forms. Nor do they respond effectively to the calls by the disability rights movement to have the voices of people with disabilities themselves heard in processes of decision making that affect their lives.

One of the major complaints of the disability rights movement is that professional interests in special education prevent the development of an understanding of the complex relationships between disability and other ways in which identity may be conceptualised. The exclusive focus on disability inhibits, for example, an exploration of the ways in which sexual and gendered discrimination, or racism, impact on people with disabilities. Dominated as they are by technical and operational concerns, disability professionals often fail to recognise that disability represents a socially constituted and reproduced set of relationships through which people with disabilities experience society in a variety of complex but unequal ways. Various educational practices in special education, for example, assume categorisations which can have the effect of dividing and separating people with disabilities into mutually antagonistic blocs.

DILEMMAS OF JUSTICE AND DIFFERENCE

The concerns we have raised throughout this chapter highlight the issues of the politics of difference in ways that are applicable to all social groups. Educational policies and programmes which target particular social groups often risk becoming too deterministic, causing people to draw stereotyped conclusions which fail to take account of the factors, not common to all members of a group, which also contribute to their educational experience and disadvantage. Indeed, in Australia there have emerged parallel bureaucratic structures for programmes designed to meet the needs of different groups classified as disadvantaged, often oblivious of other initiatives taking place in the same system. Thus gender equity initiatives have not, for example, always built upon the achievements of the Disadvantaged Schools Programme, which has been assumed to relate more to the issues of socio-economic disadvantage. Nor have they focussed much attention on the issues of the relationship between class and gender.

The Canadian feminist sociologist Mary O'Brien (1984) has referred to this phenomenon as the 'commatisation of difference'. Writing in the early 1980s, O'Brien was highly critical of a marked tendency in social theory and public policy for treating social categories as if they were distinct, as if the relationship between them could easily be described by the use of commas – race comma, gender comma, class comma, disability comma, rural disadvantage comma and so on. Such a 'commatised' view, O'Brien maintained, was reinforced by the talk of double and triple oppression, which did little to enhance an understanding of actual lived social experiences.

Ten years later, it is now recognised that issues of race, class, disability and gender cannot be so easily separated. Theories that privilege class relations and socio-economic factors have been undermined by the development of the new social movements among subordinated groups. As women, gays, ethnic minorities and others have begun to mobilise around these movements, it has become clear that the familiar social categories cannot be treated in homogeneous ways. Differences within groups cannot be as easily disregarded as some policies have done. Similarly, a number of recent black feminist authors have criticised the tendency of white feminism to privilege gender over issues of race and racism. They have pointed to the ethnocentric nature of Western feminism in positing certain priorities for struggle that do not take into account the experiences of indigenous, minority and third world women.

However, this recognition of difference raises a range of dilemmas for public policy in relation to education because most equity policies operate on the assumptions of uniformity and universal provision of services. In his book *Spheres of Justice*, Walzer (1983) has posed an issue critical to

our attempt to develop a new model for securing social justice in education around the recognition of difference: how should educational policy
and practice best respond to a society that is both heterogeneous and, it
is to be hoped, committed to social justice and democracy? In a complex
society, asserts Walzer, the idea of 'simple equality', defined as access so
that everyone gets the same thing in the same form, is neither achievable
nor desirable. It is not achievable because people do not have the same
means and capacities, and it is not desirable because people do not have
the same needs. This has been historically demonstrated in Australia and
elsewhere, in that centralised uniformity of educational provision was
never sufficient for achieving social justice. Consequently, for example, a
system that encourages integration of students with disabilities should
not continue to work on the assumptions of uniformity. Relevant differences in relative power, capacities and aspirations of students and parents must be acknowledged without risk to the notion of social justice.

Taking into account such heterogeneity, Walzer argues for a 'complex
equality', which involves the distribution of different social goods
according to different criteria. But this involves the old Aristotelian problem of how to determine what might count as 'relevant difference'.
Clearly, some criteria are required to determine which differences are relevant in which situation. The requirements of a particular context and
the different interests, capacities and histories of individuals need to be
taken into account. Yet the question of how we might compare different
interests and capacities is a difficult one. Short, then, of invoking normative principles which might apply to all cases – either in terms of the
rights of individuals or those based on the promise of universal emancipation – we are left with no other choice than to negotiate the relevance
of differences as particular claims arise in particular circumstances.
According to Walzer, this means that we need to generate general principles of social justice which are broad enough to allow for specific adaptation in different contexts.

Walzer's is a significant step forward in its recognition of the contemporary politics of difference – in the diversity that can be found within
any category, be it class, gender, sexuality, ethnicity or people with disabilities. Within each category, there is a diversity of interests. In this,
Walzer takes the political claims of the contemporary social movements
seriously. However, he does not recognise the extent to which social
movements have changed both the conception and the politics of social
justice. As Nancy Fraser points out:

> the struggle for recognition is fast becoming the paradigmatic form of
> political conflict in the late twentieth century. Heterogeneity and plu-
> ralism are now regarded as the norms against which demands for jus-
> tice are now articulated. Demands for 'recognition of difference' fuel

struggles of groups mobilised under the banners of nationality, ethnicity, race, gender and sexuality. Group identity has supplanted class conflict as the chief medium of political mobilisation. Cultural domination has supplanted economic exploitation as the fundamental injustice. And cultural recognition has displaced social-economic redistribution as the remedy for injustice and the goal of political struggle.

(Fraser 1995: 68)

Of course, material inequality has not disappeared but is now seen as articulated with demands for recognition of difference. What is also clear is that the distributive paradigm, as Iris Marion Young (1990) calls it, within which the major traditions of thinking about social justice are expressed, is no longer (if it ever was) sufficient to capture the complexities of injustice. This observation is consistent with the analysis presented above of the limitations of the policies of access and equity.

The distributive paradigm is concerned with the morally proper distribution of benefits and burdens among society's numbers. Paramount among these are wealth, income and other material resources. This definition, however, is often also stretched to include non-material goods such as rights, opportunities, power and self respect. These are treated as if they were material entities subject to the logic of a zero-sum game. So what marks the distributive paradigm is a tendency to conceive social justice and distribution as coextensive concepts. Young has identified two major problems with this way of thinking about social justice. First, she has argued that it tends to ignore, at the same time as it often presupposes, the institutional context that determines material distribution. Its focus is on consumption rather than on mode of production. As a consequence, it cannot account for those injustices that occur in the processes of social exchange and cultural formation. Second, in treating non-material goods like power, values and respect as if these were commodities, the distributive paradigm tends to misrepresent them. It obscures issues of decision making power and procedures as well as divisions of power and culture which can often lead to the perpetuation of gross injustices.

With the work of feminist scholars like Nancy Fraser and Iris Marion Young, a new mode of thinking about social justice is clearly emerging. While the distributive paradigm was associated with concepts like interest, exploitation and redistribution, this new paradigm is concerned to focus attention also on issues of identity, difference, cultural domination and recognition. The distributive paradigm saw injustice as being rooted in the political-economic structure of society which results in economic marginalisation and exploitation and denial of access and equity, and often inadequate material standards of living. The remedy was assumed to require political-economic restructuring – at least greater access and equity. The recognition paradigm does not dismiss these concerns as irrelevant, but suggests that they do not exhaust the range of injustices that occurs in human societies. Chief among these is the injustice resulting from cultural disrespect. Fraser (1995) argues that injustice can also be rooted in social patterns of representation, interpretation and communication, which result in cultural domination, non-recognition and disrespect.

The issues of representation, interpretation and communication are highly relevant to the concerns for justice in education because it is in education that students learn to develop their sense of self-worth and acceptable modes of social communication. As we have already pointed out, practices of integration, for example, have only promoted access for students with disabilities – they have done very little in changing the culture of schooling so that those with disabilities feel recognised and valued. Pedagogic and curriculum practices have remained largely unchanged with respect to the need to cater for the wide range of differences which are now acknowledged to exist in schools. Schools are still based on the assumptions of homogeneity and uniformity. They still require conformity and obedience to rules that are based on the requirements of administrative convenience rather than moral principles.

Clearly, if we are to resolve the dilemmas of justice and difference in education then policies must demand cultural and symbolic changes to the ways schools are structured. According to Fraser (1995), the politics of recognition requires social transformation in ways that would change *everybody's* sense of self. But the most significant insight that has emerged from this discussion is that policies for educational justice embrace complex issues. These involve not only the political economy of schooling – of concerns of access and equity – but also issues of identity, difference, culture and schooling. That is, the way things are named and represented, the manner in which difference is treated and the way in which the values and norms which govern life in schools are negotiated and established – these are all matters central to the concerns both of social justice and of education.

Chapter 8

The politics of educational change

> Policies, as we've seen, are useful, but blunt, instruments. Under the best of circumstances, they can influence the allocation of resources, the structure of schooling, and the content of practice; but those changes take time and often have unexpected effects.
>
> (Richard Elmore and Milbrey McLaughlin 1988: 60)

INTRODUCTION

The notion of change has been a recurring theme throughout this book. However, as the various policy case studies and other examples of policies we have referred to throughout the book show, attempting to judge the nature and extent of changes which have occurred is a difficult and complex task. Take, for example, the new policies in vocational education and training. How are these to be judged? In some areas there have been very marked changes, for example in the creation of an open training market. In other areas, little seems to have changed, for example the continuing division between academic and vocational education. Yet again, there are instances where apparent changes masked underlying inertia, seen for example in the quite elaborate mechanisms put in place to improve the position of girls in non-traditional areas of vocational education and training which failed to achieve any significant shifts in gender patterns. Some changes were momentary, for example the attempt to create a new credentialling system in place of the existing apprenticeships and traineeships. Other changes may yet evolve much more slowly, as we have seen, for instance, with advances in girls' education over time. But now we have introduced new complexities. What do we mean by 'advances' in this case? And however defined, to what extent have they been attributable to policy intervention?

Clearly these are essentially normative questions, returning us to the point we made at the beginning of the book about the significance of the position of the analyst. So any evaluations we now make of educational change and the role of policy in contributing to change, have to be seen

in terms of our position as critical policy analysts, and our interest in progressive change and the power plays involved in achieving – or inhibiting – such change. Additionally, then, our discussion contains strategic
as well as normative elements, reaffirming our earlier observations that
policy analysis and advocacy cannot be easily separated.

The relationship between policy and change, as we indicated above, is
an ambiguous one, given that change certainly occurs regardless of policy interventions, and that policy can result (intentionally or otherwise) in
little or no change. So: why does policy matter at all? Why are we so
interested in policy questions? What do we hope to achieve via policy?

We suggested in Chapter One that, given the logic of our times, governments typically use public policy for the management of change –
recognising Elmore and McLaughlin's (1988) observation that policy has
to be seen as a rather blunt instrument for this purpose. However, questions remain as to how and to what ends change is managed, and in
whose interests. These are central questions, especially for critical policy
analysis with its particular focus on progressive change. But what do we
mean by progressive change? More specifically, how do socially progressive tendencies translate into progressive educational outcomes via policy intervention?

First to the more general question of progressive change. Our view of
progressive change departs markedly from the kind of individualism
that has become dominant in recent policies. We argue that this individualism is anti-educational because education is at core a social activity
with social purposes. Of course, education can, and perhaps must, promote the development of the individual, but when policies champion
individual self-interest over social connectedness and collective well-
being they cannot be regarded as progressive.

We argue that one of the most important functions of education is to
help create what Eva Cox (1995) has called 'a truly civil society' in which
people relate to each other on terms of reciprocity and equality. As Cox
argues, 'The term "civil" offers alternative paradigms to counter the current public policy assumptions about competition and privatisation
which are unravelling the social fabric' (1995: 70). If we are to counter the
postmodern tendencies of fragmentation of society, then progressive policy must work against this trend. We must resist forms of social disintegration that reduce society simply to a sum of individuals in which social
relations are defined only in terms of competition and market-
individualism.

However, we must be careful about making assumptions about the
existence of a universal ethic – a notion predicated on the assumption
that all people are essentially the same, with the same set of needs and
interests, with the same capacities and advantages. The new social movements have demonstrated that old state structures which appeared to

work towards solidarity actually favoured middle-class white males. The new politics of difference require a reconceptualisation of how the notions of a truly civil society and collective well-being might now be negotiated through modes of democratic participation.

Of course, we know that such negotiation will always be skewed in favour of the powerful, unless material and cultural conditions for participation are genuinely free and equal (Norman 1987). Minimally, in our view, this requires a commitment to what has been called the social democratic notion of social justice, rather than those individualistic views of justice that are derived from liberalism. A social democratic notion of social justice rejects moral universalism, but none the less accepts the idea that we need to create conditions in which injustices can be morally assessed, and where political claims can be made upon the state for their redress. As Yeatman has pointed out:

> If universalism does not reside in what is, or even in what could be, but lies instead in a political, contestatory space that opens up in relation to existing wrongs and those who contest them in the name of equality, it is clear that this has radical implications for the nature of political vision.
>
> (Yeatman 1994: ix)

This implies the need to create material circumstances, as well as cultural and political spaces, which enable people to engage effectively in civic life. Such spaces are necessary if attempts to resolve the uneasy tension between equality and difference are to prove effective. Given this position, then, educational policies are progressive to the extent that they contribute to creating a truly civil society in which both equality and difference are valued simultaneously.

How might all of this apply to progressive outcomes in education, and to the role of policy in contributing to those outcomes? One way to explore the rather complex issues involved here is to look at some examples of how particular education policies have played out over time. We will look at four such examples, drawn from the Australian context. Some of the issues raised by these examples may be policy specific, relating to particular contexts at particular times. But in other ways, as we shall see, the examples raise more general issues of the relationships between policy, politics and change in education.

POLICIES AND CHANGE: SOME EXAMPLES

The intention in presenting these rather abbreviated sketches of policies in action is not so much to provide a comprehensive analysis as to highlight some pertinent aspects of change. In the latter part of the chapter, and drawing on the insights provided by these examples, we will explore in more analytical terms the policy ingredients which may contribute to, or hinder, the achievement of progressive educational outcomes.

The Disadvantaged Schools Programme: twenty years down the track

As discussed in Chapter Seven, the Disadvantaged Schools Programme (DSP) is noteworthy in that – despite periods when it has been under threat – it has survived in Australia for over twenty years. The Program aims to improve schooling for socio-economically disadvantaged students by the injection of additional funds into the schools they attend. It has been notable for its school-based focus and its attempts to improve the relationship between schools and their communities. As a result of this community focus, the particular needs of Aboriginal students, ethnic minority students and working-class girls who are living in poverty have also been given attention.

Within the Programme's history, there was initially a focus on resources, but later a move to emphasise staff development and whole school planning was made possible by the catch up in resources which helped to reduce the gap between rich and poor schools (White and Johnston 1993). Later still there was an emphasis on developing programmes which would directly impact on teaching and learning. For example, the 'Koorie Kit' was developed by participating schools with significant numbers of Aboriginal students in the Sydney inner-city area – illustrating the collaborative work between schools which went on as a result of the DSP. This collaborative work and networking contributed to the development of a 'DSP culture' among committed activist teachers.

So how are we to evaluate the success of the DSP? Certainly in terms of its longevity the Programme can claim some success, but this does not tell us much about its impact in terms of progressive change. Despite its longevity, the Programme has never attained a high profile, though it is clear that it has been a catalyst for innovative school-based change – 'It has enriched offerings and stimulated imaginative teaching and community projects across a broad front' (Connell et al. 1991: 263). And given that this change was concerned about improving participation and outcomes of schooling for disadvantaged students it can be considered to be progressive change – albeit on a fairly small scale.

What were some of the features of the DSP as a policy which facilitated change? Probably the most significant aspect of the DSP's success was that it was a *bottom-up policy* which had a *school and community focus*, built on teacher expertise. Funding for the Programme was submission based and although documents and guidelines for the Programme were produced by the Schools Commission, they were sufficiently flexible to accommodate a range of approaches and were able to be responsive to

local community needs. There was a conscious intention to devolve policy decisions to practitioners – with decisions being made at the level of
the school – and by regional and State committees. The Programme drew
on considerable experience of dealing with poverty issues, including
overseas experience, and White and Johnston refer to 'a history of strategic thinking and action which is at the heart of policy making in the
Programme' (1993: 125). However, not much of the innovative work
which has gone on in DSP schools and their communities has been well
disseminated and the Programme could probably have been more effective with more coordination at the national level.

Also significant in relation to our consideration of policy and *progressive change* is *the way the issues were framed* in the DSP, that is, how educational disadvantage was understood. White and Johnston (1993) outline
the three main discursive approaches to this issue: the discourse of individual needs, focussed on social needs of students; the discourse of community and parental involvement, focussed on the culture of students;
and the discourse of social class and collective action. They emphasise
the importance of this last approach:

> This formulation of disadvantage, although never a dominant strand
> in the Program, has been an undercurrent from the beginning. It sees
> the DSP as a strategy for collective social change rather than one
> which rescues individuals from poverty and equips them to be social-
> ly mobile.
>
> (White and Johnston 1993: 113)

As we showed in Chapter Seven, the DSP has tended to adopt a welfare
approach to poverty issues, with poverty seen as a minority problem
experienced by a small, discrete group of students – the 'ghetto
approach'. In contrast to this view, Connell *et al.* (1991), in their comprehensive review of the DSP, emphasised the scale and importance of class
inequalities in education. They argued that poverty needs to be seen as a
problem of the education system as a whole, and affecting a much larger
group of students than the 14 per cent funded under the DSP in 1991.
Instead of this welfare approach to the operation of the Programme they
advocate a system-wide approach to social justice. Recent economic pressures and high unemployment mean that an even greater proportion of
students are living in poverty and the need for a system-wide approach
is increasingly urgent. However, these same economic pressures and
stringencies mean that the Programme's funding is not secure. Thus a
question mark remains over the long-term future of the Programme as
well as its impact on progressive change in the longer term.

Developments in multicultural education: a problematic ideal?

As we noted in Chapter Seven, as an educational policy multiculturalism advocates a new approach to curriculum, pedagogy and evaluation through the promotion of a specific set of cultural attitudes to difference, and through the creation of a participative school environment. But to what extent have these policy aspirations been realised? In our view, while the rhetoric of multiculturalism has become quite strong, the changes it has been able to effect in schools have been at best limited. It has not succeeded in tackling the problems of racism which exist in Australian society. Few schools can thus claim to have translated the principles of multiculturalism into effective practice. As a result, what we find in schools are disjointed *ad hoc* activities, most of which focus on celebration of various ethnic traditions, leaving the structures of racism and inequalities largely unchallenged and unchanged.

A wide variety of reasons have been offered to explain the failure of schools to develop practices of multiculturalism in anything but the most minimal sense (see Kalantzis *et al*. 1989), including the lack of support that schools have been given, the problems concerning the inadequacies of curricular resources, the lack of in-service programmes, poor teacher education and so on. Nor have schools been entirely sure about the level of government commitment to multiculturalism. Australian society, too, remains deeply divided about multiculturalism, pointing perhaps to the failure of governments to clearly explain what they mean by the concept.

Part of the problem has thus resided in the state's *formulation* of multiculturalism itself. There have been no mandatory system-wide changes or legislation, and multicultural education policy has been stated in such a general way – as a series of platitudes – that schools have been able to refract its principles in a variety of contradictory ways. As a result, it has mostly been schools with a large proportion of ethnic minority students which have regarded multicultural education as relevant. Even in these schools, multiculturalism has been framed as a solution to a set of problems that ethnic diversity represents, rather than as something more positive which might contribute to *all* Australians developing a different sense of themselves.

There is yet another problem with the formulation of multiculturalism: the assumptions it makes about teachers and teaching. Multicultural education policy cannot realise its potential without an adequate theoretical understanding of the various ways in which teachers conceptualise their social world, and the ways these conceptualisations serve to define their pedagogy. Teaching is not a culturally neutral activity, but is itself grounded in particular cultural traditions which need to be *deconstructed* if we are to see how pedagogic relations are ethnically and racially formed. Many ethnic minority students find schooling an alienating

ience, not because they are not interested in education, but because
ɔls do not adequately deal with the problems of racism that these
ents confront. Feminist educators have been able to show how gendered and sexist teaching really is, but there has been no parallel
Australian movement associated with multiculturalism, which might
demonstrate the role curriculum and pedagogy play in the perpetuation
of racism.

Unlike the civil rights movement in the US, there has been no coherent
social movement in Australia to argue for anti-racism. Ethnic communities
do not therefore represent a major political force which might relate
directly with teachers and schools. The links that schools do have with
members of ethnic communities are often on the terms of the schools
themselves – mostly on occasions when parents are called in to discuss a
particular educational or behaviour problem or student progress.
Multicultural education policy is unlikely to be an effective instrument
for progressive change unless it is based on genuine consultation with
ethnic communities, and what is also needed is political commitment
and a significant sharpening of the focus of the policy.

The Social Justice Strategy in Queensland education: one step forward . . . ?

In late 1989 a Labour government came to power in Queensland after
twenty-three years of conservative governments which had continually
opposed progressive change in education. There was much optimism
amongst those concerned with education that new progressive policies
would be introduced. Following a restructuring of the Department of
Education, a new Directorate of Social Justice (workforce and studies)
was established with responsibility for social justice in a range of
employment practices, as well as in relation to schools. Its Director also
had responsibility for implementing policies concerning anti-discrimination and equal employment opportunity.

The Director had a long history of involvement with progressive educational politics and the women's movement, and quickly developed a
very high profile within the education community in Queensland.
Importantly, she was also a member of the executive management committee (EMC) – the most powerful policy making body within the
department, responsible for strategic decision making relating to developments across the department. This meant that a social justice perspective was brought to bear on all departmental decisions.

The Social Justice Strategy developed for the years 1992–3 was incorporated within the strategic plan of the department, by then run along
corporate managerialist lines. The Strategy set out twelve objectives to be
achieved in the first twelve months of its operation, a manifestation of

managing by objectives central to corporate managerialism. The Strategy was about embedding social justice across the departmental structures and was perceived to be the first step of a long-term strategy in relation to social justice. As such, the Strategy assumed the need for short-term achievable objectives, rather than a fully expressed philosophy of social justice. The approach to policy development was very much top-down and thus, by and large, the Strategy languished in schools. However, it did provide legitimation for activists committed to social justice across the system, and the Strategy itself was given some legitimation by the fact that knowledge of equity issues became an employment criterion for teachers and for promotion.

With a change of Minister and subsequent resignation of the Director, disillusioned with the slow pace of change, a new Director was appointed but located in a different structural position within the department, with workforce responsibilities removed. The new appointment – now Assistant Director level – was no longer a member of the EMC. The revised Social Justice Strategy (1994–8) focussed more directly on school practices rather than systemic structures. However, with yet another change of Minister there appeared to be a further weakening of commitment to social justice and this second stage of the Strategy, while distributed to schools, was never formally endorsed. When the Assistant Director was subsequently promoted, her position was never advertised or formally filled.

In early 1996 there was a change of government with the new conservative Minister indicating that social justice was no longer to be a priority of the new government. Furthermore, a demonstrable commitment to social justice was no longer a criterion for appointment or promotion. Immediately, many workers within the State department started searching for words to use other than social justice – an indication of the significance of policy language. The new Minister's statement had clearly given a signal to the education community, so that the continuation of the Social Justice Strategy in schools became dependent upon the extent to which the earlier developments had been institutionalised within the schools.

How, then, might we evaluate the successes of the Social Justice Strategy and what does its trajectory tell us about educational policy and progressive change? Clearly a *key player* – the first Director of Social Justice – was very important in giving legitimacy to the Strategy, and a Labour government after the long period of conservative rule was important to the establishment of social justice policy – an indication of the significance of *political context* to policy development and effectiveness. The effects of subsequent changes of Minister and the return to a conservative government also serve to confirm this point.

The *structural location* of the Director's position within the State

Department was important in influencing and legitimising social justice matters. This became patently obvious after the downgrading and reduction in the responsibilities of the position. *Legislation* was also important in relation to matters of social justice and equal employment opportunity – indeed, it is these legislated changes which are more likely to survive a change of government.

In the first instance, the approach to policy production was very *top-down* – perhaps appropriate for the implementation of legislative reforms, but not effective for changing school practices. Initially there was limited teacher professional development, necessary to the long-term *institutionalisation* of policy goals, but professional development was an early resourcing casualty of educational cutbacks. Initially the Strategy was framed by a managerialist approach, emphasising short-term achievable goals through clearly specified accountability procedures. For example, specific individuals at various levels within the department were responsible for monitoring and reporting their achievements at the end of twelve months. However, the possibility of a long-term approach was always contingent upon continuing political support which could be weakened by a change of Minister, and even more so by a change in government.

The social justice agenda in Queensland was extremely broad-ranging because of the years of neglect, even obstinate opposition, to such matters by previous conservative governments. This meant that commitment to the matters traversed in the Strategy was very uneven across the system, reinforcing the need for widespread teacher in-service programmes as a precondition for effective implementation of the agenda. However, it is possible that there is now a broader constituency for social justice within the system than there was prior to 1989. The fate of the Social Justice Strategy and its effects none the less remain in the balance.

The restructuring of higher education: the baby and the bath water

The creation of the unified national system (UNS) of higher education in Australia in the late 1980s, driven by the restructuring imperatives noted in Chapter Four, aimed to provide an expanded, more diverse and flexible, equitable and efficient system of higher education in Australia. Via a mix of regulatory sticks and deregulatory carrots, the government exercised both a tighter control over the priorities and funding of the university sector, at the same time as establishing the circumstances for greater entrepreneurialism within universities than had hitherto been possible. To what extent have the broad goals of the UNS been met, almost a decade later? At one level, quite successfully. In the past decade, the throughput of students – to use the jargon of the times – expanded over 70 per cent, while in relative terms staffing levels dropped by almost a third. University income from external sources – fee-paying students, consultancies, joint ventures and so forth – increased substantially. And while little real diversity between universities has been achieved in terms of priorities and range of offerings, students are able to mix and match more easily than before.

How do we evaluate these changes in terms of their progressive impact? One thing to note is that the outcomes are not evenly distributed. Some institutions have done better out of the changes than others. For example, most of the older, traditional universities and former technological institutes were able to capitalise on their more lucrative links with industry, their substantial endowment base and a long tradition of research and/or consultancy in order to generate the financial and cultural capital necessary to participate as effective players in the new education market. These universities were able to capture the bulk of research and consultancy monies, and some, led by particularly zealous chief executive officers (aka vice-chancellors), were able to seize the moment to establish niche monopolies in the export of educational services or in the potential gold-mine of the multi-media open learning industry. By contrast, a number of the former colleges of advanced education, either because of their regional location, the lack of a so-called research culture or sheer bad financial management floundered in the competitive context of the unified national system.

Within institutions, too, another divide surfaced, between a female-dominated lecturing staff, often casual and part-time, carrying the burden of the large classes and inadequate facilities, and a male-dominated core of tenured academics and administrators. Still others found new and relatively pleasant pastures in well-paid consultancies, funded research projects and lucrative senior executive positions. In this, the academic workforce reflected the hour-glass polarisation of more general labour market trends. Corporate bonding was ostensibly promoted through modern management techniques of mission statements, joint goal setting and staff development programmes. However, collegiality, if it were ever present, was replaced by an industrial divide between management and workers, by the individual competitiveness bred in the new market-tempered climate and by the sheer *anomie* induced by ever-mounting workloads and multiple demands on time and energy. Course planning became more difficult in the new client-responsive climate, though for some staff and students increased flexibility was a boon. Students exercising consumer choice were tempted towards more marketable areas of study – for example in counselling or business administration where enrolments boomed – hence creating new divisions between resource-rich and resource-poor departments.

From our point of view, the gains were highly ambivalent. For example, while elaborate accountability mechanisms aimed at improving participation patterns in universities existed, there was some evidence to suggest that those universities generating the most income were the least concerned with making their institutions more accessible and equitable. More generally, it seemed, expanded opportunity to participate in higher education to a large extent simply contributed to credentials creep, reinforcing the already existing high degree of instrumentalism in most students.

Certainly the combination of a more diverse student body, higher staff-student ratios, inadequate facilities and loss of collegiality contributed to a diminishing intellectual climate – quality reviews notwithstanding. Hence for us, the government's vaunted equity and efficiency gains were in many respects hollow, despite good initiatives in individual institutions. And as for the future? Higher education has been made one of the major targets for the new conservative coalition's spending cutbacks. The 'gang of eight' (Lowe 1996) – Australia's self-defined high profile universities – have mobilised to attain special research (and funding) status, hence in effect reconstituting a divide the UNS was created to eradicate. They may not formally succeed, but in many ways they have achieved their goal despite the massive policy intervention which the UNS represents.

Why did these outcomes emerge? This is obviously a complex matter but for our purposes two factors in particular would seem to be important: tensions between *regulatory and deregulatory* elements; and the capacity for old *vested interests* to continue to steer that agenda. The UNS was in many ways a centralist and top-down policy initiative, and the welter of reporting requirements involved in the accountability mechanisms which DEET established to monitor the system drew heavy criticism from supporters and opponents alike. But in the broader economic and ideological climate, formal accountability procedures were not too difficult to subvert – glossy documents of statistical compilations revealed little about institutional practices. And the logic of entrepreneurialism drove those institutions able to play the market towards a greater preoccupation with growth and profit than with DEET's formal priorities. Such a context which, as we saw, privileged the already established institutions, meant that in the politics of implementation old vested interests were able to assert themselves, albeit in harder times.

THE RELATIONSHIP BETWEEN POLICY AND CHANGE: A FRAMEWORK FOR ANALYSIS

So what do these examples tell us about the relationship between policy and change? In what follows, we discuss this question by considering more systematically circumstances and factors relevant to considering the role of policy in progressive change. Our discussion is structured around three general categories: issues pertaining to *external* pressures for change, including the impetus and context for change; issues concerning the *internal dynamics* of change, including the role of leadership in the change process and the strategies employed within organisations to facilitate change; and issues related to the *institutionalisation* of change as it is expressed through a dialectic between external pressures and internal dynamics. We conclude with some brief comments on issues to do with the *politics* of educational change. Before we do this, it is perhaps appropriate that we consider the manner in which the traditional policy literature deals with the question of the relationship between policy and change.

The traditional view of policy analysis, as we have already noted, makes a sharp distinction between policy development and implementation. Once the policies have been developed they have to be implemented in and by organisations. The focus of the traditional view thus is not so much on how change is affected but on organisational change. The issues considered include: how organisations implement policies by designing and structuring change, what strategies they should follow, what resistance they are likely to encounter, and how resistances can be minimised. Note that there is no mention here of the content of change (and its desirability or otherwise) – it is the strategic issues of implementation that are highlighted.

The term traditionally associated with planned organisational change is *organisational development* (OD). In education, its principles are best exemplified in the idea of the 'self-managing school' (Caldwell and Spinks 1988). Huse defines OD as 'the application of behavioural science knowledge in a long-term effort to improve an organisation's capacity to cope with changes in its external environment and increase its internal problem-solving capabilities' (1982: 555). Advocates of OD invariably use the rhetoric of collaborative management, stressing the importance of the work of the 'change agent' – normally an external consultant – whose task it is to enhance the processes of organisational learning, taking members of the organisation through a number of distinct stages, from the exploration of the organisational context, to the identification of problems, to problem solving, to the evaluation of changes achieved. OD is based on the assumption that organisational efficiency and effectiveness can only be increased when workers have been given every opportunity to internalise the nature of organisational changes required by policy shifts (Dunford 1992: 301–2).

Now, from our point of view, there are a number of problems associated with the ideas and practices of OD. First, as we have already argued, the distinction between policy development and implementation cannot be made as neatly as OD supposes. Many policies acquire their specific form only during the processes of implementation, as people debate their

ιg and significance and trial ideas, sometimes along the lines sug-
ιd by the policies, but sometimes also in opposition to them. Second,
participation in decision making that OD offers is a sham – it is
ghly undemocratic, managed by the change agent whose responsibility
it is to bring workers into line with the policies already determined elsewhere. Third, OD pays little attention to organisations as arenas within
which power operates. Nor does it consider the issue of the way in
which power may have already been exercised in policy formulation.
Fourth, OD is presented as a generic technology of change and does not
permit the evaluation of the policies themselves. And finally, it does not
make problematic the politically and historically constituted nature of
both the policies and the people who are given responsibility to implement them. In this way, OD is both *apolitical* and *ahistorical*. In contrast,
our view of policy analysis conceptualises the relationship between policy and change as historically specific and politically charged, involving
opposition, contestation and power. To describe policy historically is to
understand its context and the ways in which it responds to pressures for
change.

The impetus and context for change

In several of the case studies throughout the book we have outlined the
significance of contextual factors in placing policy issues on the agenda.
We have discussed the impact of economic pressures on education policy
agendas, for example in the shift towards a focus in Australia on the
development of skills for the 'clever country'. And we have noted the
influence of social movements in the development of social justice policies, such as the civil rights movement in the US, and the women's
movement in many parts of the world.

Though the economic, social, political and cultural aspects of the context are interrelated they may be separated analytically. Elmore and
McLaughlin comment that 'the political culture of some settings makes
them immune to certain reforms and highly susceptible to others' (1988:
12). We could say the same about the broader policy context in relation to
educational change. Various contextual factors together provide the
impetus for progressive change, or alternatively may make progressive
change an uphill struggle. However, the situation may be more complex
than this, with contradictory pressures either supporting or inhibiting
progressive change, pressures which must on the one hand be *managed*
by governments, and on the other be strategically *used* by activists.

We now turn to the different aspects of context which we have identified. We will begin with the economic context, highly significant in influencing the direction of educational policy making and increasingly
dominant in many countries of the world as a result of globalisation

pressures. As well as the more obvious influence on allocation of resources, economic prosperity facilitates a climate for progressive policies, a climate which tends to dissipate in times of recession. This point was explored in *Schooling Reform in Hard Times* (Lingard *et al.* 1993) in relation to the impact of economic goals on Labour's reformist educational agenda in Australia. Although a market approach to education has not been taken up in Australia as completely as in the UK, it has still had a profound effect on education. Equity and economic concerns have been linked together in policy – an approach which is in fact consistent with Australian traditions of reform where social justice has been provided *through* rather than *in opposition to* the market (Cass 1989).

Thus the traditions of reform in a particular country, region or State are also a significant aspect of the policy context relevant to our consideration of the politics of change. In Australia, the historical pattern of federalism is also relevant in policy making. Policies have had to be negotiated through the complexities of the relationship between central and State governments in ways which do not apply to unitary states where there is only one level of government. This means that it is more difficult for the Commonwealth to achieve acceptance of its interventions in State policy jurisdictions such as schooling.

The development of legislation and other related policies, reflecting prevailing political ideologies, may provide added impetus for change. For example, in the case of the Queensland Social Justice Strategy, the enactment of State anti-discrimination legislation and broad social justice policies in other government departments were conducive to progressive policy developments in education. The Commonwealth Affirmative Action Act, which requires that universities – as well as businesses – must report annually on progress relating to equal employment opportunity in their workplaces, has been a catalyst for progressive change in many universities. Similarly, the signing of international conventions – for example the United Nations Convention on the Rights of the Child – has provided an impetus for legislation or policy development among the countries which are signatories.

The political context also conditions how policy processes work. For example, pressure groups are significant in lobbying for – or resisting – change. During the period of the conservative National Party governments in Queensland, fundamentalist Christian groups opposed non-sexist education because it supposedly conflicted with traditional family values (Lingard *et al.* 1987). In contrast, teacher unions and professional organisations lobbying for policy on the education of girls in that State were active in pressuring successive governments. However, after the election of the first Labour government for many years in 1989, the state became more proactive, some former activists were appointed as policy officers within the bureaucracy, and some of the extra-state pressures collapsed. This is consistent with Elmore and McLaughlin's observation that educational change occurs in broad patterns of reform, quiescence and re-reform. First comes 'an upsurge of public concern' followed by some kind of policy response. Then 'the pressure for reform – political and professional – trails off, leaving traces of best practice in textbooks, teacher education, local structure, and state law; finally an upsurge of public concern starts the process again' (1988: 12).

These issues are related to the social and cultural context – crucial in influencing which issues get a place on the policy agenda – as well as to the various social movements which significantly contribute to the impetus for progressive change. We have mentioned several times the influence of the women's movement in the development of policies relating to the education of girls, but other social movements have been important in influencing education policy development. For example, despite the differences in culture, language and lifestyle, Aboriginal and Torres Strait Islander groups have been involved in a unified struggle for justice – particularly during the Bicentennial celebrations in 1988. This has helped to bring about cultural change and developments in policies, including in education. Indigenous education first appeared on the policy agenda in the early 1970s, ultimately resulting in the *National Aboriginal and Torres Strait Islander Education Policy* (DEET 1989) during the period of the Hawke Labour government. This policy was developed and later reviewed after extensive consultation with community groups and has been an important step forward in progressive reform in this area. This contrasts with the situation in multicultural education where there was no similar unified pressure for change, and where to date a national multicultural or anti-racist education policy does not exist.

Both multicultural education and indigenous education policies have met with some opposition, reminding us that policy is a contested field, as we have emphasised throughout this book. Thus, as well as understanding how context can provide a climate for change, it is useful to also consider how the context may work against progressive change. This was seen particularly clearly in relation to education policy in the UK under the Thatcher government. Thatcher's hegemonic project sought to fundamentally change society, with education playing a central role in 'the moral regeneration of a nation' (Dale 1989). Under the influence of new right pressures, equal opportunities policy was portrayed as a 'loony left' issue and Labour local education authorities – such as the Inner London Education Authority – who were committed to such policies were discredited. The media were central in these 'discourses of derision' (Ball 1990). The British experience shows the importance of the cultural, or 'common sense', level in influencing how popular prejudices are taken up and articulated in policies: the Conservatives 'were able to draw on the deep seated conservatism in British culture to marginalise anti-sexist and anti-racist education and to construct their new policy agenda' (Taylor 1993: 38).

An understanding of the way in which discourses available in the wider cultural context become articulated in policies, as demonstrated in this example, is important in relation to the politics of change. These discourses are linked to local traditions of reform, which may be reinforced or challenged by the media – with implications for progressive change. There are regular media-generated calls, for example, for 'back to the basics' in education policy in the UK and the US, as well as in Australia. Though on occasions, of course, the media do play a more sympathetic role in their presentation of education policy issues. For example, mooted savage cutbacks to higher education by the incoming conservative coalition in Australia in 1996 were portrayed by the media in somewhat critical terms.

But progressive change is always precarious because of the presence of oppositional discourses. It is in this context that political will and leadership become significant. A good example of this point is the leadership which was provided by the Keating Labour government regarding the Reconciliation process with Aboriginal people. The celebrated Redfern speech, addressed as much to the wider white community as to the Aboriginal people present at the time, was an attempt to take the lead in changing wider community attitudes.

Players and approaches to policy

We have considered various ways in which contextual imperatives establish parameters for policy making. We also need to consider the internal dynamics of policy making, deriving from the interactions of key players and interests involved in policy processes, and the implementation approaches adopted.

Elmore and McLaughlin's discussion of the relationship between policy and reform provides a useful starting point for thinking about these dynamics. They point to three 'loosely connected' levels of policy, administration and practice, suggesting that: 'If channels aren't open among the actors at each level, policy, administration and practice will never connect in a useful way' (1988: 11). Now while in Chapter Two we pointed to problems with formulations of policy which artificially distinguish these arenas, the fact also remains, as Susan's story in Chapter One indicated, that bureaucracies typically approach the business of policy making in just such a so-called rational manner. The fact also remains, as all our examples above showed, that policies unravel over a very long span of time, so that making distinctions between formally stated policy objectives, the procedures used to administer policies and the ways in which policies translate – or fail to translate – into changed practices does provide some analytical purchase on the relationship between policy and change. As Elmore and McLaughlin go on to acknowledge (1988: 47), given the differing locations of key people involved in policy making processes and the conflicting interests they often represent, making connections between policy, administration and practice remains a precarious business. We would add that this has significant implications for the extent to which the aims of potentially progressive policies may be realised.

The ways in which the goals of Queensland's Social Justice Strategy were frustrated over time is a case in point. On the one hand, the experience, expertise and political nous of the initial Director produced a sophisticated conceptualisation of the policy issues and a comprehensive implementation strategy containing both long- and short-term elements. On the other hand, the equity interests she represented – requiring material rather than simply symbolic commitment – conflicted deeply with other interests on the Executive Management Committee, reflecting in part the broader conflict of interests identified by Pusey (1991) between market-oriented and programme- and service-oriented departments within government. Here equity interests also conflicted with the interests and knowledge-base of what Lipsky (1980) refers to as street-level bureaucrats, in this case, teachers in schools. As a result, and with some notable exceptions, the Strategy by and large met with either indifference or positive resistance. The same tendency was discerned in the diminution of the progressive objectives of the new policies in vocational education and training over time, described in Chapter Six. Here we saw a vanguard of key players at the national level setting out a complex and ambitious policy agenda, while 'on the ground' key committees and other groups of players, whose interests often pulled in different directions, crafted the policies into a particular shape to fit local circumstances and ambitions.

Now, 'loose connections' between policy, administration and practice are of course endemic to policy making processes, though, as we suggested above, the discursive and material context at any given time provides some clues as to what kinds of connections are likely to be made and which interests are more likely to be realised. So for us the issue of 'making connections' is more of a strategic than a technical question, to do with maintaining a momentum for an explicitly progressive policy agenda – for example the *National Aboriginal and Torres Strait Islander Education Policy*, the *Disadvantaged Schools Program*, the *National Policy for the Education of Girls* – or with extracting the progressive potential from a mixed policy bag – for example, the training reform agenda in Australia, multiculturalism policy or even a school discipline policy.

These are political questions in which matters of power are centrally implicated, a point worth elaborating upon briefly. Lukes' (1974) discussion of three dimensions of power is useful here. The first, he suggests, 'occurs in observable overt conflicts between actors over key issues' (Ham and Hill 1993: 70). So, for example, when governments are able to enforce grudging compliance with their reporting requirements they are exercising power in this sense. The second dimension refers to the ways in which dominant groups are able to inhibit issues from reaching policy agendas, so that conflict remains covert. Bachrach and Baratz (1963) coined the term 'non decision making' to refer to this dimension of power. The exclusion of so many voices in the construction of multiculturalism policy, or the caution revealed in Shakila's story in Chapter One in producing an anti-racism policy because of the potentially explosive cultural and political issues involved, or the avoidance of issues of sexuality in early anti-discrimination legislation and, indeed, in the *National Policy for the Education of Girls* are all examples of this dimension of power. Lukes goes on to suggest that 'the most effective and insidious use of power is to prevent . . . conflict from arising in the first place' (1974: 23). This is his third dimension of power, where potential issues fail to reach the policy agenda because they remain beyond the realm of consideration, so that conflict remains latent. The failure to conceptualise multiculturalism policy in terms other than a celebration of culture, or the failure to conceptualise poverty as integrally related to privilege in many compensatory education programmes, are cases in point. Changing policy agendas, therefore, as have occurred in some anti-racism policies in the UK, and in some of the DSP approaches in Australia, constitutes a priority for those trying to achieve progressive ends from policy making.

What we are discussing here, then, are questions of the politics of policy making, from the gestation or conceptualisation of policy through to the kinds of implementation and monitoring procedures adopted. We will try to give this discussion some shape by focussing on what, from the examples throughout the book, appear to be three significant elements of such a politics. They relate to matters of the structural location of key players; to the approaches to policy implementation that they adopt; and to processes of resistance, marginalisation and cooption that they frequently invoke.

As Lingard (1995) pointed out in his discussion of micropolitics within the state, *structural location* within the bureaucratic hierarchy is a key factor in influencing policy agendas. With seniority comes the capacity to participate in, and influence, decisions at highest levels, including decisions about the constitution of key committees and implementation procedures (Cockburn 1991). The Director's clout to push Queensland's Social Justice Strategy, or Maria's (whose story appeared in Chapter One) capacity as principal to manipulate the system even given the constraints she faced, is testament to this. At the same time of course, policy processes are influenced at many levels and in many different arenas. The use by academic unions and women's groups of Affirmative Action and Equal Employment Opportunity legislation in universities to extract some benefits from restructuring is illustrative of this point.

But policy agendas are also influenced through manoeuvrings of groups outside the state. The mobilisation of community groups in Victoria together with teachers and students to stop the closure of a small school with a high Aboriginal and Torres Strait Islander enrolment (part of the Schools of the Future rationalisation project), culminating in a victory in the courts, is an example of this.

How do progressive policy makers negotiate the path between *top-down and bottom-up* policy imperatives? In the discussion of the training reform agenda in Chapter Six, we noted how the tools of corporate management were appropriated as one means of gaining compliance with equity objectives. We saw there, and also in the example of the Social Justice Strategy above, the potential but also the limitations of this top-down approach. At the same time, the example of the Disadvantaged Schools Program showed how its grass-roots emphasis, while effectively garnering support from a significant number of committed teachers, perhaps achieved less than it could have because of a lack of overarching mechanisms for coordinating and disseminating ideas. There appear to be no easy answers to this conundrum, though a key element in tempering authoritarian forms of top-down policy making may lie in approaches to consultation – a problem confronting Susan in Chapter One.

In explicitly top-down models, often associated with notions of 'strong leadership', consultation may be non-existent – the introduction of *Schools of the Future* in Victoria being a case in point. More often, consultative processes are formally built into policy processes but in seemingly tokenistic ways. Criticisms of ritual consultation are often confirmed when final policy documents look suspiciously like their prior Discussion Papers – seen for example in the Green and White Papers accompanying the formation of the Unified National System of higher education. More participatory forms of consultation were seen in the development of policies such as the National Policy for the Education of Girls in Australian Schools and the National Aboriginal and Torres Strait Islander Education Policy. From our point of view, these more robust consultative approaches tend to achieve greater commitment for their policy prescriptions from the communities they are designed to serve, with concomitantly improved chances for the long-term survival of those policies and more progressive educational outcomes.

Processes of *resistance and marginalisation* refer to those overt and covert blocking and stalling tactics identified, for example, by Cynthia Cockburn (1991) in her discussion of men's resistance to women in the workplace and seen in the implementation of equity policy more generally (Apelt 1995). Resistance and marginalisation processes were evident, too, in the collective inertia in implementing and monitoring equity requirements of the AVTS pilot projects described in Chapter Six. More insidious perhaps are processes of *cooption* through which the radical objectives which key players often bring on behalf of the interests they represent are undermined by the bureaucratic structures in which they work. Penny Tripcony muses on the dilemma:

> To work within a system might provide opportunities to influence policy-makers and strategists, but to join the public service might be viewed as a rejection of Aboriginal values and aspirations. Was I being coopted to be later used in a coercing, controlling role in dealings with Aboriginal community groups? Would I be in a position to work towards social justice and equity for Aboriginal people? In so doing, would I maintain my integrity as an Aboriginal woman and a member of that Aboriginal community?
>
> (Tripcony 1995: 122)

Femocrats – feminists with allegiances to women's groups working within the bureaucracy – have faced similar dilemmas (Franzway 1986), as have academics undertaking critical policy work within government – as mentioned in Chapter One.

Institutionalising change

Effective change in educational practices requires more than positive hopes and aspirations, though these are very important in mobilising initial and continuing support for change. Long-term effective change of a progressive kind in education requires the operationalisation of ideas and, more importantly, their institutionalisation in structures, cultures and practices. However, institutionalisation does not mean a closing off of debate. One thing we need to recognise is that we never reach the ideal situation – it always remains an aspiration. Research and better ways of conceptualising the issues in policy are developing all the time. Further, the broader contexts of policy also continue to change.

What, then, are the central elements with which those concerned with change in education ought to work? In common with much of the organisational change literature (for example, Wilenski 1986: 176–83), we would suggest a need to consider changes in organisational structures and culture as well as changes in individual attitudes, behaviours and practices. Likewise, Rizvi and Kemmis (1987: 338) speak of the need to focus on structures, discourses and practices. A focus on all three is necessary, though experience has shown that it is perhaps easier to change structures than effect broad cultural change or changes in individual attitudes and behaviour. None the less, legislative demands and structural rearrangements do impact on behaviour – seen, for example, in the impact of sexual harassment or racial discrimination legislation on public behaviour.

Wilenski (1986: 179–83) suggests a number of 'levers of change'. These include legislation, the creation of new institutional or structural arrangements, changes in formal processes involving new coordination mechanisms, as well as new budgetary processes, and the appointment of new people. The changes Wilenski brought to the structure and operation of the public service in Australia to some extent exemplify his policy approach in practice. However, more is required for the institutionalisation of long-term change than simply the utilisation of particular levers. As Harvey and Hergert point out, 'Whether the program, practice or policy sticks after attention has been directed elsewhere depends largely on what occurs during the institutionalisation phase' (1986: 295). Thinking about the organisational, cultural and individual complexities involved in implementing a top-down policy in a State system of schooling gives us some idea of the range of matters which need to be considered to ensure institutionalisation. Daws picks up on this complexity when she observes: 'At each point, policy is a response to complex and diverse elements, including a range of constraints imposed by other levels of public and educational policy, different administrative contexts, varying ideologies and the personal idiosyncrasies of the people involved' (1995: 129). To ensure institutionalisation of progressive change, considerable thought needs to go into how change can be effected in relation to these structural, cultural, administrative, ideological and personal elements of the system into which policy is introduced. This is particularly necessary given the endemic tensions between long-term institutionalisation processes and the short time-frames of electoral cycles. However, as Wilenski (1986) has noted, often more effort and politicking are put into achievement of the policy statement than in considering these matters central to effective implementation and institutionalisation. Wilenski also points to the reality that new policies are usually implemented by those individuals in structures that the policies aim to change!

While structural change is a useful focus and essential to institutionalisation, in-service or professional development is also important to effect change in both organisational culture and practices. As McLaughlin (1987) has noted, in education the smallest unit – the classroom – will ultimately determine the effectiveness of a policy. Elsewhere, she has also observed that: 'We have learned that we can't mandate what matters to effective practice: the challenge lies in understanding how policy can enable and facilitate it' (McLaughlin 1991: 155).

Applied to change in schools, this means we need to consider teachers' interests, as Connell (1985) notes in his study of teachers' work.

Much educational policy does not deal with teaching and learning processes. Rather, the implications of policies for these practices, particularly in relation to matters of social justice, are often left unstated and certainly under-theorised. There are also important lessons here for policy production. Elmore and McLaughlin (1988) have noted how many policy processes tend to substitute external authority for the expertise of educational practitioners. However, as we saw in the example of the DSP, the involvement of teachers and school communities which was built into the Programme was a major factor in its success. Furthermore, as the quote at the beginning of this chapter states, often policies 'communicate hostility or indifference to the very people whose commitment is required to make them work'. This point also alerts us to the significance of the language in which a particular policy is couched. Mark's story in Chapter One indicated how as a classroom teacher he felt very much as if teachers had been excluded from, or indeed even frozen out of, contemporary policy processes.

As we have suggested earlier, exclusion from policy processes will often precipitate resistances. These may take a number of forms and stem from a number of motivations – stretching from straightforward individual and organisational inertia, to more deep-seated and organised ideological and political opposition. Wilenski (1986: 172–6), in considering opposition to reform in public administration, suggests that opposition takes three basic forms: first, that resulting from genuine value differences and ideologies; second, the reluctance to relinquish power by those who benefit most from current arrangements; and third, psychological opposition to change – sometimes stemming from the implied criticisms of older practices implicit in the new policy frameworks.

The mobilisation of support for progressive change, as already noted, is central to institutionalisation of policies over time, a process which operates at a number of levels. We have already pointed to the significance of developing support at the local sites of practice, for example schools and other institutions. Dealing strategically with bureaucracies at both State and national levels is also important, as Penny Tripcony (1995) found in her experiences as an Aboriginal woman working in a state bureaucracy in an area crossing State and federal boundaries. Mobilisation beyond the state and in international domains has also proved useful strategically in progressive politics, as we pointed out in Chapter Four in relation to indigenous and environment politics. Possibilities also exist for this in education. For example, the Australian Education Union is considering the use of the external affairs power in the constitution to press for funding guarantees for Australian schooling (Borgeest 1994). This view of an interconnected politics perhaps distinguishes our position from that of some postmodernist politics which would simply emphasise political engagement at local sites. As we have ied to show throughout the book, it is no longer possible to separate out the local from the national from the global.

Finally, and to reiterate our earlier point, change is not simply linear in character. Gains can never be taken for granted and not all change contributes to outcomes which we would regard as progressive. For example, market 'reforms' of schooling in the UK have reversed the incremental developments towards comprehensive education across the postwar period. In Australia, Liberal State governments have unravelled many progressive elements of Labour-initiated education policies – for example, assessment policy in New South Wales, social justice in Queensland and participative decision making in Victoria. The new federal conservative coalition government may well unravel the unified national system of higher education in ways which may not be progressive. There is also the potential for the bureaucratisation of a policy to domesticate it, or sap it of its vitality, as it were, as Rizvi and Kemmis (1987: 302–3) so clearly demonstrated in relation to the implementation of the Participation and Equity Programme in Victoria. Progressive change tends to be achieved in an incremental fashion and is always open to challenge – two steps forward and one step back perhaps best encapsulates the reality.

CONCLUSION

In this chapter, we have discussed some of the ways in which policies impact on the processes of change. We have noted that the relationship between policy and change is multiple, complex and often contradictory. The examples we have considered have shown that change cannot be produced by government edict alone; and that although government legislation, policies and programmes are important, they can be interpreted in a variety of ways. Not only do they articulate with a range of cultural, social, economic and political considerations but also with the specificities of local circumstances – of local agendas and the interests of individuals and groups.

Traditionally, policy analysis has been viewed either as an academic exercise or an exercise in the service of the state bureaucracies. In both of these guises, policy analysis is assumed to be separate from questions of political advocacy. We have rejected this view, arguing instead that policy analysis is always inherently political. If this is so, then critical policy analysts have an important role to play in relation to educational change. If policies are judged to be progressive then critical policy analysis can contribute to enhancing people's understandings of the origins of the policies, of their political context, of their moral bases and of the ways in which they relate to the progressive purposes of education in creating a more equal and caring society. If, on the other hand, policies are assessed to be regressive then critical policy analysis can help provide intellectual and political resources with which to establish patterns of opposition and resistance. If, however, policies are an amalgam of progressive and regressive elements, as is so often the case, then the task of critical policy analysis is to help to develop strategies to harness their progressive potential.

References

Adams, F. (ed.) (1986) *Special Education*, London: Longmans.

Alexander, D. and Rizvi, F. (1993) 'Education, markets and the contradictions of Asia-Australia relations', *The Australian Universities' Review* 36, 2: 16–20.

Allen, J. (1990) 'Does feminism need a theory of the state?', in S. Watson (ed.) *Playing the State: Australian Feminist Interventions*, Sydney: Allen and Unwin, pp. 21–37.

Anderson, B. (1983) *Imagined Communities*, London: Verso.

Anderson, J. E. (1975) *Public Policy Making*, London: Nelson.

Angus, L. (1993) 'Democratic participation or efficient site management: The social and political location of the self-managing school' in J. Smyth (ed.) *A Socially Critical View of the Self-managing School*, London: Falmer Press, pp.11–33.

Angus, M. (1990) 'Making *Better Schools*: Devolution the second time around', paper presented to American Educational Research Association Conference, Boston.

Anyon, J. (1980) 'Social class and the hidden curriculum of work', *Journal of Education* 162, 1: 67–92.

Apelt, L. (1995) 'Organisational culture and the maintenance of male privilege', in B. Limerick and B. Lingard (eds) *Gender and Changing Educational Management*, Sydney: Hodder, pp. 198–202.

Apple, M. (1988) 'Equality and the politics of commonsense', in W. Secada (ed.) *Equity in Education*, London: Falmer Press, pp. 7–25.

—— (1992) Review of *Education and the Economy in a Changing Society* (OECD 1989a), *Comparative Education Review* 36, 1: 127–9.

—— (1993) 'Thinking "Right" in the USA: Ideological transformations in an age of conservatism', in B. Lingard, J. Knight and P. Porter (eds) *Schooling Reform in Hard Times*, London: Falmer Press, pp. 49–62.

—— (1994) *Official Knowledge*, New York: Routledge.

Archer, C. (1994) *Organizing Europe: The Institutions of Integration*, second edition, London: Edward Arnold.

Archer, M. (1985) 'Educational politics: A model for their analysis', in I. McNay and J. Ozga (eds) *Policymaking in Education: The Breakdown of Consensus*, Oxford: Pergamon Press, pp. 39–64.

Australian Centre for Industrial Relations Research and Teaching (1994) *Draft Progress Report of the Systemic Review of the Australian Vocational Certificate Pilot Program*, Sydney: ACIRRT.

Australian Council of Trade Unions/Trade Development Commission (1987) *Australia Reconstructed: A Report by the Mission Members to the ACTU and the TDC*, Canberra: AGPS.

Australian Education Council (1989) *Common and Agreed National Goals for Schooling in Australia*, Melbourne: Curriculum Corporation. (Hobart Declaration)

—— (1993) *National Action Plan for the Education of Girls 1993–97*, Melbourne: Curriculum Corporation.

Australian Education Council Review Committee (1991) *Young People's Participation in Post-compulsory Education and Training*, Canberra: AGPS. (Finn Report)

Australian Education Council/Ministers of Vocational Education, Employment and Training (1992) *Putting General Education to Work: The Key Competencies Report*, Canberra: AGPS. (Mayer Report)

Australian National Training Authority (ANTA) (1994a) *Towards a Skilled Australia: A National Strategy for Vocational Education and Training*, Brisbane: ANTA.

—— (1994b) *Description of the National Training Reform Agenda* (draft), Brisbane: ANTA.

—— (1994c) *Draft Guidelines for the Development of 1996 State Training Profiles*, Brisbane: ANTA.

—— (1995) *An Access and Equity Planning Model*, Brisbane: ANTA.

—— (undated, circa 1995) *Corporate Directions*, Brisbane: ANTA.

Australian Teaching Council (1994) *What Do Teachers Think?*, Sydney: Australian Teaching Council.

Bachrach, P. and Baratz, M. (1963) 'Decisions and non decisions: An analytical framework', *American Political Science Review* 57: 632–4.

Ball, S. J. (1990) *Politics and Policy Making in Education: Explorations in Policy Sociology*, London: Routledge.

—— (1993) 'Culture, cost and control: Self-management and entrepreneurial schooling in England and Wales', in J. Smyth (ed.) *A Socially Critical View of the Self-managing School*, London: Falmer Press, pp. 63–82.

—— (1994a) *Education Reform: A Critical and Post-structural Approach*, Buckingham: Open University Press.

—— (1994b) 'Researching inside the state: Issues in the interpretation of elite interviews', in D. Halpin and B. Troyna (eds) *Researching Education Policy: Ethical and Methodological Issues*, London: Falmer Press, pp. 107–20.

Barnett, K. and Wilson, S. (1995) *Separate Responsibilities: A Comparative, Equity Focused Study of Commercial and Community Providers*, Canberra: AGPS.

Barry, B. (1973) *The Liberal Theory of Justice*, Oxford: Clarendon Press.

Bartlett, L., Knight, J., Lingard, B. and Porter, P. (1994) 'Redefining a national agenda in education: The states fight back', *Australian Education Researcher* 21, 2: 29–44.

Beilharz, P. (1989) 'Social democracy and social justice', *Australian and New Zealand Journal of Sociology* 25, 1: 85–99.

Beilharz, P., Considine, M. and Watts, R. (1992) *Arguing about the Welfare State: The Australian Experience*, Sydney: Allen and Unwin.

Blackmore, J. (1995) 'Where's the level playing field? A feminist perspective on educational restructuring', paper presented to Australian Association for Research in Education Conference, Hobart.

Blackmore, J. and Kenway, J. (eds) (1993) *Gender Matters in Educational Administration and Policy*, London: Falmer Press.

Borgeest, T. (1994) *Public Education and the Constitution: Constitutional Guarantees for Public Education*, Melbourne: Australian Education Union.

Bourdieu, P. and Passeron, J. (1977) *Reproduction in Education, Society and Culture*, London: Sage.

Bowe, R., Ball, S. J. and Gold, A. (1992) *Reforming Education and Changing Schools: Case Studies in Policy Sociology*, London: Routledge.

Bowles, S. and Gintis, H. (1976) *Schooling in Capitalist America*, London: Routledge and Kegan Paul.

Braverman, H. (1974) *Labor and Monopoly Capital: The Degradation of Work in the Twentieth Century*, New York: Monthly Review Press.

Brieschke, P. A. (1989/90) 'The surprise side of policy analysis', *Policy Studies Journal* 18, 2: 305–23.

Broadband Services Expert Group (1994) *Networking Australia's Future*, Canberra: AGPS.

Buchbinder, H. and Newson, J. (1990) 'Corporate-university linkages in Canada: Transforming a public institution', *Higher Education* 20, 4: 355–79.

Burton, C. (1993) 'Equal employment opportunity and corporate planning', in J. Blackmore and J. Kenway (eds) *Gender Matters in Educational Administration and Policy: A Feminist Introduction*, London: Falmer Press, pp. 157–64.

Caldwell, B. and Spinks, J. (1988) *The Self-managing School*, London: Falmer Press.

Carley, M. (1980) *Rational Techniques in Policy Analysis*, Aldershot: Gower.

Carmichael, L. (1992) 'Key note address', conference on the Australian Vocational Certificate Training System, Sydney University, 19 June.

Cass, B. (1989) 'Defending and reforming the Australian welfare state: Some ideas for the next decade', in L. Orchard and R. Dare (eds) *Markets, Morals and Public Policy*, Sydney: Federation Press, pp. 134–56.

Castles, F. (1988) *Australian Public Policy and Economic Vulnerability*, Sydney: Allen and Unwin.

—— (1994) 'On the credulity of capital, or why globalisation does not prevent variation in domestic policy-making', in Public Sector Research Centre, University of New South Wales, *A Global State? Implications of Globalisation and Challenges for the Public Sector in Australia*, conference proceedings.

Castles, S. (1987) 'A new agenda for multiculturalism', paper presented at the conference Whither Multiculturalism?, Melbourne: La Trobe University, April.

Castles, S. and Wustenberg, W. (1979) *The Education of the Future: An Introduction to the Theory and Practice of Socialist Education*, London: Pluto Press.

Cerny, P. (1990) *The Changing Architecture of Politics: Structure, Agency and the Future of the State*, London: Sage.

Chomsky, N. (1993) *Year 501: The Conquest Continues*, London: Verso.

Cibulka, J. G. (1994) 'Policy analysis and the study of education', *Journal of Education Policy* 9, 5–6: 105–25 (special issue: *The Study of Educational Politics*, Politics of Education Association Yearbook 1994).

Civics Expert Group (1994) *Whereas the People: Civics and Citizenship Education*, Canberra: AGPS.

Cockburn, C. (1991) *In the Way of Women: Men's Resistance to Sex Equality in Organizations*, New York: ILR Press.

Codd, J. (1985) 'Images of schooling and discourses of the state', in J. Codd, R. Hawker and R. Nash (eds) *Political Issues in New Zealand Education*, Palmerston North: Dunmore Press, pp. 23–41.

—— (1988) 'The construction and deconstruction of educational policy documents', *Journal of Education Policy* 3, 3: 235–47.

Commission on Global Governance (1995) *Our Global Neighbourhood: The Report of the Commission on Global Governance*, Oxford: Oxford University Press.

Commonwealth of Australia (1994a) *Creative Nation: Commonwealth Cultural Policy*, Canberra: AGPS.

—— (1994b) *Working Nation*, Canberra: AGPS.

Commonwealth Schools Commission (1984a) *Girls and Tomorrow: The Challenge for Schools*, Canberra: AGPS.

—— (1984b) *Participation and Equity in Australian Schools*, Canberra: AGPS.

—— (1987) *The National Policy for the Education of Girls in Australian Schools*, Canberra: AGPS.

Connell, R.W. (1985) *Teachers' Work*, Sydney: Allen and Unwin.

Connell, R.W., Ashenden, D., Kessler, S. and Dowsett, G. (1982) *Making the Difference: Schools, Families and Social Division*, Sydney: Allen and Unwin.

Connell, R. W. and White, V. (1989) 'Child poverty and educational action', in D. Edgar, D. Keane and P. McDonald (eds) *Child Poverty*, Sydney: Allen and Unwin, pp. 104–22.

Connell, R. W., White, V. and Johnston, K. (1991) *'Running Twice as Hard': The Disadvantaged Schools Program in Australia*, Geelong: Deakin University Press.

Connors, L. and McMorrow, J. (1988) 'National policy development: The significance of the National Policy for the Education of Girls', *Unicorn* 14, 4: 256–65.

Considine, M. (1988) 'The corporate management framework as administrative science: A critique', *Australian Journal of Public Administration* 47, 1: 4–19.

—— (1994) *Public Policy: A Critical Approach*, Melbourne: Macmillan.

Council of Australian Governments (1994) *National Asian Languages and Cultures Strategy*, Canberra: AGPS.

Cox, E. (1995) *A Truly Civil Society*, Sydney: ABC Books.

Crook, S., Pakulski, J. and Waters, M. (1992) *Postmodernization*, London: Sage.

Cunningham, G. (1963) 'Policy and practice', *Public Administration* 41: 229–38.

Curtain, R. (1992) 'The New Industrial Relations in Australia', in D. Riley (ed.) *Industrial Relations in Australian Education*, Sydney: Social Science Press, pp. 1–23.

Dale, R. (1989) *The State and Education Policy*, Milton Keynes, UK: Open University Press.

—— (1992) 'Whither the state and education policy? Recent work in Australia and New Zealand', *British Journal of Sociology of Education* 13: 387–95.

—— (1994) 'Applied education politics or political sociology of education?', in D. Halpin and B. Troyna (eds) *Researching Education Policy: Ethical and Methodological Issues*, London: Falmer Press, pp. 31–41.

Dale, R., Esland, G. and MacDonald, M. (eds) (1976) *Schooling and Capitalism: A Sociological Reader*, London: Routledge and Kegan Paul.

Davis, G., Wanna, J., Warhurst, J. and Weller, P. (1993) *Public Policy in Australia*, second edition, Sydney: Allen and Unwin.

Dawkins, J. (1987) *Higher Education: A Policy Discussion Paper*, Canberra: AGPS.

—— (1988a) *Higher Education: A Policy Statement*, Canberra: AGPS.

—— (1988b) *Strengthening Australia's Schools*, Canberra: AGPS.

Dawkins, J. and Holding C. (1987) *Skills for Australia*, Canberra: AGPS.

Daws, L. (1995) 'From Chalky Towers to Class 10 B Plain Street: Policy construction at different sites', in B. Limerick and H. Nielsen (eds) *School and Community Relations: Participation, Policy and Practice*, Sydney: Harcourt Brace, pp. 119–31.

―― (1996) 'National Policy for the Education of Girls: The quiet achiever', in B. Lingard and P. Porter (eds) *Australian Schooling: The State of National Developments*, Canberra: Australian College of Education.

Deleon, P. (1994) 'Reinventing the policy sciences: Three steps back to the future', *Policy Sciences* 27: 77–95.

Department of Employment, Education and Training (DEET) (1989) *National Aboriginal and Torres Strait Islander Education Policy*, Canberra: AGPS.

―― (1993a) *AVC Pilots National Evaluation Strategy*, Canberra: AGPS.

―― (1993b) *Access and Equity: Explanatory notes for AVC Pilot Proposals*, Canberra: AGPS.

―― (1994) *Australian Vocational Certificate Training System. Pilot Projects 1994–94. Project Descriptions*, Canberra: AGPS.

―― (undated) *Draft Equity Strategy*, Canberra: AGPS..

Department of Prime Minister and Cabinet / Office of the Status of Women (1988) *A Say, a Choice, a Fair Go: The Government's National Agenda for Women*, Canberra: AGPS.

Dewey, J. (1958) *Philosophy of Education*, New Jersey: Littlefield, Adams and Co.

Dudley, J. and Vidovich, L. (1995) *The Politics of Education: Commonwealth Schools Policy 1973–1995*, Melbourne: Australian Council for Educational Research.

Dunford, R. W. (1992) *Organisational Behaviour: An Organisational Analysis Perspective*, Sydney: Addison-Wesley.

Dye, T. (1992) *Understanding Public Policy*, seventh edition, Englewood Cliffs, N.J.: Prentice-Hall.

Easton, D. (1953) *The Political System*, New York: Knopf.

Edwards, T., Fitz, J. and Whitty, G. (1989) *The State and Private Education: An Evaluation of the Assisted Places Scheme*, London: Falmer Press.

Elmore, R. F. and McLaughlin, M. (1988) *Steady Work: Policy Practice, and the Reform of American Education*, The RAND Corporation, Report for the National Institute of Education, R–3574–NIE / RC.

Employment and Skills Formation Council (ESFC) (1992) *Australian Vocational Certificate Training System*, Canberra: AGPS. (Carmichael Report)

Falk, R. (1993) 'The making of global citizenship', in J. Brecher, J. B. Childs and J. Cutler (eds) *Global Visions: Beyond the New World Order*, Montreal: Black Rose Books, pp. 39–50.

Faraclas, N. (1993) 'Critical literacy in PNG: Give praxis a chance', paper presented at the Critical Literacy Conference, Griffith University, Brisbane.

Fay, B. (1975) *Social Theory and Political Practice*, London: Allen and Unwin.

Finch, J. (1984) *Research and Policy: The Uses of Qualitative Methods in Social and Educational Research*, London: Falmer Press.

Finegold, D., McFarland, L. and Richardson, W. (eds) (1993) *Something Borrowed, Something Learned? The Transatlantic Market in Education and Training Reform*, Washington: The Brookings Institution.

Fischer, F. (1989) 'Beyond the rationality project: Policy analysis and the post positivist challenge', *Policy Studies Journal* 17, 4: 941–51.

Fooks, D. (1996) 'Training frustrated at every point by self-serving parties', *The Australian* 2 May: 12.

Foucault, M. (1980) *Power/Knowledge: Selected Interviews and Other Writings 1972–1977*, ed. C. Gordon, Brighton: Harvester Press.

Franzway, S. (1986) 'With problems of their own: Femocrats and the welfare state', *Australian Feminist Studies* 3: 45–57.

Franzway, S., Court, D. and Connell, R.W. (1989) *Staking a Claim: Feminism, Bureaucracy and the State*, Sydney: Allen and Unwin.

Fraser, N. (1995) 'From redistribution to recognition: Dilemmas of justice in a "post-socialist" society', *New Left Review*, July–August: 68–93.

Freeland, J. (1981) 'Where do they go after school? A critical analysis of one education program for unemployed youth', *The Australian Quarterly* Spring: 351–73.

—— (1986) 'Australia: The search for a new educational settlement', in R. Sharp (ed.) *Capitalist Crisis and Schooling: Comparative Studies in the Politics of Education*, Melbourne: MacMillan, pp. 212–36.

—— (1992) 'Education and training for the school to work transition', in T. Seddon and C. Deer (eds) *A Curriculum for the Senior Secondary Years*, Melbourne: ACER, pp. 64–88.

Fulcher, G. (1989) *Disabling Policies? A Comparative Approach to Education Policy and Disability*, London: Falmer Press.

Galbally Report (1978) *Report of the Review of Post-arrival Programs for Migrants*, volume 1, Canberra: AGPS.

Gee, J. and Lankshear, C. (1995) 'The new work order: Critical language awareness and "fast capitalism" texts', *Discourse* 16, 1: 5–20.

Gender Equity Taskforce (1996) *Gender Equity: A Framework for Australian Schools*, prepared for the Ministerial Council for Employment, Education and Training and Youth Affairs, draft for consultation, ACT.

Gewirtz, S. and Ozga, J. (1990) 'Partnership, pluralism and education policy: A reassessment', *Journal of Education Policy* 5, 1: 37–48.

Gewirtz, S., Ball, S. J. and Bowe, R. (1995) *Markets, Choice and Equity in Education*, Buckingham: Open University Press.

Giddens, A. (1990) *The Consequences of Modernity*, Cambridge: Polity Press.

—— (1994) *Beyond Left and Right: The Future of Radical Politics*, Cambridge: Polity Press.

Gil, D. (1989) *Unravelling Social Policy: Theory, Analysis, and Political Action Towards Social Inequality*, fifth edition, Rochester, Vermont: Schenkeman Books.

Gilbert, P. (1996) *Talking About Gender: Terminology Used in the Education of Girls Policy Area and the Implications for Policy Priorities and Programs*, a WEETAG Project, Canberra: AGPS.

Glenn, C.L. (1993) 'Creating an irresponsible school choice program', in C. Marshall (ed.) *The New Politics of Race and Gender*, Washington: Falmer Press.

Gordon, I., Lewis, J. and Young, R. (1977) 'Perspectives on policy analysis', *Public Administration Bulletin* 25: 26–35.

Green, M. (1995) *Releasing the Imagination: Essays on Education, the Arts and Social Change*, San Francisco: Jossey-Bass Publishers.

Griffin, C. (1993) *Representations of Youth: The Study of Youth and Adolescence in Britain and America*, Cambridge: Polity Press.

Hall, S. (1991) 'Ethnicity, identity and difference', *Radical America* 23, 2: 3–14.

—— (1992) 'The question of cultural identity', in S. Hall, D. Held and T. McGrew (eds) *Modernity and its Futures*, Cambridge: Polity Press, pp. 297–316.

Halpin, D. (1994) 'Practice and prospects in education policy research', in D. Halpin and B. Troyna (eds) *Researching Education Policy: Ethical and Methodological Issues*, London: Falmer Press, pp. 198–206.

Halpin, D. and Troyna, B. (eds) (1994) *Researching Education Policy: Ethical and Methodological Issues*, London: Falmer Press.

Ham, C. and Hill, M. (1993) *The Policy Process in the Modern Capitalist State*, second edition, Brighton: Wheatsheaf Books.

Harman, G. (1984) 'Conceptual and theoretical issues', in J. R. Hough (ed.) *Educational Policy: An International Survey*, London: Croom Helm, pp. 13–29.

Harrington, M. (1963) *The Other America: Poverty in the United States*, Baltimore: Penguin.

Harvey, D. (1989) *The Condition of Postmodernity*, Oxford: Blackwell.

Harvey, G. and Hergert, L. (1986) 'Strategies for Achieving Sex Equality in Education', *Theory into Practice* 25, 4: 290–99.

Harvey, L. (1990) *Critical Social Research*, London: Allen and Unwin.

Hatcher, R. and Troyna, B. (1994) 'The "policy cycle": A ball by ball account', *Journal of Education Policy* 9, 2: 155–70.

Hawkesworth, M. E. (1988) *Theoretical Issues in Policy Analysis*, New York: State University of New York Press.

Held, D. (1995a) 'Democracy and the new international order', in D. Archibuigi and D. Held (eds) *Cosmopolitan Democracy: An Agenda for a New World Order*, Cambridge: Polity Press, pp. 96–120.

—— (1995b) *Democracy and the Global Order: From the Modern State to Cosmopolitan Governance*, Cambridge: Polity Press.

Heller, A. (1987) *A Theory of Needs*, Cambridge: Polity Press.

Henry, M. (1993) 'What is policy? A response to Stephen Ball', *Discourse* 14, 1: 102–5.

Henry, M. and Franzway, S. (1993) 'Gender, unions and the new workplace: Realising the promise?', in B. Probert and B. Wilson (eds) *Pink Collar Blues: Work, Gender and Technology*, Melbourne: Melbourne University Press, pp. 126–53.

Henry, M. and Taylor, S. (1993) 'Gender equity and economic rationalism: An uneasy alliance', in B. Lingard, J. Knight and P. Porter (eds) *Schooling Reform in Hard Times*, London: Falmer Press, pp. 153–75.

—— (1995a) 'Equity and the AVC pilots in Queensland: A study in policy refraction', *Australian Education Researcher* 22, 1: 85–106.

—— (1995b) 'The AVC work-based pilots: Opportunities and barriers for women in vocational education and training', *Melbourne Studies in Education* 29, 1: 55–70.

Hinkson, J. (1991) *Post-modernity, State and Education*, Geelong: Deakin University Press.

Hobsbawm, E. (1994) *Age of Extremes: The Short Twentieth Century 1914–1991*, London: Michael Joseph.

Hoffman, J. (1995) *Beyond the State: An Introductory Critique*, Cambridge: Polity Press.

Hogwood, B. and Peters, G. (1983) *Policy Dynamics*, Brighton: Wheatsheaf.

Hogwood, B.W. and Gunn, L.A. (1984) *Policy Analysis for the Real World*, Oxford: Oxford University Press.

Horsman, M. and Marshall, A. (1995) *After the Nation-state: Citizens, Tribalism and the New World Order*, London: Harper Collins.

Huse, E. F. (1982) *Management*, second edition, St Paul, Minnesota: Westview.

Jakubowicz, A. (1981) 'State and ethnicity: Multiculturalism as ideology', *Australian and New Zealand Journal of Sociology* 17, 3: 4–13.

Jameson, F. (1991) *Postmodernism or the Cultural Logic of Late Capitalism*, Durham: Duke University Press.

Jayasuriya, L. (1987) 'Ethnic Minorities and Social Justice in Australia', *Australian Journal of Social Issues* 22, 3: 481–97.

Jessop, B. (1990) *State Theory: Putting the Capitalist State in its Place*, Cambridge: Polity Press.

Johnson, W. (1992) 'South Australia: From good school practices to effective policy', in R. Slee (ed.) *Discipline in Australian Public Education: Changing Policy and Practice*, Hawthorne: ACER, pp. 79–104.

Johnston, K. (1993) 'Inequality and educational reform: Lessons from the Disadvantaged Schools Program', in B. Lingard, J. Knight and P. Porter (eds) *Schooling Reform in Hard Times*, London: Falmer Press, pp. 106–19.

Kalantzis, M., Cope, B. and Slade, D. (1989) *Minority Languages and Social Equity*, London: Falmer Press.

Kemmis, S. (1990a) *The Curriculum Corporation: Observations and Implications*, Melbourne: Australian Curriculum Studies Association.

—— (1990b) *Curriculum, Contestation and Change*, Geelong: Deakin University, School of Education.

Kenway, J. (1990) *Gender and Education Policy: A Call for New Directions*, Geelong: Deakin University Press.

—— (1992) 'Feminist theories of the state: To be or not to be', in M. Muetzenfeldt (ed.) *Society State and Politics in Australia*, Sydney: Pluto Press, pp. 108–44.

—— (1995) 'Technological trends: Issues for schooling', in R. Lingard and F. Rizvi (eds) *External Environmental Scan*, Department of Education, Queensland, pp. 20–26.

Kenway, J., Bigum, C., Fitzclarence, L. and Collier, J. (1993) 'Marketing education in the 1990s: An introductory essay', *The Australian Universities' Review* 36, 2: 2–6.

Kickert, W. (1991) 'Steering at a distance: A new paradigm of public governance in Dutch higher education', paper presented to European Consortium for Political Research, University of Essex.

Knox, M. and Pickersgill, R. (1993) *Women and Training: Education in the Workforce*, literature review, ACIRRT Working Paper 29, Australian Centre for Industrial Relations Research and Teaching, University of Sydney.

Kulwaum, G. (1995) *Problems of Devolution in Papua New Guinea Education*, unpublished PhD thesis, University of Queensland.

Le Compte, M. D., Millroy, W. and Preisle, J. (eds) (1992) *The Handbook of Qualitative Research in Education*, San Diego: Academic Press.

Limerick, B. and Lingard, B. (eds) (1995) *Gender and Changing Educational Management*, Sydney: Hodder.

Lingard, B. (1993a) 'Corporate federalism: The emerging approach to policy-making for Australian schools', in B. Lingard, J. Knight and P. Porter (eds) *Schooling Reform in Hard Times*, London: Falmer Press, pp. 2–35.

—— (1993b) 'The changing state of policy production in education: Some Australian reflections on the state of policy sociology', *International Studies in Sociology of Education* 3, 1: 25–47.

—— (1995) 'Gendered policy making inside the state', in B. Limerick and B. Lingard (eds) *Gender and Changing Educational Management*, Sydney: Edward Arnold, pp. 136–49.

Lingard, B., Henry, M. and Taylor, S. (1987) ' "A girl in a militant pose": A chronology of struggle in girls' education in Queensland', *British Journal of Sociology of Education* 8, 2: 135–52.

Lingard, B., Knight, J. and Porter, P. (1995) 'Restructuring Australian schooling: Changing conceptions of top-down and bottom-up reforms', in B. Limerick and H. Nielsen (eds) *School and Community Relations: Participation, Policy and Practice*, Sydney: Harcourt Brace, pp. 81–99.

—— (eds) (1993) *Schooling Reform in Hard Times*, London: Falmer Press.

Lingard, B. and Limerick, B. (1995) 'Thinking gender, changing educational management', in B. Limerick and B. Lingard (eds) *Gender and Changing Educational Management*, Sydney: Hodder, pp. 1–10.

Lingard, B., Porter, P., Bartlett, L. and Knight, J. (1995) 'Federal/State mediations in the Australian national education agenda: From the AEC to MCEETYA 1987–1993', *Australian Journal of Education* 39, 1: 41–66.

Lipsky, M. (1980) *Street Level Bureaucracy*, New York: Russell Sage.

Lowe, I. (1996) 'The empire strikes back', *NTEU Advocate* 3, 2: 29.

Luke, A., Nakata, M., Singh, M. and Smith, R. (1993) 'Policy and the politics of representation: Torres Strait Islanders and Aborigines at the margins', in B. Lingard, J. Knight and P. Porter (eds) *Schooling Reform in Hard Times*, London: Falmer Press, pp. 139–52.

Luke, C. (1996) 'ekstasis@cyberia' *Discourse* 17, 2: 187–207.

Lukes, S. (1974) *Power: A Radical View*, London: Macmillan Press.

Mac an Ghaill, M. (1991) 'State-school policy: Contradictions, confusions and contestation', *Journal of Education Policy* 6: 299–314.

McFarland, L. and Vickers, M. (1994) 'The context and rationale for the reform of vocational and technical education', in OECD *Vocational Education and Training: Towards Coherent Policy and Practice*, Paris: OECD, pp. 7–18.

McHoul, A. W. (1984) 'Writing, sexism and schooling: A discourse analytic investigation of some recent documents on sexism and education in Queensland', *Discourse* 4, 2: 1–17.

MacIntyre, S. (1985) *Winners and Losers*, Sydney: Allen and Unwin.

McLaughlin, M. (1991) 'The Rand Change Agent study: Ten years later', in A. R. Odden (ed.) *Education Policy Implementation*, Albany, NY: State University of New York Press, pp. 143–55.

McLaughlin, M.W. (1987) 'Learning from experience: Lessons from policy implementation', *Educational Evaluation and Policy Analysis* 9, 2: 171–8.

McPherson, A. and Raab, C. (1989) *Governing Education: A Sociology of Policy Since 1945*, Edinburgh: Edinburgh University Press.

Milligan, S. and Thomson, K. (1992) *Listening to Girls*, Curriculum Corporation: Melbourne.

Maguire, M. and Ball, S. (1994) 'Researching politics and the politics of research: Recent qualitative studies in the UK', *International Journal of Qualitative Studies in Education* 7, 3: 269–85.

Marginson, S. (1993) *Education and Public Policy in Australia*, Cambridge: Cambridge University Press.

Marginson, S., Martin, R. and Williamson, J. (1995) *Creating an Education Nation for the Year 2000*, Melbourne: Australian Education Union.

Marshall, C. (ed.) (1993) *The New Politics of Race and Gender*, London: Falmer Press.

Mathews, J. (1989) *Tools of Change: New Technology and the Democratisation of Work*, Sydney: Pluto Press.

Neave, G. (1991) 'On programmes, universities and Jacobins: Or, 1992 vision and reality for European higher education', *Higher Education Policy* 4, 4: 37–41.

Nicholls J. (1992) 'Competencies, training and higher education', *Journal of Higher Education* 15, 2: 2–4.

Norman, R. (1987) *Free and Equal*, Oxford: Oxford University Press.

Nozick, R. (1976) *Anarchy, State and Utopia*, Oxford: Blackwell.

O'Brien, M. (1984) 'The commatisation of women: Patriarchal fetishism in the sociology of education', *Interchange* 15, 2: 43–60.

Offe, C. (1975) 'The theory of the capitalist state and the problem of policy formation', in L. Lindberg, R. Alford, C. Crouch and C. Offe (eds) *Stress and Contradiction in Modern Capitalism*, Boston: Lexington Books, pp. 125–44.

—— (1984) *Disorganised Capitalism: Contemporary Transformations of Work and Politics*, Cambridge: Cambridge University Press.

Office of Multicultural Affairs (1989) *The National Agenda for a Multicultural Australia*, Canberra: Australian Government Printing Service.

Organisation for Economic Co-operation and Development (OECD) (1979) *Future Educational Policies in the Changing Social and Economic Context*, Paris: OECD.

—— (1989a) *Education and the Economy in a Changing Society*, Paris: OECD.

—— (1989b) *Pathways for Learning: Education and Training from 16 to 19*, Paris: OECD.

—— (1994a) *Vocational Education and Training for Youth: Towards Coherent Policy and Practice*, Paris: OECD.

—— (1994b) *Women and Structural Change: New Perspectives*, Paris: OECD.

—— (1995) *Governance in Transition: Public Management Reforms in OECD Countries*, Paris: OECD.

—— (undated) *OECD*, brochure outlining the functions and structure of the OECD, Paris: OECD.

Ozga, J. (1987) 'Studying education through the lives of policy makers: An attempt to close the micro-macro gap', in S. Walker and L. Barton (eds) *Changing Policies: Changing Teachers*, Milton Keynes: Open University Press, pp. 138–50.

Ozga, J. and Gewirtz, S. (1994) 'Sex, lies and audiotape: Interviewing the education policy elite', in D. Halpin and B. Troyna (eds) *Researching Education Policy: Ethical and Methodological Issues*, London: Falmer Press, pp. 121–35.

Painter, M. (1988) 'Australian federalism and the policy process: Politics with extra vitamins', *Politics* 23, 2: 57–66.

Papadopoulos, G. (1995) *Education 1960–1990: The OECD Perspective*, Paris: OECD.

Pijl, S. (1994) 'United States', in C. Meijer, S. Pijl and S. Hegarty (eds) *New Perspectives in Special Education: A Six-country Study of Integration*, London: Routledge, pp. 55–78.

Pocock, B. (1992) *Women in Entry Level Training: Some Overseas Experiences*, Canberra: AGPS.

Prunty, J. (1984) *A Critical Reformulation of Educational Policy Analysis*, Geelong: Deakin University Press.

—— (1985) 'Signposts for a critical educational policy analysis', *Australian Journal of Education* 29, 2: 133–40.

Pusey, M. (1991) *Economic Rationalism in Canberra: A Nation-building State Changes its Mind*, Cambridge: Cambridge University Press.

Queensland Department of Education (1981) *Equality of Opportunity in Education for Girls and Boys*, Brisbane: Government Printer.

Raab, C. D. (1994) 'Where we are now: Reflections on the sociology of education policy', in D. Halpin and B. Troyna (eds) *Researching Education Policy: Ethical and Methodological Issues*, London: Falmer Press, pp. 17–30.

Raffe, D. (1994) 'Compulsory education and what then? Signals, choices, pathways', in OECD *Vocational Education and Training for Youth: Towards a Coherent Policy and Practice*, Paris: OECD, pp. 41–67.

Rawls, J. (1972) *A Theory of Justice*, Oxford: Clarendon Press.

Rein, M. (1983) *From Policy to Practice*, London: Macmillan.

Rizvi, F. (1994) 'Devolution in education: Three contrasting perspectives', in R. Martin, J. McCollow, L. McFarlane, G. McMurdo, J. Graham and R. Hull (eds) *Devolution, Decentralisation and Recentralisation: The Structure of Australian Schooling*, Melbourne: Australian Education Union, pp. 1–5.

Rizvi, F. and Kemmis, S. (1987) *Dilemmas of Reform: The Participation and Equity Program in Victorian Schools*, Geelong: Deakin Institute for Studies in Education.

Rizvi, F., Lingard, B., Taylor, S. and Henry, M. (1995–7) Globalisation and education policy: An exploration of the role of the OECD in shaping Australian education (1984–present). Project conducted under the auspices of the Australian Research Council.

Roberts, H. (ed.) (1981) *Doing Feminist Research*, London: Routledge and Kegan Paul.

Robertson, R. (1992) *Globalization*, London: Sage.

Ruby, A. (1992) ' "If Freeman Butts calls tell him we might be changing course": A perspective on the notion of competency and Australia's schools', in D. Anderson *et al. Higher Education and the Competency Movement: Implications for Tertiary Education and the Professions*, conference proceedings, Centre for Continuing Education, ANU, Canberra, pp. 15–23.

Rudd, K. (1994) *Asian Languages and Australia's Economic Future: A Report Prepared for the Council of Australian Governments on a Proposed National Asian Languages/Studies Strategy for Australian Schools*, Brisbane: Queensland Government Printer.

Ryan, M. (1971) *Blaming the Victim*, New York: Pantheon Books.

Samuel, M. (1996) 'Language policies in Malaysian education: Some recent developments', unpublished paper.

Sawer, M. (1989) 'Efficiency, effectiveness and equity?', in G. Davis, P. Weller and C. Lewis (eds) *Corporate Management in Australia*, Melbourne: Macmillan, pp. 138–53.

Schools Commission (1973) *Schools in Australia: Report of the Interim Committee for the Australian Schools Commission*, Canberra: AGPS. (Karmel Report)

—— (1975) *Girls, School and Society*, Canberra: AGPS.

Schram, S. F. (1993) 'Postmodern policy analysis: Discourse and identity in welfare policy', *Policy Sciences* 26: 249–70.

Scott, R. (1995) 'Mayer's unfinished eighth: Cultural understanding as a key competency', in C. Collins (ed.) *Curriculum Stocktake*, Canberra: Australian College of Education, pp. 46–58.

Seddon, T. (1989) 'Which way for schooling?', *Australian Teacher* 24: 18–19.

—— (1992/3) 'An historical reckoning: Education and training reform', *Education Links* 44: 5–9.

—— (1994) *Context and Beyond: Reframing the Theory and Practice of Education*, London: Falmer Press.

Shilling, C. (1989) *Schooling for Work in Capitalist Britain*, Lewes: Falmer Press.

Sinclair, A. (1989) 'Public sector culture: Managerialism or multiculturalism?', *Australian Journal of Public Administration* 48, 4: 382–97.

Sivanandan, A. (1989) 'New circuits of imperialism', *Race and Class* 30, 4: 1–19.

Slee, R. (1993) 'The politics of integration: A critical analysis of professional culture and school organisation', *Disability, Handicap and Society* 8, 4: 351–60.

Sloan, J. (1996) 'Training agenda is off-course', *The Australian* 25 April.

Smith, R. (1982) 'Policy studies in education: Problems and prospects', in R. Young, M. Pusey, and R. Bates (eds) *Australian Education Policy: Issues and Critique*, Geelong: Deakin University Press, pp. 143–67.

Smyth, J. (1993) 'Introduction', in J. Smyth (ed.) *A Socially Critical View of the Self-managing School*, London: Falmer Press, pp. 1–9.

Solity, J. (1992) *Special Education*, London: Cassell.

Spender, D. (1995) *Nattering on the Net: Women, Power and Cyberspace*, Melbourne: Spinifex.

Storey, R. (1996) 'Curtin rises on institutional marriage vows', *The Australian* 26 April.

Symes, C. (1995) 'A post-fordist reworking of Australian education: The Finn, Mayer and Carmichael reports in the context of labour reprocessing', *The Vocational Aspect of Education* 47, 3: 247–71.

Symes, C. and Hopkins, S. (1994) 'Universities Inc.: Caveat emptor', *The Australian Universities' Review* 37, 2: 47–51.

Tannock, P. and Birch, I. (1976) 'Constitutional responsibility for education in Australia: The federal government's latent power', in G. S. Harman and C. Selby-Smith (eds) *Readings in the Economics and Politics of Australian Education*, Melbourne: Pergamon Press, pp. 32–9.

Taylor, S. (1993) ' "Equal opportunities" policies and the 1988 Education Reform Act in Britain: Equity issues in cultural and political context', *Discourse* 14, 1: 30–43.

Taylor, S. and Henry, M. (1994) 'Equity and the new post-compulsory education and training policies in Australia: A progressive or regressive agenda?', *Journal of Education Policy* 9, 2: 105–27.

—— (1996, in press) 'Reframing equity in the training reform agenda: Implications for social change', Australian Vocational Education Review.

Teese, R., Davies, M., Charlton, M. and Polesel, J. (1995) *Who Wins at School? Boys and Girls in Australian Secondary Education*, Melbourne: Department of Education Policy and Management, Melbourne University.

ten Dam, G. and Volman, M. (1995) 'Feminist research and educational policy', *Journal of Education Policy* 10, 2: 209–20.

Torres, C. A. (1995) 'State and education revisited: Why educational researchers should think politically about education', in M. W. Apple (ed.) *Review of Research in Education 21*, Washington: American Educational Research Association, pp. 255–331.

Tripcony, P. (1995) 'Barely scratching the surface: An indigenous experience of education administration', in B. Limerick and B. Lingard (eds) *Gender and Changing Educational Management*, Sydney: Edward Arnold, pp. 121–34.

Troyna, B. (1994) 'Critical social research and education policy', *British Journal of Educational Studies* 42, 2: 70–84.

Troyna, B. and Williams, J. (1986) *Racism, Education and the State*, Beckenham: Croom Helm.

Vickers, M. (1994) 'Cross-national exchange, the OECD, and Australian education policy', *Knowledge and Policy* 7, 1: 25–47.

Victorian Ministry of Education (1980) *Equal Opportunity and the Elimination of Sexism*, policy statement.

Walzer, M. (1983) *Spheres of Justice*, Oxford: Blackwell.

Waters, M. (1995) *Globalization*, London: Routledge.

Watt, J. (1989) 'Devolution of power: The ideological meaning', *Journal of Educational Administration* 27, 1: 19–28.

Weiss, C. H. (1986) 'The circuitry of enlightenment: Diffusion of social science research to policy makers', *Knowledge: Creation, Diffusion, Utilisation* 8, 2: 274–81.

—— (1989) 'Congressional committees as users of analysis', *Journal of Policy Analysis and Management* 8, 3: 411–31.

Weller, P. and Lewis, C. (1989) 'Corporate management: Background and dilemmas', in G. Davis, P. Weller and C. Lewis (eds) *Corporate Management in Australian Government*, Melbourne: MacMillan, pp. 1–16.

White, V. and Johnston, K. (1993) 'Inside the disadvantaged schools program: The politics of practical policy-making', in L. Angus (ed.) *Education Inequality and Social Identity*, London: Falmer Press, pp. 104–27.

Wilenski, P. (1986) *Public Power and Public Administration*, Sydney: Hale and Iremonger.

—— (1988) 'Social change as a source of competing values in public administration', *Australian Journal of Public Administration* 47, 3: 213–22.

Williams, B. (1979) *Education, Training and Employment: Report of the Committee of Inquiry into Education and Training*, Canberra: AGPS. (Williams Report)

Williams, F. (1989) *Social Policy: A Critical Introduction*, Cambridge: Polity Press.

Williams, R. (1961) *The Long Revolution*, Harmondsworth: Penguin.

—— (1981) *Culture*, London: Fontana.

Willis, P. (1990) *Common Culture: Symbolic Work at Play in the Everyday Cultures of the Young*, Milton Keynes: Open University Press.

Wise, A. 1984), 'Why educational policies often fail: The hyperrationalisation hypothesis', in J. J. Prunty (ed.) *A Critical Reformulation of Educational Policy Analysis*, Geelong: Deakin University Press, pp. 72–86.

World Bank (1991) *Vocational and Technical Education and Training: A World Bank Policy Paper*, Washington: World Bank.

Yates, L. (1993) *The Education of Girls: Policy, Research and the Question of Gender*, Hawthorn: ACER.

Yeatman, A. (1987) 'The concept of public management and the Australian state in the 1980s', *Australian Journal of Public Administration* 46, 4: 339–53.

—— (1990) *Bureaucrats, Technocrats, Femocrats: Essays on the Contemporary Australian State*, Sydney: Allen and Unwin.

—— (1994) *Postmodernist Revisionings of the Political*, New York: Routledge.

Young, I. M. (1990) *Justice and the Politics of Difference*, Princeton, N.J.: Princeton University Press.

Young, M. (1993) 'A curriculum for the 21st century? Towards a new basis for overcoming academic/vocational divisions', *British Journal of Educational Studies* 41, 3: 203–22.

Index